WILFRED THESIGER was born in 1910 at the British Legation in Addis Ababa, and spent his early years in Abyssinia. He was educated at Eton and Oxford. In the Second World War, serving under Orde Wingate in Abyssinia, he was awarded a DSO. He later served with the SOE in Syria and the SAS in the Western Desert.

Thesiger's journeys have won him the Founder's Medal of the Royal Geographical Society, the Lawrence of Arabia Medal of the Royal Central Asian Society and the Burton Memorial Medal of the Royal Asiatic Society.

His writing has won him the Heinemann Award, Fellowship of the Royal Society of Literature, and an Honorary D.Litt. from Leicester University and an Honorary D.Litt. from the University of Bath.

In 1968 Thesiger was made CBE. He is Honorary Fellow of the British Academy and Honorary Fellow of Magdalen College, Oxford. He was honoured with a KBE in 1995.

For over twenty years, until 1994, he lived mostly among the pastoral Samburu at Maralal in north Kenya. He now lives permanently in Surrey.

WILFRED THESIGER

MY LIFE AND TRAVELS

An Anthology, Edited by
Alexander Maitland

Flamingo
An Imprint of HarperCollins*Publishers*

Flamingo
An imprint of HarperCollins*Publishers*
77–85 Fulham Palace Road,
Hammersmith, London W6 8JB

Flamingo is a registered trade mark of
HarperCollins Publishers Limited

www.harpercollins.co.uk

Published by Flamingo 2003
9 8 7 6 5 4 3 2 1

First published in Great Britain by
HarperCollins*Publishers* 2002

ISBN 0 00 655212 9

Typeset in Sabon

Printed and bound in Great Britain
by Clays Ltd, St Ives plc

CONTENTS

ILLUSTRATIONS

Thesiger's parents, 1909.
Thesiger's birthplace, 1910.
Thesiger photographed by Umar, his Somali headman.
Thesiger with hand-reared lion cubs, Sudan.
Thesiger's Nuer porters.
Thesiger in Arab dress in the Empty Quarter.
Shibam, Hadhramaut.
Salim bin Ghabaisha, during second crossing of the Empty
    Quarter.
Wilfred Thesiger, during second crossing of the Empty
    Quarter, 1947–8.
Salim bin Kabina in the western Sands, 1948.
A Kuwaiti *boom* returning from Zanzibar.
Bin Kabina and bin Ghabaisha in Oman, 1950.
Salim bin Kabina riding a camel.
Bin Ghabaisha in 1950.
Mud-roofed village, Iraqi Kurdistan, c.1950.
Qandil Range, Kurdish mountains.
Start of journey to Kachi Kuni Pass, Chitral.
Baroghil Pass, northern Chitral, 1952.
Rakaposhi mountain, Hunza, 1953.

*In lasting memory
of my brother, Dermot*

INTRODUCTION

Wilfred Patrick Thesiger was born in 1910 at Addis Ababa, Abyssinia, where his father, Captain The Hon. Wilfred Gilbert Thesiger, was Consul-General and Minister in charge of the British Legation.

As a boy, Thesiger had longed to hunt big game and travel among tribes living in remote areas. A hunting trip which followed the coronation of the Abyssinian emperor, Haile Selassie, in 1930, led to Thesiger's first important journey when he traced Abyssinia's unmapped Awash river to its end, thereby solving one of Africa's last geographical mysteries.

Between 1919 and 1933, Thesiger was educated at an English preparatory school, followed by Eton and Oxford. After five years as an Assistant District Commissioner in the Sudan, Thesiger served in Abyssinia, the Middle East and North Africa during the Second World War. In Cairo, in 1945, a decisive chance encounter gave Thesiger the opportunity of twice crossing the Empty Quarter of Arabia: epic journeys which established his reputation as a traveller and an explorer.

Including seven years spent with the Marsh Arabs in Iraq, Thesiger continued to travel on foot using animal transport, for a further thirty years, in little-known areas of the Middle

East, Africa and western Asia. From 1968 until 1994, he lived mainly in northern Kenya, while travelling at intervals in India, Indonesia, Trans-Jordan, Yemen and Ladakh.

Had Thesiger never written anything, had he never taken up photography, he would still have been famous and highly respected as a great traveller and explorer. But it is improbable – in his lifetime at any rate – that he would have achieved the degree of fame worldwide that resulted from his books and photographs.

Thesiger's first book, *Arabian Sands*, published in 1959, heralded him as an exceptionally gifted writer. His second book, *The Marsh Arabs*, published five years later, confirmed this. Thesiger has told and retold many times how he had been persuaded to write *Arabian Sands*, yet he has never really attempted to explain why he began to write. Nor, for that matter, has he explained why he went on writing.

Companionship and conversation – the kind Thesiger describes as 'hard talking' among friends – were vitally important to him. Although he was by nature reserved, all his life Thesiger desperately needed to communicate with people. It may be that writing had been another, extended means of satisfying this chronic need; that, by reliving and writing down what he had experienced and deeply felt, he purged his memory of images, sensations and impressions that were disturbingly, almost unbearably real. Thesiger's vivid memories of his five years in Arabia, for instance, were to remain for him, in some ways, more real than reality itself. Yet a delay of seven years before he began to write *Arabian Sands* edited even those precious memories.

Until 1957 Thesiger had never contemplated writing a book. Even then he found himself being urged to write, as if by accident, when a literary agent, Graham Watson, came to look at his photographs. At that instant, in the words of V. S. Pritchett, the opportunity presented itself 'to disclose the extraordinary experience, physical and mental ... shut up in himself with stern determination for half an active lifetime'.

Although Thesiger had never travelled with the intention of writing about a journey, over two decades he had published about twenty articles, including several describing his main journeys in Ethiopia and Arabia which discreetly acknowledged their importance. Throughout his travels he had kept diaries and had photographed 'as a record' thousands of tribal people in their remote desert, marsh or mountain worlds. His diaries and photographs, together with letters he wrote to his family, provided Thesiger with information for articles in *The Times*, the *Geographical Magazine* and the Royal Geographical Society's *Journal* between 1934 and 1958. Years later they helped him to recall no less vividly much of the authentic detail he needed to write his books.

Two childhood essays, based on a family visit to India in 1917, are the earliest known examples of Thesiger's prose. In one, he tells how Geoffrey Archer, Commissioner of what was then British Somaliland, took him and his younger brother, Brian, to shoot seabirds at Berbera, on the Somali coast. In the other, aged seven, Wilfred describes thrilling scenes from a vice-regal tiger shoot in the Jaipur forests of Rajasthan.

In 1919, at the end of Captain Thesiger's posting at Addis Ababa the family returned to England from Abyssinia. The following year his father died suddenly in Brighton. Wilfred's mother moved from Sussex to a Welsh farmhouse; then to The Milebrook, in Radnorshire, which remained the family's home until the Second World War. In a series of matching notebooks (each fitted with a brass lock and key), Wilfred kept meticulous records of shooting, fishing and natural history at

The Milebrook, where he and his three younger brothers spent most of their school and university holidays from 1922.

Six months after he had left Oxford, in December 1933, Thesiger set out on his first major expedition, across a remote area of northeast Abyssinia, inhabited by warlike Danakil tribesmen, to discover where the mysterious Awash river ended. Using his expedition diary and field-notes of Danakil customs, he reported this dangerous journey in four consecutive articles, published in *The Times* between 31 July and 3 August 1934.

In January 1935 Thesiger joined the Sudan Political Service. From then until 1939, he corresponded at regular intervals with his mother and brothers about his big game hunting adventures and life as an Assistant District Commissioner in Northern Darfur and the Western Nuer Province. In his 1938 diary (the only diary Thesiger kept during those years) he documented a camel journey from the Sudan to Tibesti in the French Sahara. Fifty years later, Thesiger included an account of this journey in his bestselling autobiography, *The Life of My Choice*.

After the Second World War, his diaries recorded the now-famous journeys across Arabia's Empty Quarter and Oman, followed by seven years when he lived for long periods among the Marsh Arabs of southern Iraq. Between 1950 and 1983, in notebooks or pocket-diaries, he described successive travels in Kurdistan, the Hindu Kush, the Karakorams and the Atlas mountains of Morocco, northern and southern Ethiopia, northern Kenya, Tanzania, India and Ladakh.

Thesiger spent the winter months of 1957 alone in Denmark, – a stark contrast to the climate and people of Arabia – writing *Arabian Sands*. He used his 1945–50 diaries and photographs to describe with absolute precision his desert journeys, the desert tribes and their unforgiving landscape. Even so, Thesiger wrote *Arabian Sands* largely from memory, working for up to fourteen hours a day at the Park Hotel in Copenhagen. He recalled occasions when 'I felt as if my Bedu companions, bin Kabina and bin Ghabaisha, were there with me'. Or else, 'I'd be searching for just the right adjective to describe exactly what I meant. I would go out and walk round the Tivoli Gardens near the hotel, thinking, thinking what could it be? Then the word would come to me and I'd get back to my room and carry on writing till bedtime.'

Thesiger's book enshrined his 'five most important years' and paid tribute to the Bedu who had accompanied him. His crossings of Arabia's vast southern desert gave *Arabian Sands* its epic dimension, theme and title. In *Arabian Sands* Thesiger recreated not so much a literal impression as an intensely personal vision of Arabia. His ability to express or suppress powerful emotion, to evoke atmosphere, to portray character and mood, to mine rich, complex veins of personal experience, raised an already engrossing narrative of exploration and travel to the highest realms of modern literature. *Arabian Sands* could hardly have differed more from the prosaic recollections of the Empty Quarter published by Bertram Thomas and H. St John Philby in the early 1930s. As a literary phenomenon, it can only be compared with classics of the genre such as C. M. Doughty's *Arabia Deserta* or T. E. Lawrence's *Seven Pillars of Wisdom*.

Based upon Thesiger's experiences in southern Iraq in 1951–8, his next book, *The Marsh Arabs* (1964), offered a supremely authoritative account of the Marshmen and their little-known surroundings. Today, this important, beautiful work immortalizes a vanished, centuries-old way of life observed at first hand by only a very few Europeans.

In *Arabian Sands*, Thesiger had dealt with the constant physical and mental challenge of desert travel, accompanied by small parties of nomadic tribesmen. In *The Marsh Arabs*, by converse, he portrayed a settled, communal life shared with the Marshmen in their photogenic wilderness of reeds, sky and water.

Widely acclaimed as Thesiger's finest work and one of the greatest travel books of all time, *Arabian Sands* has remained continuously in print since it was first published in 1959. Inevitably every book Thesiger produced during the next forty years, including *The Marsh Arabs*, would be judged against the nearly flawless perfection of *Arabian Sands*.

After he had completed *The Marsh Arabs*, Thesiger decided that he had written enough for the time being. He commented: 'Writing was hard work and I preferred to be off somewhere travelling in places which interested me.' Eventually, in 1979, a large-format book appeared, its enthralling text lavishly illustrated with Thesiger's magnificent photographs. Simply, evocatively titled, *Desert, Marsh and Mountain*, this new book included journeys Thesiger had made in western Asia between 1952 and 1965.

Visions of a Nomad, published in 1987, was devoted almost entirely to Thesiger's black-and-white photography. Also published in 1987, after years of hard work in England, India and Kenya, Thesiger's long-awaited autobiography, *The Life of My Choice*, became an immediate bestseller. This monumental work, which Thesiger liked to describe, tongue-in-cheek, as a 'fragment', was developed from the opening chapter of *Arabian Sands*. In due course, Thesiger brought *The Life of My Choice* up to date by producing three illustrated postscripts: *My Kenya Days* (1994), which he dictated at Maralal in Kenya after his sight had begun to fail; *The Danakil Diary* (1996); and *Among the Mountains* (1998). The last two were compiled in London from his diaries of journeys in Ethiopia, Iraqi Kurdistan and Asia.

Aged ninety, Thesiger confirmed without hesitation: 'The books that have really mattered to me have been *Arabian Sands*, *The Marsh Arabs* and *The Life of My Choice*. When I sat down to write, I never thought: will this next book be as successful as the previous ones? I just wrote what I wanted, when I wanted and I said to myself – they can make of this what they like.'

Thesiger's straightforward, uncompromising approach to more than fifty years of travel is thus reflected in his attitude toward writing and, for that matter, to photography. It is interesting to observe how his style varies: the quality of his mature prose compared with the untouched, spontaneous writing taken from early diaries; and, more recently, his skill overcoming the many difficulties of writing by dictation.

For the first time, Wilfred Thesiger's fascinating life-story has been compiled from his original works published over some thirty-five years. While newcomers to Thesiger's life and travels will read these extracts as a prelude to discovering the books from which they were taken, readers better acquainted with Thesiger's writing will find again many tantalizing glimpses or reminders of journeys among landscapes and people already familiar to them. From an editorial viewpoint the book's contents inevitably reflect some degree of personal bias. Indeed it would be surprising if this were not so.

The anthology has been divided into three parts. Part One (1910–45) begins with the arrival of Thesiger's parents in Ethiopia (then Abyssinia) where he was born and brought up. It ends with the Second World War and his return to Ethiopia as the Crown Prince's Political Advisor.

The second part (1945–60) includes Thesiger's five 'most memorable' years in Arabia, followed by seven years which he spent mainly with the Marsh Arabs in southern Iraq. During this period, he travelled at intervals in Morocco and among the mountains of western Asia.

Part Three (1960–94) describes Thesiger's life and travels in northern Kenya, Tanzania, Iran and Yemen. From 1978 to 1994 he lived with the pastoral Samburu near Maralal, a small township which he had first visited in 1961. It was there, among his adoptive African 'families', that Thesiger had hoped to end his days.

Above all, these selected passages celebrate the great traveller's finest writing illustrated with many of his superb photographs – a fitting testimony to the legendary journeys Wilfred Thesiger has made throughout his long and remarkably adventurous life.

Alexander Maitland
London, 2002

BIOGRAPHICAL SUMMARY and LIST OF PRINCIPAL TRAVELS, 1910–2001

1910	*June*	Born at the British Legation, Addis Ababa.
1910–19		Mainly in Addis Ababa.
1911	*February-March*	Journey by mule and camel to Diredawa, then by train to Jibuti on the coast; leave in England.
1914		Leave in England.
1916		Rebellion in Abyssinia.
	October	Battle of Sagale.
1917	*February*	Coronation of the Empress Zauditou.
	December	Leave. Berbera, British Somaliland.
1918	*January*	Leave. Berbera; Aden; India; Delhi and Jaipur.
	April	Return to Addis Ababa.
1919	*May*	Back to England.
	September	Started at preparatory school, Sussex.
1919–23		Preparatory school.
1924–28		Eton.

1929–33		Magdalen College, Oxford.
1930	*June-July*	Worked passage as fireman on S.S. *Sorrento* to Constantinople and Constanza.
	October-November	Attached to the Duke of Gloucester's Mission to Abyssinia for the Coronation of Emperor Haile Selassie.
	December	Journey in the Danakil country of Abyssinia.
1931	*January*	Back at Oxford.
	July	Worked on a trawler off Iceland.
1933	*June*	Went down from Oxford.
	August-December	To Addis Ababa; journey through the Arussi mountains; exploration of the Awash River and to Bahdu in Danakil country.
1934	*February-May*	Addis Ababa to Bahdu; exploration of Aussa (Danakil); then through French Somaliland to the coast at Tajura; then to England.
	December	Cairo, Egypt.
1935–40		Mainly in the Anglo-Egyptian Sudan.
1935	*January*	Sudan Political Service; Kutum, Northern Darfur.
1936	*June*	Syria and Palestine (on leave).
1937	*November*	Morocco (on leave). Posted to Western Nuer District, Upper Nile.
1938	*August-November*	Journey to Tibesti (on leave), in French Equatorial Africa.
1939	*July*	England (on leave). Returned to Sudan on outbreak of war.

1940	*June*	With Sudan Defence Force at Galabat, fighting against the Italians.
1941	*January-June*	With 101 Mission in Gojam, Abyssinia; and with Wingate's Gideon Force, campaign to liberate Abyssinia.
	July-mid 1942	Syrian campaign with Druze Legion at Jebel Druze; then with Special Operations Executive (SOE) in Syria.
1942	*June*	To Egypt, with SOE.
	December	To Western Desert and Tripolitania with Special Air Service (SAS).
1943	*June*	To Palestine, with SAS.
1944	*February*	Dessie, northern Abyssinia, as Political Advisor.
1945–50		A substantial part of each year spent in Arabia.
1945	*February*	Left Abyssinia.
	April-June	Saudi Arabia with Desert Locust Unit.
	July-September	England.
	September	Western Aden Protectorate.
	October	Dhaufar; Salala and Qarra Mountains.
	November-December	Southern edge of the Empty Quarter.
1946	*January-March*	Salala to the Hadhramaut.
	April-July	The Hejaz; the Tihama; the Assir; England.
	October-December	Dhaufar; first crossing of the Empty Quarter.
1947	*January-February*	Return to Salala via Inner Oman.
	March-May	Salala to Mukalla (Hadhramaut).
	May-August	The Hejaz; the Tihama; the Assir; Najran.

	September-October	England. Declined permanent Locust Control appointment in the Hejaz.
	November	Hadhramaut; preparations for second crossing of the Empty Quarter.
	December	Began approach to second crossing, from Shibam.
1948	*January-March*	From Manwakh to Sulaiyil. Thence across to Abu Dhabi, Trucial Coast.
	April-May	Buraimi; Sharja; Dubai; by dhow to Bahrain.
	June-September	England.
	October-December	Dubai; by launch to Abu Dhabi; Buraimi; Liwa oasis.
1949	*January-April*	Journeys through Inner Oman; back to Trucial Coast.
	May	By boat via Kuwait to Bushire (Persia); by road through Persia; thence to Iraqi Kurdistan; to Baghdad; later to England.
	November	Back to Trucial Coast.
1950	*January-April*	Second journey into Inner Oman. Left Trucial Coast, by air from Sharja.
	July-September	Iraqi Kurdistan.
	October	The Marshes of Iraq.
	November	Meshed, in Persia.
1951–58		A substantial part of each year except 1957 spent in the Marshes of Iraq.
1951	*February*	The Marshes.
	May-September	Iraqi Kurdistan.
	October	The Marshes.
1952	*February*	The Marshes.
	July-October	Pakistan; North West Frontier Province; Swat and Chitral.

12

1953	*February*	The Marshes.
	August-October	Pakistan; Hunza.
1954	*February*	The Marshes.
	August-September	Afghanistan; the Hazarajat.
1955	*February*	The Marshes.
	August	Morocco; the High Atlas.
1956	*February*	The Marshes.
	July-August	Afghanistan; Nuristan.
	September	The Marshes.
1957		Writing *Arabian Sands*.
1958	*January-June*	The Marshes.
1959		Abyssinia; with mules from Addis Ababa to the Kenya border (Moyale) and back.
1960	*February*	Abyssinia; with mules from Addis Ababa to Lake Tana; the Simien Mountains; back to Addis Ababa. Back to England.
	December	Kenya; Nairobi; safari with camels in Northern Province.
1961		Safari on foot in Kenya.
1961–2		Writing *The Marsh Arabs*.
1962		Safari on foot in Kenya. Climbed Mt Kilimanjaro (Tanganyika).
1963		Tanganyika; donkey journey through the Maasai country.
1964	*June-December*	Persia. Elburz Mountains; with Bakhtiari migration through Zagros Mountains; Dasht-i-Lut.
1965	*June-September*	Afghanistan; Nuristan and Badakhshan; later by road from

		Kabul via Balkh and Herat to Meshed (Persia).
1966	*May*	To Addis Ababa: ceremony for 25th anniversary of its liberation.
	June-November	With the Royalist forces in the Yemen. Then to England.
1967	*November*	Again with the Royalists in the Yemen.
1968	*January*	Back to England.
1968–76		Kenya, nine months each year, mainly on safari.
1977	*January-March*	From Kenya, via Ethiopia (Addis Ababa and Danakil country), to revisit the Yemen (Yemen Arab Republic), Oman (Muscat, Inner Oman and Dhaufar) and Abu Dhabi (United Arab Emirates).
	March-June	England; later by air to the Far East.
	July-December	Voyage by ketch: Bali, Kalimantan (Borneo), Sulawesi (Celebes), Sarawak, Brunei; visited Royal Geographical Society expedition to Mt Mulu in Sarawak for two weeks. Then by ketch to Singapore. Later to Malay Peninsula; Kuala Lumpur.
1978	*January-March*	India; Delhi; Hyderabad. Began to write *Desert, Marsh and Mountain*.
	March-June	England.
	June-December	Kenya, mainly on safari.
1979	*January-March*	Kenya.
	March-June	England and France.
	June-September	Kenya.
	September	England; *Desert, Marsh and Mountain* published.
	September-December	Kenya.

1980	*January-March*	Kenya.
	March-June	England via Egypt.
	June-December	Kenya.
1981	*January-March*	Kenya.
	March-June	England via Egypt.
	June-December	Kenya via Egypt.
1982	*January-April*	Kenya.
	April-June	England (Lawi with WT in England May/June).
	July-December	Kenya.
1983	*January-April*	Kenya.
	April-July	England.
	July-August	Yugoslavia; Bosnia.
	August	India.
	September-October	Ladakh via Kashmir.
	October-December	India – Delhi, Jaisalmer, Bandhavgarh.
1984	*January-February:*	India – Hyderabad. Writing *The Life of My Choice*.
	February-March	Bandhavgarh.
	March-April	Nepal – Kathmandu; Annapurna Range.
	April-July	England.
	July-December	Kenya.
1985	*January-April*	Kenya.
	April-July	England.
	July-December	Kenya. Writing *The Life of My Choice*.
1986	*January-April*	Kenya.
	April-September	England.
	September-December	Kenya.
1987	*January-March/April*	Kenya.
	April-August	England.
	August-November	Kenya.

	November-December	England (*Visions of a Nomad* published).
1988	January-February	England.
	February-June	Kenya.
	June-September	England.
	September-December	Kenya.
1989	January-March	Kenya.
	March-June	England.
	June-October	Kenya.
	October-November	England.
	November-December	Kenya.
1990	January	Kenya.
	February	United Arab Emirates.
	February-April	Kenya.
	April-June	England.
	June-July	Kenya.
	July-August	Zimbabwe; Malawi.
	August-December	Kenya.
1991	January-April	Kenya.
	April-June	England.
	June-July	Kenya.
	July	Botswana; Okavango Swamps.
	July-October	Kenya.
	October	United Arab Emirates; Oman.
	October-December	Kenya.
1992	January-June	Kenya.
	June-July	England.
	July-December	Kenya. Began to dictate *My Kenya Days*.
1993	January-May	Kenya.
	May-June	England.
	June-October	Kenya.
	October	England.
	November	Kenya via United Arab Emirates.
	November-December	Kenya.

1994	*January-April*	Kenya.
	April-May	England.
	May-June	United Arab Emirates.
	June-October	Kenya.
	October	Left Kenya to settle permanently in England.
1995	*January-December*	England. Knighthood. Began editing *The Danakil Diary*.
1996	*May-June*	Ethiopia, centenary celebrations at Addis Ababa.
	June-July	Spain – Seville, Algeciras.
	December	United Arab Emirates.
1997	*February*	Began compiling *Among the Mountains*.
	April	South Africa – Zululand.
	May	Selected photographs for *Crossing the Sands*.
1998	*June*	Moved from London to live in Surrey.
1999		Working on *A Vanished World*.
2000	*January*	Gibraltar.
	February-March	United Arab Emirates.
	June	Paris.
2001		*A Vanished World* published.

PROLOGUE

A cloud gathers, the rain falls, men live; the cloud disperses without rain, and men and animals die. In the deserts of southern Arabia there is no rhythm of the seasons, no rise and fall of sap, but empty wastes where only the changing temperature marks the passage of the year. It is a bitter, desiccated land which knows nothing of gentleness or ease. Yet men have lived there since earliest times. Passing generations have left fire-blackened stones at camping sites, a few faint tracks polished on the gravel plains. Elsewhere the winds wipe out their footprints. Men live there because it is the world into which they were born; the life they lead is the life their forefathers led before them; they accept hardships and privations; they know no other way. Lawrence wrote in *Seven Pillars of Wisdom*, 'Bedouin ways were hard, even for those brought up in them and for strangers terrible: a death in life.' No man can live this life and emerge unchanged. He will carry, however faint, the imprint of the desert, the brand which marks the nomad; and he will have within him the yearning to return, weak or insistent according to his nature. For this cruel land can cast a spell which no temperate clime can match.

from *Arabian Sands*

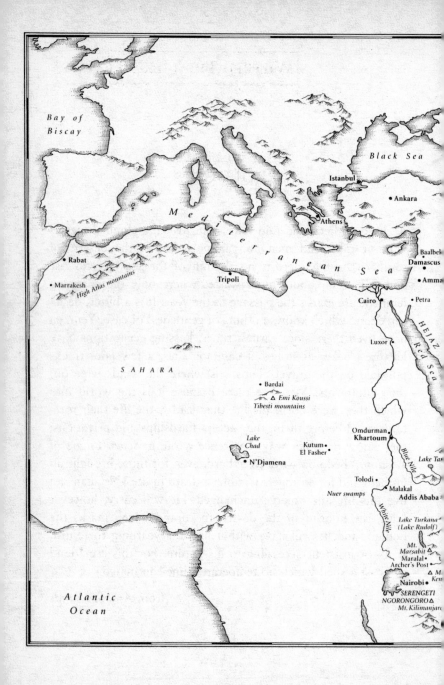

WILFRED THESIGER'S TRAVELS

Caspian Sea

Aral Sea

Lake Van

Elburz mountains

Tehran

Baghdad

Isfahan

Dasht-i-Lut

Marshes

Basra

Yazd

Zagros mountains

Persian Gulf

Riyadh

Dubai

Abu Dhabi

Liwa Oasis

Muscat

Umm al Samim
(quicksands)

RUB AL KHALI
(Empty Quarter)

OMAN

HADHRAMAUT

Salala

Sana'a

Aden

Djibouti

Berbera

Dire Dawa

Harar

ogadishu

ro R.

Hindu Kush range

Rakaposhi

Karakoram range

Puchal

Gilgit

Kabul

Srinagar

Leh

HAZARAJAT

Simla

Himalaya

Annapurna range

Delhi

Kathmandu

Jaisalmer

Jaipur

Bandhavgarh

Arabian
Sea

Hyderabad

Bay of
Bengal

Indian
Ocean

PART ONE
1910–45

I have sometimes wondered what strange compulsion has driven me from my own land to wander in the deserts of the east, living year after year among alien peoples, often in great hardship, with no thought of material reward. The urge to travel and explore probably originated in my childhood. Certainly it was an unusual childhood.

I was born in 1910, the eldest of four brothers, in one of the mud buildings which initially housed the Legation at Addis Ababa where my father was British Minister. Indistinct recollections of camels and of tents, of a river and men with spears, and one vivid picture of my father shooting an oryx when I was three – these are among my earliest memories. But these early memories of desert travel are almost gone, overlaid by later ones of the Abyssinian highlands, for it was there I lived till I was nearly nine.

The golden broom in the garden, iridescent sunbirds among the flowers, the juniper bushes and red gullies behind the house, our *syce* waiting with the ponies, a camp by a waterfall, the dipping flight of green and chestnut bee-eaters, and the crimson flash of a touraco's wings among the trees – these are a few pictures that spring to mind from scores of others. I remember sitting beside my father in the twilight above a gorge, hoping he would get a shot at a leopard; I remember looking for blood-stains and cartridge cases near a small bridge where there had been a fight; listening to my father as he read to me of big game hunting and ox wagons and Zulus, from *Jock of the Bushveld*, as the sun went down behind Wochercher; watching in shocked disbelief the lance head come out through the shoulder of our favourite *sowar* when he had an accident getting on his horse, his grey face and closed eyes as I sat miserably beside him after my brother Brian had galloped off for help. He had dismounted to show us a bird's nest. I can see again the white-robed priests dancing in line before the Ark of the Covenant to the beat of silver drums, surrounded by other priests in richly coloured robes, holding silver crosses in their hands. Above all I can remember some of the events during the Rebellion of 1916 when Lij Yasu was deposed: watching the armies going forth to fight, a seemingly chaotic flood of warriors, mounted and on foot; jostling women driving mules and donkeys laden with pots and sacks of grain; all moving inexorably northward; over-hearing the news that Ras Lul Seged's army had been wiped out and that Negus Michael, Lij Yasu's father and king of the north, was advancing on Addis Ababa; seeing Ras Tafari, later to become Haile Selassie, walk up the Legation steps when he brought his infant son to my father for safekeeping, before he went north to give final battle; hearing the mass rifle-fire in the town, celebrating the news of overwhelming victory.

Two days later the army came in. Throughout the day they poured past the Royal Pavilion to the thunder of war drums and the blare of trumpets. They were still frenzied with the excitement of that desperate battle, when sixty thousand men fought hand-to-hand on the plains around Sagale. The blood on the clothes they had stripped from the dead was barely dry. All of them carried shields and brandished rifles, spears or naked swords. Most of them were in white, but the chiefs were in full panoply of war, lion-mane head-dresses, velvet cloaks of many colours, long silken shirts; their shields were embossed with silver or gilt as were the scabbards of their swords. Above this endless tide of men the banners dipped and danced, red, gold and green, the colours of the Empire. Wave after wave, horsemen and men on foot, mixed in seeming confusion, they surged past throughout the day, thrusting close to the steps of the Pavilion to boast of their prowess, while the Court Chamberlains beat them back with wands. Negus Michael was led past with a stone on his shoulder in token of submission, an old man in a black *burnous* with a white cloth wrapped about his head. Ras Lul Seged's young son came past at the head of a few hundred men, all that were left of the five thousand who had fought beside his father at Ankober. I remember the excited face of a boy, seemingly little older than myself, who was carried past in triumph. He had killed two men. At last it was over – a small English boy had watched a sight as barbaric and enthralling as was ever seen in Africa.

from *Desert, Marsh and Mountain*

In the summer of 1924, during my first year at Eton, Ras Tafari, later to be Emperor Haile Selassie but at that time Regent, paid a State Visit to England and invited my mother and me to call on him in London. I had seen him on a number of occasions during my childhood in Abyssinia where my father had been British Minister at Addis Ababa, but this was the first time I spoke to him. Wearing a black, gold-embroidered silk cloak over a finely woven *shamma*, he came across the room to greet us, shook hands and with a smile and a gesture invited us to be seated. He was very small but even then to my mind his slight body and lack of height emphasized his distinction, drawing attention to the sensitive and finely moulded face.

My first and lasting impression was of dignity, a dignity entirely unassumed; then I was conscious of his kindness. In years to come I was to appreciate his inflexible will, his intense patience, his courage, his horror of cruelty, his dedication to his country and his deep religious faith.

27

We spoke in French, the foreign language in which he was fluent. He expressed at once his sorrow for my father's death. 'I shall never forget', he said, 'the support and help he gave me during the critical months of the revolution in 1916. He was a friend on whose advice I could always count. Such friends are few.'

My mother enquired after Ras Tafari's wife and family, especially after his eldest son, Asfa Wossen, who as a baby at the time of the battle of Sagale had sheltered with us in the Legation; then they spoke of mutual friends, and recalled events that had occurred while we were in Abyssinia. Meanwhile tea and cakes were brought in. Later, as we took our leave, I told Ras Tafari how I longed above all to return to his country.

'You will always be very welcome. One day you must come as my guest.'

When my father arrived in Abyssinia in mid-December 1909 to take up his post as British Minister in charge of the Legation, the Emperor Menelik, the greatest ruler the country had known for centuries, was reported to be still alive; but no one knew for certain, and all men asked what would happen when he died.

For a year or more Menelik had lain in the palace, a living corpse, paralysed and speechless. He lived for another four years while his empire lapsed into chaos. He is said to have rallied before he died and to have whispered, 'My poor people', as the tears ran down his face. A few years earlier he had been the undisputed master of the empire: two hundred thousand of his warriors had paraded before him while a hundred thousand others guarded the marches of the north or fought the Somalis in the deserts to the east. He had founded Addis Ababa, 'the New Flower', below the Entoto mountains. Before his reign the site would have been on the southernmost borders of the empire; when he died it was at the empire's heart.

My father and mother had travelled by train from Jibuti, on the coast of French Somaliland, to Dire Dawa, the railhead in Abyssinia. They had brought all that they would require in Abyssinia: provisions, clothes, books, pictures, furniture, tents, saddlery. There were scores of boxes and crates, all to be checked and loaded before they left Dire Dawa.

My mother had been married only a few months, and had never previously been further abroad than Italy. She was now faced with an arduous journey into a remote country where there might well be anarchy when Menelik died. It was enough to daunt most people, but she once told me that the only thing that dismayed her was sorting out their incredible mass of luggage, making sure that the right things went by the right route and that nothing was left behind. The heavier loads were being sent to Addis Ababa on camels by the desert route, where the Danakil, always dangerous, were said to be giving more trouble than usual. My parents, using mule transport, travelled to Addis Ababa through the Chercher mountains, by way of Harar, that ancient walled city which Burton had reached fifty-four years earlier.

There my father was anxious to meet Dedjazmatch Balcha, Governor of the Muslim city of Harar and one of the most powerful men in Abyssinia. Balcha was a Gurage by origin; as a boy he had been wounded and castrated in one of the many battles which Menelik had fought while subduing the southern tribes. When the fighting was over Menelik noticed the boy and told his servants to tend him. Balcha recovered, grew up as a page in Menelik's household and later fought with distinction at Adua, where in 1896 the Abyssinians destroyed an Italian army. As Governor of Harar he had a well-merited reputation for ruthlessness, brutality and avarice, and was hated and feared by his subjects.

Two days after leaving Dire Dawa my parents camped in the highlands beside Haramaya Lake, a small stretch of water teeming with wildfowl, not far from Harar. Next day Balcha sent a force to escort my father to the town: my mother, who was pregnant and tired, remained in camp – and would regret it all her life.

The long, winding column of armed men, on horses, on mules and on foot, was an unforgettable sight as it moved across the plain in a haze of dust under a blazing sky. I wish my father had left a description of his encounter with Balcha but I can find none in his letters or despatches. That remarkable man was to play an important part in forthcoming events and twenty-six years later was killed fighting against the Italians once more.

A month later my parents were met on the open plain outside Addis Ababa by Lord Herbert Hervey, the Consul, and a deputation of Abyssinian notables who escorted them to the Legation, at some distance to the east of the town, in an extensive compound at the foot of the Entoto hills. The Legation consisted of connecting wattle-and-daub *tukuls*, each circular and thatched with grass. These buildings were comfortable and spacious, and had great charm. I was born in one of them in June 1910, the first British child born in Abyssinia. Not until the following year was the stone-built Legation completed, which houses the Embassy today.

In those days Great Britain was represented by an Ambassador in Paris, Berlin, St Petersburg, Rome, Constantinople and Washington, but in most other countries by a Minister Plenipotentiary in a Legation.

A few days after his arrival my father was received in

audience. In full diplomatic uniform he rode to the palace on a richly caparisoned mule sent to him by Menelik: in Abyssinia mules were more highly esteemed than horses. With him was my mother, the Consul and the mounted escort of Sikhs, and a small army even more colourful and far more numerous than the escort provided by Dedjazmatch Balcha. The palace was several miles from the Legation and every time they topped a rise my parents saw the whole procession spread out in front and behind.

By now Menelik was totally incapacitated and my father never met him. Instead he was greeted by Ras Tasamma, the Regent, and by Lij Yasu, the Emperor's fifteen-year-old grandson and heir. In a letter to his mother he described the day's events:

> At the main gate of the palace officials drove back the unauthor-ized with the unsparing use of long bamboos to clear a passage-way. Inside the large first court musicians blew on long, straight trumpets and negroes with long flutes added to the din which was very thrilling and appropriate.

They rode through another crowded court and came to the inner court lined only by chiefs. There they dismounted.

Lij Yasu sat on a dais in front of the throne. At that first meeting my father can have had no idea of the troubles this boy would bring upon his country.

Such was my father's introduction to Abyssinia where, except for three periods of leave, he was to remain for the next ten years.

My father was intensely and justifiably proud of his family, which in his own generation produced a viceroy, a general, an admiral, a Lord of Appeal, a High Court judge and a famous actor. Intelligent, sensitive and artistic, with a certain diffidence which added to his charm, he was above all a man of absolute integrity. He enjoyed sketching, writing verse and playing music. The faint sound of his cello, as I lay tucked up in bed, is woven into my childhood memories. He had an abiding love of the English countryside, loved horses and greatly enjoyed fox-hunting, the theme of several of his poems. With the Yeomanry in South Africa he had acquired much experience in horse management. In Addis Ababa he kept a large stable, trained the horses carefully, played polo with enthusiasm and won many races against the other Legations.

He was a natural games player; he had been a notable cricketer like several of his family, and had captained the school XI at Cheltenham. He had always been drawn to the sea, as is also evinced by his poems; at Taranto he became a keen yachtsman. In the Congo he had hunted big game for the first time and in Abyssinia he took every opportunity to do so, and conveyed his enthusiasm to me when I was only a small boy. I was known as Billy, and was three when he wrote to his mother:

> Billy goes out shooting every day but does not get much as his only weapons are a tennis bat and empty cartridge case which he hits at the birds. He says he can't get them flying but if they would only sit for him he is sure he could kill one. His sporting instincts are very strongly developed.

Kathleen Mary, my mother, was a Vigors from County Carlow where her family had long been established at Burgage, their ancestral home. She was the second of four children, two boys and two girls. When she was seven her parents separated and her mother took the children to England. My maternal grandmother was an undemonstrative and rather prudish woman, whereas my grandfather was rather a rake, a confirmed gambler and obviously excellent company. My mother remembered him with affection all her life. As she grew up she often visited relations in Ireland and she developed a lifelong romantic passion for that country, originating in her childhood adoration of Burgage.

Naturally adventurous, she loved the life in Abyssinia, where nothing daunted her. She shared my father's love of horses and enjoyed to the full the constant riding. Like him, she was an enthusiastic and skilful gardener: from a bare hillside they created the garden which is today such a delightful feature of the British Embassy in Addis Ababa. Since she was utterly devoted to my father, her children inevitably took second place. In consequence in my childhood memories she does not feature as much as my father; only later did I fully appreciate her forceful yet lovable character.

The ten years my parents spent in Abyssinia were undoubtedly the happiest of their lives.

from *The Life of My Choice*

When my father arrived there, Addis Ababa consisted of a series of scattered villages grouped on hillsides with open, uncultivated spaces in between. Menelik's palace crowned the largest hill; nearby a jumble of thatched huts and some corrugated-iron-roofed shacks clustered round the large open market. Nowhere were there any proper roads.

Abyssinians of any standing travelled everywhere on mule-back, followed by an armed mob of slaves and retainers, varying in number according to the importance of their master. Galla,

Somali, Gurage, people from the subject kingdom of Kaffa, negroes from the west, mingled on the streets with their Amhara and Tigrean overlords; but it was these latter who dominated the scene, imposed their stamp upon the town and gave it its unique character. Wrapped in white toga-like *shammas* worn over long white shirts and jodhpurs, they set a fashion which over the years was copied by an increasing number of their subjects.

The clothes, the buildings, the pitch and intonation of voices speaking Amharic; the smell of rancid butter, of red peppers and burning cow dung that permeated the town; the packs of savage dogs that roamed the streets and whose howling rose and fell through the night; an occasional corpse hanging on the gallows-tree; beggars who had lost a hand or foot for theft; debtors and creditors wandering round chained together; strings of donkeys bringing in firewood; caravans of mules; the crowded market where men and women squatted on the ground, selling earthen pots, lengths of cloths, skins, cartridges, bars of salt, silver ornaments, heaps of grain, vegetables, beer – all this combined to create a scene and an atmosphere unlike any other in the world.

On 10 April 1911 Ras Tasamma, the Regent, died of a stroke. My father had judged him 'to stand for everything that was most corrupt in officialdom'. He had, however, possessed authority. As soon as the Rases heard of his death they congregated in Addis Ababa, which soon resembled an armed camp. All normal business came to a standstill. At this critical moment my father had to escort an Abyssinian Mission, headed by Ras Kassa, to England to attend King George V's coronation. He set off for Dire Dawa by caravan on 4 May and arrived in England on 15 June. The five Abyssinian notables, in their full regalia, created a stir in the Abbey.

In order to avoid the hot weather my mother had preceded my father to England, escorted as far as Jibuti by an official from the Sudan who was temporarily serving at the Legation. My father was due four months' leave and this they spent at Beachley, his attractive house near Chepstow at the mouth of the Severn. In the family album are some photographs of me on the lawn with Susannah, my Indian *ayah*, to whom I was devoted. I was then a year old and she was with us till I was nearly four. With her I could do no wrong. When my mother remonstrated she would answer, 'He one handsome Rajah – why for he no do what he want?' I apparently walked at an unusually early age but was slow learning to speak. My mother always maintained that the first words I said were 'Go yay,' which meant 'Go away' and showed an independent spirit.

My brother Brian was born in October 1911, and my parents engaged Mary Buckle to look after us. She was eighteen and had never been out of England, yet she unhesitatingly set off for a remote and savage country in Africa. She gave us unfailing devotion and became an essential part of our family. As children we called her Minna, and she has been known to us and to our friends as Minna ever since. Now, after more than seventy years, she is still my cherished friend and confidante, the one person left with shared memories of those far-off days.

While my father was on his way to England, Lij Yasu, with the support of the Fitaurari Habta Giorgis, Menelik's commander-in-chief, seized the palace and assumed control of the country. He schemed to be proclaimed Emperor, but as long as Menelik was known to be alive this was impossible. Even after Menelik's death Lij Yasu was never crowned, possibly because he believed a prophecy that if he was crowned he would die. This omission certainly weakened his position during the struggle that lay ahead.

The situation in Abyssinia was becoming increasingly chaotic when my father returned there in January 1912. This was due in large part to the character of Lij Yasu. From the day he seized power in 1911 he thought of nothing but his own amusement and he was frequently absent from Addis Ababa, which he detested, for months on end. During his absence all government business, even the most trivial, came to a stop, since no minister was willing to make a decision while Lij Yasu was away.

Cruelty and arrogance predominated in his nature. He would watch an execution or a flogging with evident enjoyment. A story was even current that to prove his manhood he had killed and castrated a boy belonging to the palace.

In 1913, the year of Menelik's death, Lij Yasu wantonly attacked some Danakil encampments and massacred three hundred men, women and children. My father's explanation was that 'It was simply because he liked the sight of blood'. He had apparently adopted the Danakil custom of castrating the dead and dying. Count Colli, the Italian Minister, quoted one of Lij Yasu's officers as saying on his return from this expedition that Lij Yasu cut the breasts off a girl who had refused his advances, after he had watched her being raped by his soldiers.

By 1913 conditions on the boundary between Abyssinia and the British East Africa Protectorate, later known as Kenya, had become worse than usual, with frequent incursions by well-armed gangs of Abyssinians raiding for slaves and ivory. My father was therefore anxious to travel to Nairobi and discuss with the Governor measures to prevent these raids, as well as the possibility of delimiting the frontier and finding an answer to the demand by the Abyssinian Government for the return of the Boran and Gabbra tribesmen who had migrated in large

36

numbers into East Africa after Menelik's conquest of their homelands.

In November 1913 he accompanied his family on their way to England as far as the railhead, which had now reached the Awash river, and then returned to Addis Ababa. From there he set off with a caravan of mules on a journey of some eight hundred miles to Nairobi. His letters evince the excitement he felt at undertaking this journey, one which few Europeans had as yet made, and his anticipation of getting plenty of big game hunting on the way.

My father travelled to Nairobi by way of Mega, Moyale, Marsabit, Laisamis and Nyeri, all places with which I was to be familiar some fifty-five years later. After several days in Nairobi he took the train to Mombasa where he caught a ship to England; there, soon after my brother Dermot was born, he rejoined my mother. He was still on leave in England when war was declared on 4 August 1914. An accomplished linguist, fluent in German and French, he was accepted by the Army, given an appointment as a captain in the Intelligence Branch, and sent to France, where he arrived on 23 September. This posting was a remarkable achievement, considering the number of regular officers trying desperately to get to the front, dreading that the war would be over before they could take part. He was attached to the 3rd Army Corps, and while serving in France he earned a mention in despatches. The Foreign Office had only given him permission to join the Army on the understanding that he would return to Abyssinia when his leave expired. He returned to Addis Ababa with his family in January 1915.

Susannah had gone back to India in 1913 when we sailed from Jibuti to England. I suspect that in the excitement of going on board I hardly realized she was leaving me for good. In

England my parents engaged an elderly trained nurse to look after Dermot. We all called her Nanny; I never knew her name. She had charge of Dermot, and of Roderic, born a year later in the Legation.

On 27 October 1916 the armies of the north and south had joined battle on the plain of Sagale, sixty miles north of Addis Ababa, and there they fought hand-to-hand throughout the day. Finally Negus Michael was captured, and his army was routed and largely destroyed. Forty-four years later I visited the battlefield and saw skulls and bones in crevices on the rocky hillock where Negus Michael had made his final stand.

A few days later the victorious army entered Addis Ababa and paraded before the Empress Zauditu on Jan Meda, that great open space where Menelik had reviewed his troops.

Early that morning my father and mother, with Brian and me, preceded by the Legation escort with their red and white pennoned lances, rode down the wide lane between Balcha's troops to the royal pavilion. The war drums throbbed, a muffled, far-carrying, never-ceasing sound that thrilled me to the core; the five-foot trumpets brayed. Above the lines of waiting troops a host of banners fluttered in the breeze.

I can recall almost every detail: the embroidered caps of the drummers decorated with cowries; a man falling off his horse as he charged by; a small boy carried past in triumph – he had killed two men though he seemed little older than myself; the face of Ras Lul Seged's young son, and the sheepskin over his shoulder. I had been reading *Tales from the Iliad*. Now, in boyish fancy, I watched the likes of Achilles, Ajax and Ulysses pass in triumph with aged Priam, proud even in defeat. I believe that day implanted in me a life-long craving for barbaric splendour, for savagery and colour and the throb of drums, and that it gave me a lasting veneration for long-established custom and ritual, from which would derive later a deep-seated resentment of Western innovations in other lands, and a distaste for the drab uniformity of the modern world.

By December 1917 my father badly needed leave. The altitude of Addis Ababa, at eight thousand feet, was affecting his heart. He had been short-handed, overworked and under considerable strain as a result of the events leading to the Revolution, well aware of the importance of its success to the Allied cause, and the danger to his family if the Revolution failed. On being granted leave, he decided to take us to India and visit his brother, Lord Chelmsford, the Viceroy.

At Viceregal Lodge we were housed in palatial tents luxuriously carpeted and furnished, and were looked after by a host of servants. There were rows of similar tents on the lawns, for the accommodation in the Lodge itself was limited. The Government of India had only moved to Delhi from Calcutta in 1911, and the magnificent Lutyens buildings which today dominate New Delhi were still being built.

From the moment I arrived I was immensely impressed by the pomp and the ceremony which surrounded my uncle as Viceroy, fascinated by the splendour of the bodyguard, and the varied liveries and elaborate turbans of the doorkeepers, messengers, coachmen, household servants and other functionaries.

I had grown up in Addis Ababa where there were few permanent buildings other than the Legations. I had only the vaguest recollections of England. I therefore associated towns with tin roofs and thatched huts; in Jibuti, Berbera and Aden I had seen no memorable buildings. I was totally unprepared for Delhi, yet old enough to understand what I saw. The Moghul tombs, the Red Fort, the towering minarets of the Jami Masjid, made me aware for the first time of the significance of civilization, and the meaning of history.

One afternoon we were taken to the Ridge above Delhi where British troops had held out against constant attacks during the Mutiny. We were shown a bullet-ridden orb, lying on the ground, that had once decorated the church spire. My father described to me how the Guides had arrived and gone straight into action after marching day and night from the Punjab; how Nicholson had been killed leading the troops as they stormed the ramparts of Delhi. He told me that my grandfather had fought in the Mutiny, and that Mrs Inglis, daughter of my great-grandfather Chelmsford, had been in Lucknow through the siege, where her husband commanded the troops.

My parents went to visit the Rajput States while we boys continued to go for rides in the mornings and picnics in the afternoons. Perhaps a fortnight later Brian and I were sent with Minna to join them at Jaipur, where they were guests of the Maharajah. We travelled there by train; I remember herds of blackbuck grazing near the line and bullock-carts lumbering along in clouds of dust.

When we arrived at Jaipur my father told us that he had sent for us so that we could go with him tiger-shooting. I could hardly believe what I heard. I do not remember how long we stayed at Jaipur but every day was packed with excitement. From the backs of elephants we watched pig-sticking, and went out after blackbuck in a bullock-cart; my father shot two, each with a good head. Then the great day dawned.

Soon after breakfast we set off into the jungle. We saw some wild boar which paid little attention to our passing elephants, and we saw several magnificent peacock and a number of monkeys; to me the monkeys were *bandar log*, straight out of

Kipling's *Jungle Book*. It must have taken a couple of hours or more to reach the *machan*, a platform raised on poles. We climbed up on to it; someone blew a horn and the beat started. After a time I could hear distant shouts. I sat very still, hardly daring to move my head. A peacock flew past. Then my father slowly raised his rifle and there was the tiger, padding towards us along a narrow game trail, his head moving from side to side. I still remember him as I saw him then. He was magnificent, larger even than I had expected, looking almost red against the pale dry grass.

My father fired. I saw the tiger stagger. He roared, bounded off and disappeared into the jungle. He was never found, though they searched for him on elephants while we returned to the palace. I was very conscious of my father's intense disappointment. Two days later we went on another beat, this time for panther, but the panther broke back and we never saw it. However, a great sambhur stag did gallop past the *machan*. Scenes such as this remained most vividly in my memory.

Before Brian and I went to school we had hardly met any other English boys; I remember only one, Standish Roche, who lived nearby while we were in Ireland. Gerald Campbell, Consul in Addis Ababa during our last years there, had two children, a little younger than me, but they were girls and had no part in our lives. There had been no other English children in Abyssinia, none in Somaliland, none at Aden, and in Delhi I can only remember meeting girls.

Suddenly at St Aubyn's we found ourselves in a crowd of seventy boys, nearly all older. There was no privacy anywhere; we were always among others; whether in classrooms, dining room or gymnasium, on the playing fields or in the dormitory at night. School-boys are very conventional and quick to gang

41

up on any boy who in behaviour or dress does not conform. With our extraordinary background, Brian and I lacked the ability to cope with our contemporaries; as English boys who had barely heard of cricket we were natural targets.

Soon after we arrived I was interrogated about my parents and our home life. At first I was a friendly, forthcoming little boy, very ready to talk, perhaps to boast about journeys I had made and things I had seen. My stories, however, were greeted with disbelief and derision, and I felt increasingly rejected. As a result I withdrew into myself, treated overtures of friendship with mistrust, and was easily provoked. I made few friends, but once I adapted to this life I do not think I was particularly unhappy. I could comfort myself, especially at night, by re-calling the sights and scenery of Abyssinia, far more real to me than the cold bleak English downs behind the school.

St Aubyn's had a good reputation when my father decided to send us there. Unfortunately, just before we arrived, a new headmaster, R. C. V. Lang, took over. He was unmarried; his sister looked after him. He was a large, imposing man who had been a noted athlete and I am sure he created a favourable impression on my parents. In fact he was a sadist, and after my father's death both Brian and I were among his victims. The school motto was 'Quit you like men: be strong', an exhor-tation not without relevance to some of us boys. He beat me on a number of occasions, often for some trivial offence. Sent up early to the dormitory, I had to kneel naked by the side of my bed. I remember crying out the first time, 'It hurts!' and Lang saying grimly, 'It's meant to.'

For two or three days after each beating, I was called to his study so that he could see I was healing properly. Though I had never been hurt like this before, strangely enough I bore him no resentment for these beatings, accepting them as the penalty for what I had done. It never occurred to me how disproportionate was the punishment to the offence.

I was an unreceptive boy to teach, disinclined to concentrate on any subject that bored me. I certainly learnt next to nothing at St Aubyn's and when I took the Common Entrance examination for Eton I failed so ignominiously that the authorities wrote to my mother that it would be futile for me to try again. Undismayed, she sent me to a first-class crammer for two terms, and Brian to another preparatory school. At my next attempt I passed into Eton a whole form from the bottom of the school.

Early in September 1923 I arrived at Windsor Station with my mother, and from there we drove in a horse-drawn cab past the Castle and across the Thames into Eton. There were twenty-four houses at Eton, each with about forty-five boys who were known as Oppidans and were distinct from the seventy Scholars who lived apart in College. Each house was run by a senior master and was known by his name. My housemaster was A. M. McNeile. We had tea with him and his wife and met the three other new boys and their parents: Harry Phillimore, small, dark-haired and bespectacled; Ronnie Chance, slim, blond and diffident; and Desmond Parsons, a tall, good-looking boy.

Harry Phillimore was to become a lifelong friend. Scholarly and intensely hard-working, his otherwise serious nature was lightened by a streak of mischief. We were an unruly lot of Lower boys at McNeile's and it was usually Harry Phillimore who instigated the disturbances we caused. He died in 1974, a Lord Justice of Appeal. Listening once to him on the Bench I recalled an occasion when the aged and formidable boys' maid who looked after our rooms had stood with arms akimbo accusing him of some peccadillo, and ended her tirade: 'Mr Phillimore, don't you stand there lying like Ananias!'

Our worst enormity was when we flushed Desmond Parsons out of his room with the fire hydrant and, having turned it on, could not turn it off. Water was soon cascading down the stairs from the top storey. Eventually McNeile appeared, holding his trousers above his knees, and muttering, 'Hooligans, damned hooligans,' he turned it off. That was one of the many occasions when we were sent for after supper and beaten by the Library (the Etonian equivalent of house prefects).

Only once did I bear resentment after being beaten. I had been selected in my second year at Eton, while I was still a Lower boy, to box against the Eton Mission from Hackney Wick in the East End of London. I was giving tea to my opponent who, though the same weight, was probably two years older, when I was sent for by Julian Hall, my fag master. He was head of the house, in the sixth form, captain of the Oppidans and in consequence in Pop (the equivalent of school prefects).

'Why have you not turned up to cook my tea?' he demanded.

'I'm sorry,' I replied, 'I forgot to tell you I'm boxing against the Eton Mission tonight and am giving tea in my room to the boy I'm boxing.'

'I'll teach you to forget. Bend over,' he said, and gave me six with his Pop cane, a stiff, knotted bamboo. I have often wondered what my guest would have thought when I got back if I had told him I had just been beaten. I never forgave Hall. Anyone else would have said, 'Good luck. Be sure to beat him.' It was an unfortunate evening for me: I was knocked out in the second round, the only time I was knocked out, either at Eton or at Oxford.

It is winter evenings at Eton that I remember most vividly: talking and arguing about anything and everything with friends in front of a coal fire; sitting in my armchair with my feet up, reading a story by Buchan, Kipling or Conrad, or something by one of the African big-game hunters whose books I was already collecting. There was a civilized comfort about these winter evenings that gained by contrast with the hardships of daytime.

Many people assume that Eton is a luxurious school. When I was there it was one of the most spartan in the country. The Thames Valley is often bitterly cold and damp. The classrooms were heated in winter, but in the houses there was no form of heating until we lit fires in our rooms at six in the evening. We were given a lot of work to prepare in our spare time and I remember trying to keep warm in the daytime in an overcoat and scarf while I wrote an essay or struggled with Latin composition. After a hard frost the passage walls sweated and water trickled down the corridors. In McNeile's there were no changing rooms or showers, only foot baths in which we could wash after games, and only two baths and five lavatories for forty-seven of us. Except for the Library, who could bath at any time, a boy was allocated two baths a week. It never occurred to us to criticize these conditions, which we accepted as a part of Eton life, like the tailcoats and top hats we wore.

I went up to Magdalen College, Oxford, in the autumn of 1929 and was there four years. Most of my Eton contemporaries at Oxford were at Christ Church, Trinity, Balliol or New College, and it was with them I spent much of my time. Nevertheless, I was always thankful that I was at Magdalen, perhaps the most beautiful of Oxford colleges. Though small it was spacious, with its deer park and Addison's Walk along the bank of the Cherwell. My memories of Oxford, unlike my memories of Eton, are summer ones: the tranquil beauty of the High Street in the early morning before the traffic; May morning and the choirboys singing on Magdalen Tower; reading in a punt on the river beneath overhanging willows; the water meadows beyond

Parsons' Pleasure, and the sound of corn-crakes; sailing with Robin Campbell on Port Meadow and then tea together at the Trout Inn; dinner parties in my rooms, with evening light on the College buildings and the scent of wallflowers from the President's garden.

During my last summer vacation from Oxford, I worked my passage in a tramp steamer bound for the Black Sea.

On 28 June 1930 in the East India Docks I climbed the gangway of the *Sorrento* and set foot on her rusty iron deck. I was thrilled at the prospect ahead of me but diffident and embarrassed at joining a community so totally unfamiliar. I need not have worried; the officers and men were welcoming and friendly. The crew consisted of the captain, first, second and third mates, chief and second engineer, wireless operator, bosun, carpenter and eighteen other hands. On board was a Maltese deck passenger who boasted he had been in nine different prisons in England; after we had sailed a friend of his was discovered stowed away in the chain locker.

I found I had the best of both worlds. I worked regular hours as an ordinary member of the crew but fed with the officers; the food was substantial and good. I was given the bosun's cabin to sleep in. I apologized to him for this but he said, 'I'm glad to be out of it. Wait till you see the cockroaches.'

During the next four weeks we steamed from one port to another, unloading and loading a variety of cargoes. I was doing my four hours on and eight off, and as a supernumerary was given a variety of jobs. Most of the time I worked in the bunkers, trying to keep the stoker supplied with enough coal to fire the furnaces; he would rattle his shovel in the hatch if I fell behind. This was hard, hot, dirty, choking work. At other times I chipped rust off the deck, painted the boats and, in harbour, helped to repaint the ship's side or check the discharge of cargo.

Sometimes during the mate's watch I took the wheel and learnt to steer. The first time or two he exclaimed, 'For God's sake, man, keep her steady. It'd break a snake's back to follow your course.'

We called briefly at Gibraltar where I just had time to walk up the Rock and see the apes. We then sailed along the African coast. The Rif mountains were clearly visible; somewhere among them Abd al Karim and his fellow tribesmen had destroyed a Spanish army of sixteen thousand men in 1921. They had then invaded French Morocco and, after desperate fighting, had threatened Fez. At Eton I had gone each day to Spottiswoode's bookshop to follow the course of this war in *The Times*. I remember my despondency in 1926 when Abd al Karim was forced to surrender to the French.

At Malta a battle cruiser, an aircraft carrier and three destroyers were anchored in the inner harbour. We were only there for twenty-four hours, working throughout the night. Our next port of call was Piraeus, which I thought a dirty, uninteresting place. In the distance I could see the rock-girt Acropolis crowned by the ruins of the Parthenon. Without any great enthusiasm I visited Athens. The weather was hot and I felt little interest in ruins; but the Parthenon proved to have a matchless beauty for which I was quite unprepared.

We were four days in Piraeus and every day I went back to the Acropolis. At that time few tourists went to Greece during the summer; some goats wandered among the fallen pillars, the goatherd dozed in the shade, otherwise I had the place to myself. It was utterly peaceful, sitting there in the hot sun with the scent of thyme around me and a view of distant Hymettos over the tiled roofs of Athens. Only a murmur rose from the town below me. Two lesser kestrels, the first I had ever seen, flew to and fro above my head.

We left for Salonika on 17 July, arrived next morning, and stayed two days, which gave me time to explore the older part of the town. From the ramparts I had a view across the bay to green marshes and, far above them, rising above a swathe of cloud, the snow-covered summit of Olympus, infinitely remote.

We sailed across the Aegean to Izmir, which till recently had been called Smyrna; and the captain told me how, a few years earlier, as he entered the port, his ship had nosed her way through the floating corpses of Greeks massacred by the Turks. The town had been largely burnt and rebuilt; it looked uninteresting and, as there was a lot of work to be done on board, I did not go ashore.

Our next port of call would be Constantinople – or, as it had just been renamed, Istanbul. We passed Lesbos, Lemnos and other Greek islands floating in the haze on a calm sea, each more beautiful than the last. Then we sailed through the Dardanelles, past beaches and rocky scrub-covered hills, once the scene of so much unavailing gallantry and sacrifice.

On the other side of the straits was Asia and the site of Troy. The sun was setting as we anchored off Constantinople; in the twilight a crescent moon hung low above a silhouette of domes and minarets. I could hardly wait to land.

In the morning I went ashore with the captain in a bumboat, passing a variety of small craft that plied to and fro across the straits. At the ship's office I was informed that Sir George Clerk, the British Ambassador, had sent a message that as soon as I landed I was to call on him at the Embassy. I knew he had been a colleague of my father; I wondered how he knew I was on the *Sorrento*.

I felt embarrassed at the prospect of meeting him. I am conventional enough to dislike appearing anywhere in unsuitable clothes. Here I was wearing a shirt and an old pair of grey flannel trousers; they were clean, for I had washed them, but they were certainly not suitable for calling on an ambassador. However, I had nothing better on board and could not ignore his summons.

I had some difficulty in securing admission to the Embassy, past a *kavas* in a spectacular scarlet uniform. A secretary showed me into an ornately furnished drawing room and a few minutes later Sir George came in. He had a distinguished air, was formally dressed in a tailcoat, and was precisely my idea of an ambassador. He accepted my apologies for my appearance and quickly put me at ease, saying he had been a close friend of my father and was delighted to meet his son.

I told him that ever since listening to my father's vivid descriptions of Constantinople I had always wanted to visit the city, but that I had been sadly disillusioned by the Turks I had seen on my way to the Embassy; they had looked so incongruous in second-hand European clothes. Sir George agreed that the place was very different now from my father's time. The Sultan had since abdicated, the Caliphate had been abolished, the Dervish orders had been suppressed and most traditional ceremonies and pageantry had been done away with. But in spite of the changes, Sir George insisted that Constantinople was still a fascinating city, superbly sited, full of interest, and worth visiting just to see Hagia Sophia.

The *Sorrento* remained four days at Constantinople. In that time I followed the course of the massive city walls which over the centuries had sustained so many assaults before falling at last to the Turkish onslaught. I wandered among turbanned headstones in the Muslim cemetery, mingled with the crowds on the Galata Bridge over the Golden Horn, and ate Turkish food in unpretentious eating-houses on the waterfront. I visited the underground cisterns, spent hours in the covered bazaar and a whole morning among the treasures of the Seraglio. But most of my time I spent in the many and varied mosques, and each day I went back to Hagia Sophia, sometimes remaining for hours. Built by Justinian as the centre of Christian worship, this miraculous embodiment of space had been converted by the victorious Turks, with only minor modifications, into their foremost mosque and had been taken as the prototype for others which they built. None, however, rivalled it. The Blue Mosque and the Mosque of Suleiman the Magnificent were more impressive from outside; but inside them I was conscious of confinement.

On a Friday I witnessed the midday prayers in Hagia Sophia. Now that religious observance was officially discouraged only a few hundred worshippers were present. A few years previously thousands would have attended. This was the first time I saw an Islamic service and I was impressed by the unhurried, synchronized movements of the worshippers and by the sonorous rhythm of their prayers.

On 28 July 1930 I disembarked from the *Sorrento* at Constanza in the Black Sea. I was touched by the good wishes of the crew when I went ashore. I had enjoyed every minute of the past month. No luxury cruise around the Mediterranean could have been half as rewarding: I should have been fed up at sea and embarrassed ashore, always conscious of the intrusion of our party as we were shown the sights.

Back at The Milebrook I found two letters waiting for me. One was an invitation from Ras Tafari to attend his coronation as the Emperor Haile Selassie. The other was a notification from the Foreign Office that I had been appointed Honorary Attaché to HRH the Duke of Gloucester who would attend the coronation as the representative of his father, King George V.

from *The Life of My Choice*

Wednesday 5th November

Dear Mother

The coronation was almost too wonderful to attempt to describe. It began at six in the morning and lasted till one.

The actual coronation was held in a canvas building added onto St George's Cathedral, which was well arranged so that it did not jar.

We were all able to get in and were not at all crowded. The Emperor and Empress (who is to have a child in a month's time and consequently has the European midwife as lady-in-waiting) had had an all-night vigil in St George's. The church was surrounded by all the chiefs and Rases in lion's mane crowns and velvet cloaks, outside them were the regular troops in khaki, and surging in apparently hopeless confusion beyond them again were the ordinary troops. The crowds were terrific, all men and all armed.

The Emperor and Empress entered the outer building accompanied by the Abuna, Patriarch of Alexandria and the Etchege and chief priests, all clothed in the most wonderful robes and with glittering crowns.

The Emperor was extremely dignified and the whole ceremony was intensely interesting. The Empress and Prince were also crowned, with rather awful European crowns.

The Cathedral of St George was filled with the rest of the priests. I went in and watched them dancing. All through the ceremony their chanting and the throbbing of their drums came faintly to our ears. In the outer church we had a special Coptic choir.

Kassa, Hailu, Seyum and Gugsa were present and wore crowns too, in their capacity of lesser kings I suppose. The church was filled with chiefs in lion's mane head-dresses, and all the European missions. The Abyssinian diplomatic corps wore European clothes and cocked hats, which was a pity.

Tafari was to have left in his state carriage, but the horses were unmanageable.

The streets were lined with troops in their native dress and every side street was packed with dense crowds. There must have been a hundred thousand people present. A wonderful spectacle.

After the ceremony the Abyssinian air force flew over the building (they have crashed two planes in the last fortnight).

In the evening Tafari gave a dinner party for the heads of missions. I went to the reception afterwards. There was a tremendous selection of fireworks, but unfortunately an accident occurred and they all went off at once.

Yesterday there was a state procession. An odd mixture of East and West. But I must say his regular troops are well disciplined and good at their drills. All the Rases and chiefs went past with their soldiers and looked very wonderful.

I had a private audience with him at six and gave him the books. He says he can never repay what you did for him. Zaff [Zaphiro, who interpreted] said I had the most cordial reception of anyone. Tafari is fixing up for me to shoot a bushbuck at Mangasha, and go down the Awash for kudu and oryx. Sandford is lending me boys and I am going to stay on the line to avoid a caravan. I am having an audience with the Empress later.

I dined with the Prince in the evening, a large party. The Emperor and Empress were present. We fed off gold plates with gold spoons and forks.

Afterwards we were to have seen King George's coronation on the cinema, but after a few flickering efforts it went out altogether.

The review is on Friday and should be quite wonderful.

The coronation and other ceremonies have had the strangest contrasts. Scenes which take you back a thousand years, and make the dead past live again. Robes and crosses, lion's mane crowns and incense, and the wail and throb of the bands; and then a dirty Greek in European clothes directing operations in the foreground, khaki-clad troops, cinema, motors and aeroplanes. In some ways it is rather pathetic, and in others it is incomparably magnificent.

I think he is staking his all on one great effort. If he fails Heaven knows what will happen. Kassa supports him, otherwise he could not hold his position. Hailu is just waiting for a chance to bid for the crown. He was only allowed to bring three hundred men in and I think the country is apathetic and would go either way. Gugsa and Seyum would probably side with the winner.

This coronation must have cost him hundreds of thousands and some one has got to pay. There are the oddest rumours afloat and Lij Yasu figures prominently in them. The country seems to be awaiting his return. They don't understand Tafari. Lij Yasu was a man and they say no man could look him in the eyes. In point of fact, he is I believe so debauched as to be barely alive – if still alive, which seems doubtful. But it shows the country is waiting for the coming of a prophet, so to speak. The Emperor looks very small and frail surrounded by great burly warriors such as Hailu and Gugsa, but he is almost inhumanly dignified. You can't help feeling he was born to be a king when you look at him.

His changes are very superficial. A thousand men in khaki, a few aeroplanes and ministers in European clothes. The crowds which line the streets are the crowds of twelve years ago.

I met Kassa, Hailu and the Minister for War at a garden

53

party here the other day, also Doctor Martin. I met Heroui yesterday. He is Minister for the Interior and a thorn in the side of the Legation, I think.

I am loving my time here, and each day brings back the old days more vividly, and so many things which I have forgotten are coming back again. I have had several lovely rides.

Dear Mother, I think of you such a lot. There has never been anyone like you and Daddy here since you left and they know it.

I am longing for a letter.

Very very much love,

Wilfred

from *The Danakil Diary*

I had brought a rifle with me to Abyssinia, determined to achieve my dream of hunting big game. I now decided that before going back to Oxford I would spend a month in the Danakil country. It was easily accessible from the Awash railway station and was one of the few areas in Abyssinia where wild animals survived in any number. The Danakil did not hunt and the Abyssinians, who had wiped out most of the game elsewhere, were afraid to venture into their country, since among the Danakil a man's standing depended on the number of men he had killed and castrated. Muslims of Hamitic origin, they were akin to the Somalis, though their language was distinct.

Much of the Danakil country was still unexplored, including the remote Aussa Sultanate where the Awash river was reputed to terminate. This considerable river rose in the highlands near Addis Ababa, flowed down into the Danakil desert but never reached the sea. My intention, however, was not to explore but to hunt, and I did not intend to penetrate far into the Danakil country. Even so, it was a challenging undertaking for a young man of twenty with no previous experience.

During this month I led the life for which I had always yearned, hunting big game on my own in the wilds of Africa; but now I realized that this expedition had meant more to me than just the excitement of hunting. I had been on the borders of a virtually unexplored land inhabited by dangerous, untouched tribes. Before I had turned back from Bilen I had watched the Awash flowing towards its unknown destination. I had felt the lure of the unexplored, the compulsion to go where others had not been.

from *The Life of My Choice*

In Addis Ababa I had heard that somewhere on the Awash was the virtually independent Danakil Sultanate of Aussa which was ruled by an autocratic Sultan who acknowledged no allegiance to the Abyssinian government. No European had as yet succeeded in setting foot in Aussa, though a number had tried. I learned that in 1875 an Egyptian army commanded by Werner Munzinger, a Swiss mercenary who had served under Gordon in the Sudan, had set out to invade Abyssinia, only to be defeated by the Danakil. Not one of his men survived; all carried on their persons trophies which the Danakil were anxious to acquire. Then, in 1881 an expedition led by Giulietti and Bigliore, accompanied by thirteen other Italians, had been wiped out somewhere to the north of Aussa. Three years later an expedition led by Bianchi with two other Italians had met a similar fate in the same area.

Ludovico Nesbitt and his two Italian companions had enjoyed greater success in 1928, travelling through the Danakil country from the Awash station to Asmara in Eritrea. I do not think that when I was there in 1930 anyone in Addis Ababa was aware that Nesbitt had made this journey – I had heard no mention of it.

Nesbitt published an account of his journey in the October 1930 issue of the Royal Geographical Society's *Journal*. Three of his servants were killed by the Danakil during the course of the journey, and when Nesbitt was in Bahdu there was every chance they would all be attacked and killed. Nesbitt then crossed to the northern side of the Awash, and kept away from the river. He rejoined the Awash at Tendaho and followed it eastwards to the border of Aussa. Here he met the Sultan and was given permission to continue northwards towards Eritrea.

When, one evening in my digs at Oxford, I read Nesbitt's description of his journey in the *Journal*, it brought home vividly to me the risks I should be taking when I made my own journey.

from *The Danakil Diary*

Three years later, accompanied by David Haig-Thomas, I returned to Abyssinia to explore the Danakil country. We travelled first with mules for two months in the Arussi mountains, for we wished to test under easy conditions the men who were going with us before we took them down into the Danakil desert. We camped high on mountain-tops, where the slopes around us were covered with giant heath, or higher still among giant lobelias where clouds formed and re-formed, allowing only glimpses of the Rift Valley seven thousand feet below.

We travelled for days through forests, where black and white colobus monkeys played in the lichen-covered trees, and rode across the rolling plains near the head-waters of the Webi Shebeli. We passed through some of the finest mountain scenery in Abyssinia. Then we dropped off the Chercher mountains to the desert's edge. Breaths of warm air played round us and rustled the dry leaves on the acacia bushes, and that night my Somali servants brought me a bowl of camel's milk from a nomad encampment near by. I was filled with a great contentment. The desert had already claimed me, though I did not know it yet.

Unfortunately, David Haig-Thomas developed acute laryngitis during our journey in the mountains. As he was too ill to accompany me into the Danakil country, I left the Awash station without him on 1 December with forty Abyssinians and Somalis, all armed with rifles. We obviously could not force our way through the country ahead of us, but I hoped that we should appear too strong a force to be a tempting prey. We had eighteen camels to carry our provisions. As I planned to follow the river, I did not expect to be short of water. We started as quickly as possible since I heard that the Ethiopian Government intended to forbid my departure.

A fortnight later we were on the edge of Bahdu district, where the country was very disturbed; the village in which we stopped had been raided two days before and several people killed. The Danakil are divided into two groups, the Assaaimara and the Adaaimara. The Assaaimara, who are by far the more powerful, inhabit Bahdu and Aussa, and all the tribes through whom we had passed were terrified of the Bahdu warriors. The Adaaimara warned us that we should have no hope of escaping massacre if we entered Bahdu, which was guarded from the south by a pass between a low escarpment and some marshes. This we picketed at dawn and were through it before the Assaaimara were aware of our movements. We then halted and, using the loads and camel-saddles, quickly built a small perimeter round our camp, which was protected on one side by the river. We were soon surrounded by crowds of excited Danakils, all armed – most of them with rifles. Two Greeks and their servants had been massacred here three years before. Expecting an attack we stood-to at dawn. Next day, after endless argument, we persuaded an emaciated and nearly blind old man, who possessed great influence in Bahdu, to provide us with guides and hostages. Everything seemed to be satisfactorily arranged, when just before sunset a letter arrived from the government. It had been passed on from one chief to another until it reached us. Its arrival roused great excitement among the Danakil, who collected in large numbers round their old chief. The letter was written in Amharic, and I had to have it translated, so there was no possibility of concealing its contents. It ordered me to return at once, since fighting had broken out among the tribes, and emphasized that in no circumstances must I try to enter Bahdu – the very place where I now was. Half my men insisted that they were going back, the others agreed to leave the decision to me. I knew that if I ignored this order and continued my journey with a reduced party we should be attacked and wiped out. I realized that I must return, but it was bitter to have my plans wrecked, especially when we had successfully entered Bahdu, and by so doing had overcome the first great difficulty in our way.

On the way back we passed the ruins of a large Adaaimara village. The Assaaimara had sent a deputation of seven old men to this village to discuss a dispute about pasturage. The villagers had feasted them and then set upon them during the night. Only one man, whose wounds I doctored in Bahdu, had escaped. The

Assaaimara then attacked the village and killed sixty-one men. It was the incident that had started the recent fighting among the tribes.

from *Arabian Sands*

Just before sunset I heard a hubbub outside where a crowd had collected. A letter had arrived from Asba Tafari addressed to the head of my escort; it had been passed from chief to chief. It ordered me to return at once and in no circumstances to try to enter Bahdu. Should I refuse to do so, the soldiers themselves were to return after announcing to the Danakil that the authorities took no further responsibility for my safety. The soldiers made no attempt to conceal their delight.

I went back to my tent and discussed the situation with Omar. He said he thought some of my men would follow me if I decided to go on. I realized, however, that to do so after we had been deprived of half our rifles and whatever security the protection of the Government afforded us would be to invite almost certain massacre. For four years I had been planning this journey, and the thought of exploring Aussa and discovering what happened to the Awash had seldom been out of my mind. I had hoped we were now beyond reach of Government interference. We had managed to enter Bahdu, had been accepted, and the road to Aussa lay open. Now everything was wrecked.

I decided I must go up to Addis Ababa and try to get permission to start again, but I had little hope of succeeding. To save time, I determined to cut straight across the desert to Afdam instead of returning by the longer route we had come by. That evening my men, led by Kassimi, came to my tent and expressed regret that we had been recalled, which I felt was the genuine sentiment of most of them.

Next morning while we were loading, Omar brought a young but responsible-looking man over to me who had just arrived from Asba Tafari. His name was Ali Wali and he was the nephew and adopted son of Miriam Muhammad, the Hanga-daala or spiritual head of Bahdu. He and his uncle had visited the Governor in Asba Tafari and there they had been detained as hostages for the good behaviour of the Asaaimara; his uncle's refusal to guarantee my safety in Bahdu had led to my recall. I was impressed by Ali Wali and told him I hoped to get per-mission to return. Omar expressed anxiety that we might be attacked as we withdrew from Bahdu, but Ali Wali guaranteed our safety.

from *The Life of My Choice*

December 23rd
Addis Ababa

Darling Mother

Everything has crashed at the moment, but I hope to be able to pull things round. When I was within a week's march of the end of the river and everything going splendidly, I received an order from the Abyssinian Governor to return. They had sud-denly got jumpy over the Asaaimara. We were through the place where any trouble might have been expected, and I have not the least doubt that I should have reached the end of the river from where I was without difficulty. You cannot imagine my bitterness. However, to have pushed on despite this order, and though my soldiers were ordered to return, would have been suicide. The men were prepared to follow me if I went on, but I came to the conclusion we should not stand a chance. We should have lost half our rifles.

We did four forced marches and struck the railway between Awash and Dire Dawa. I have left the caravan there ready to return the moment I get leave. I have seen Barton, who has returned, and I hope he will be able to obtain permission for me to go back. However, nothing can be done for a day or two and I shall go out to the Sandfords for Christmas. I had hoped to spend it at the end of the river.

Everything was going simply splendidly. We were being handed on quickly from one headman to the next, and secured hostages for good behaviour off each headman. It is infuriating that the Government should suddenly have developed an attack of nerves. Nor was there the least reason for it, beyond the usual risks inseparable from travel in such an area. These risks they knew before they gave me leave to go in England, and before they issued my pass here.

However, I still hope for the best. The Legation are out to do what they can for me.

Darling Mother I suppose it is good for our souls, but it is bitterly disappointing to be baulked like this. It makes it more bitter when it is not your fault that you have failed, and you believe that except for this you could have done it. I have staked such a lot on this venture; not only money, though there is £1500 of that, but everything. However, I shall fight desperately to get back there. I have not wired as it was impossible to put all this in a wire and a short and unintelligible wire would only have added to your anxiety.

I will write again very soon.

Love from your son,

Wilfred

61

I was in Addis Ababa for a month. Shortly after my arrival Sir Sidney Barton returned from leave, which was fortunate for me: he had approved my plans and obtained the initial permission for me to undertake the journey and now his persistence eventually obtained the permission for me to resume it. He insisted that Dr Martin, Governor of Chercher Province, should be summoned to Addis Ababa from Asba Tafari to discuss the matter. Dr Martin was an Abyssinian who had led an extraordinary life. As a small boy he had attached himself to an officer on the Magdala Expedition as it returned to the coast in 1868. The officer took him to India, educated him and gave him a medical training. Martin served for a time as a doctor in northern Burma before eventually returning to his homeland, where his European background made him easier than most Abyssinian officials for foreigners to deal with. At a meeting with Dr Martin, Sir Sidney pressed for me to be allowed to resume my journey; he also suggested that my escort should be increased but I opposed this, still sure that too large a force would risk provoking hostility. Dr Martin eventually agreed to sanction my return, but insisted that I first gave him the following letter:

January 20th, 1934
Addis Ababa

Dear Doctor Martin,

With reference to the permission given to me by the Ethiopian [*sic*] Government to travel along the Awash river to the place where it disappears in the Aussa Sultanate, I agree that the provision of an escort of fifteen men, to accompany me and remain with me until I return to the Awash station or leave Ethiopian territory at the French frontier in the Aussa country, together with letters recommending me to the tribal chiefs *en route* will constitute a discharge of the Ethiopian Government's responsibility for the taking of reasonable measures to ensure the safety of my expedition.

Yours sincerely,

Wilfred Thesiger

His Excellency Dr Martin

Governor of Chercher Province, at Addis Ababa

from *The Danakil Diary*

I wasted six weeks at Addis Ababa before I could induce the government to let me return, and then only after I had given them a letter absolving them from all responsibility for my safety. I returned [to Afdam] to find my men suffering from fever, which is prevalent along the banks of the Awash. They were demoralized, and a few of them insisted on being paid off. In return for the letter which I had given them, the government had agreed to release from prison an old man, Miriam Muhammad, and to allow him to accompany me. He was the head chief of the Bahdu tribes. Some months before, he had visited the government and had been detained as a hostage for the good behaviour of his tribes. It was his refusal to guarantee my safety while in Bahdu which had led to my recall. His presence with me ensured us a favourable reception there and at least an introduction to the Sultan of Aussa.

from *The Life of My Choice*

While we were in Bahdu, a good-looking young chief called Hamdo Ouga visited our camp. He looked about eighteen; he had a ready, friendly smile and considerable charm. His father, a renowned warrior and influential chief, had died and some of the tribe had objected to Hamdo Ouga succeeding him since he had only killed one man.

Hamdo Ouga went down to the Issa territory with some friends. When we met him he had just returned with four trophies; no one any longer questioned his right to be chief. He now sported a wooden comb in his hair, which was dressed with ghee, and five leather thongs hung from the sheath of his dagger. He struck me as the Danakil equivalent of a nice, rather self-conscious Etonian who had just won his school colours for cricket. Two days after we left, his village was surprised by another tribe, and when I asked about Hamdo Ouga I heard that he had been killed.

from *The Danakil Diary*

Six weeks later I was at Galifage on the borders of Aussa, camped on the edge of dense forest. The tall trees were smothered in creepers; the grass was green and rank; little sunlight penetrated to my tent. It was a different world from the tawny plains, the thirsty thorn-scrub, the cracked and blackened rocks of the land through which we had passed. It was here that Nesbitt had met Muhammad Yayu, the Sultan. Nesbitt had received permission to continue his journey but his object was to travel across the lava desert to the north, not to penetrate into the fertile plains of Aussa. Muhammad Yayu, like his father before him, feared and mistrusted all Europeans. This was natural enough. He had seen the French and the Italians occupy the entire coastline, which consists of nothing but lava-fields and salt-pans, and he naturally believed that any European power would desire to seize the rich plains of Aussa if it learnt of their existence. No European before Nesbitt had been given the Sultan's safe conduct and all had been massacred in consequence. Until I arrived in Aussa I had been faced with conditions of tribal anarchy, but now I was confronted by an autocrat whose word was law. If we died here it would be at the Sultan's order, not through some chance meeting with tribesmen in the bush.

I was ordered to remain at Galifage. The camp was full of rumours. On the evening of the third day we heard the sound of distant trumpets. The forest was sombre in the dusk, between the setting of the sun and the rising of the full moon. Later a messenger arrived and informed me that the Sultan was waiting to receive me. We followed him deeper into the forest, along twisting paths, until we came to a large clearing. About four hundred men were massed on the far side of it. They all carried rifles, their belts were filled with cartridges. They all wore daggers, and their loin-cloths were clean – vivid white in the moonlight. Not one of them spoke. Sitting a little in front of them on a stool was a small dark man, with a bearded oval face.

from *Arabian Sands*

The Sultan was bare-headed and dressed entirely in white, in narrow Abyssinian-type trousers, long shirt and finely woven *shamma*. He wore a superb, silver-mounted dagger, which had probably belonged to his father or grandfather, and held a black, silver-topped stick. Though he was darker, he reminded me at once of Haile Selassie: like him he was small and gracefully built, with a bearded oval face, finely moulded features and shapely hands. His expression was sensitive and proud. I was aware that his authority was absolute, that his slightest word was law. I was certain that he could be ruthless, having heard tales of his appalling prison – men said it was better to be dead than shut up there; yet he gave me no impression of wilful cruelty.

As I looked round the clearing at the ranks of squatting warriors and the small isolated group of my own men, I knew that this moonlight meeting in unknown Africa with a savage potentate who hated Europeans was the realization of my boyhood dreams. I had come here in search of adventure: the mapping, the collecting of animals and birds were all incidental. The knowledge that somewhere in this neighbourhood three previous expeditions had been exterminated, that we were far beyond any hope of assistance, that even our whereabouts were unknown, I found wholly satisfying.

The Sultan made the customary enquiries about my health, speaking in Arabic to Omar who translated to me. He then asked at some length about my journey, the route I had followed, how long it had taken me and whom I had met, mentioning several names. I realized he knew the answers to these questions. There were frequent pauses during which he eyed me intently, stroking his beard and fingering his prayer beads. The night was very still, despite the large number of men gathered around us; if they spoke at all it must have been in whispers. I remember hearing a hyena howl in the distance, probably near our camp, and the purring of nightjars as they flew overhead.

from *The Life of My Choice*

The Sultan asked me where I wished to go and I told him that I wanted to follow the river to its end. He asked me what I sought, whether I worked for the government, and many other questions. It would have been difficult to explain my love of exploration to this suspicious tyrant, even without the added difficulties of interpretation. My headman was questioned, and also the Danakil who had accompanied me from Bahdu. Eventually the Sultan gave me permission to follow the river through Aussa to its end. Why he gave me this permission, which had never before been granted to a European, I do not know.

Two days later I climbed a hill and looked out over Aussa. It was strange to think that even fifty years earlier a great part of Africa had been unexplored. But since then travellers, missionaries, traders, and administrators had penetrated nearly everywhere. This was one of the last corners that remained unknown. Below me was a square plain about thirty miles across. It was shut in on all sides by dark barren mountains. To the east an unbroken precipice fell into the water of Lake Adobada, which was fifteen miles long. The northern half of the plain was covered with dense forest, but there were wide clearings where I could see sheep, goats, and cattle. Farther south was a great swamp and open sheets of water, and beyond this a line of volcanoes.

from *Arabian Sands*

April 15
Aussa Sultanate

Darling Mother

I am now within reach of the end of the river and hope to get down there shortly. I thought it ended in a big lake by which I am now encamped. The Danakil assured me that it did not flow out again. I explored this lake however and found the exit, and they now admit that it goes down into the Issa country through three more lakes, two of which I have overlooked from a mountain here. It will probably take me some little time to get there. I don't want to spoil everything now that I have come so far by skimping the end. I cannot, I think, expect to get to Jibuti till towards the end of May. I will then catch the first boat home and be in England in early June. I will wire you at once from Jibuti.

I have written to Sir Sidney and asked him to wire you now. I have had a completely wonderful time and no trouble of any sort. The Danakil have received me most hospitably, and since I left Afdam I have been given two hundred sheep and thirty oxen besides hundreds of skins of milk. My men in consequence have had more than enough to eat. They have been splendid and will go anywhere and do anything. We have been lucky and had almost no fever, and I have kept very fit.

It is exciting to think that I have penetrated into a country where no white man has been allowed before. Nesbitt never got down into Aussa and all other expeditions have been turned back at its frontier. It is an extraordinary oasis shut in all round by sheer precipices of black rock. The Awash flows round it on three sides seeking an exit and at last finds a crack in this wall of rock, and flows down into the Issa desert where it ends in a vast lake.

Coming here we passed through a veritable land of death. Black volcanic rock tumbled and piled in every direction and not a sign of life or vegetation except on the very river's edge. If my photos come out I shall have some good ones. Then suddenly the mountains open out and you find yourself on the edge of Aussa. This is roughly square in shape and the whole plain is wonderfully luxuriant. Half of it is dense forest with clearings where they graze their flocks and cultivate some durra; the other half is extensive swamp. There are five lakes varying from five to eighteen miles in length.

I met the Sultan twice, in itself rather a feat, after nearly three weeks wasted in preliminary negotiations. We had a moonlight meeting in a big clearing surrounded by the silent forest. He had some forty of his picked troops lined up round him, and I and my small band felt rather overwhelmed as we advanced towards him. He was very friendly when once he had got over his preliminary suspicion and we met here again the next morning and had a long talk.

They want one to see as little of Aussa as possible and ever since it has been a constant battle of wits. I have however succeeded in following the river's course as far as this and they have now agreed to show me the real end. He has given me the silver baton, without which it is impossible to move a step, and thirteen *askaris* to add to our forces in the Issa country. From the end of the river to the French post of Dikil is only two days march.

I cannot hope to describe anything in a letter and am reluctant to spoil what I have to tell you by a bad description. I have kept an extremely full diary. I long to see you again and to tell you all about it. It has been wonderful, in very truth a dream come true.

There is one horror here and that is the tarantulas, large,

hairy and four inches across. They scuttle round camp as soon as the sun sets. Last night we killed twelve in camp. In my dreams they assume the most nightmarish proportions.

There are also great numbers of pythons round the lake and we usually kill two or three when out after birds. The largest was thirteen feet long. Crocodiles abound.

I have collected some six hundred birds, and have I think got a new species of Speke's gazelle. Previously it was only believed to exist in the Haud in Somaliland. It stretches all across this country at a much lower altitude. I have also mapped Aussa.

The Sultan has agreed to get this letter down to Dikil for me.

Darling Mother, I think of you endlessly and would give anything to get a letter from you. I do pray you are all well and happy. What fun we will have when I get back and it is not long now. I shall wire the boat from Jibuti so that you will know when I shall arrive. Do bring my brown suit up to London with you as I have no tidy suit with me. I long desperately to see you and the others again and shall be filled with impatience all the way back on the boat. God bless you and keep you safe and happy.

Your loving son,
Wilfred

from *The Danakil Diary*

We followed the river, through the forest, past the lakes and swamps, down to the far side of Aussa. It was fascinating country, and I would gladly have remained here for weeks, but our escort hurried us on. I had permission from the Sultan to pass through this land, but not to linger. The Awash skirted the volcanoes of Jira and re-entered the desert, and there it ended in the salt lake of Abhebad. The river had come a long way from the Akaki plains to end here in this dead world, and it was this that I myself had come so far to see – three hundred square miles of bitter water, on which red algae floated like stale blood. Sluggish waves slapped over the glutinous black mud which bordered the lake, and hot water seeped down into it from among the basaltic rocks. It was a place of shadows but not of shade, where the sun beat down, and the heat struck back again from the calcined rocks. Small flocks of wading birds only emphasized the desolation as they passed crying along the shore, for they were migrants free to leave at will. A few pigmy crocodiles, stunted no doubt by the salt water in which they lived, watched us with unblinking yellow eyes – symbolizing, I thought, the spirit of the place. Some Danakil who were with me told me it was here that their fathers had destroyed an army of 'Turks', and thrown their guns into the lake. No doubt this was where Munzinger's expedition had been wiped out in 1875.

I crossed the border into French Somaliland and stayed with Capitaine Bernard in the fort which he commanded at Dikil. He and most of his men were to die a few months later when they were ambushed by a raiding force from Aussá. From Dikil I travelled across the lava desert to Tajura on the coast. So far it had been the tribes that had threatened us, now it was the land itself. It was without life or vegetation, a chaos of twisted riven rock, the debris of successive cataclysms, spewed forth molten to scald the surface of the earth. This dead landscape seemed to presage the final desolation of a dead world. For twelve days we struggled over the sharp rocks, across mountains, through gorges, past craters. We skirted the Assal basin four hundred feet below sea-level. The blue-black waters of the lake were surrounded by a great plain of salt, white and level as an icefield, from which the mountains rose in crowded tiers, the lava on their slopes black and rusty red. We were lucky. Some rain had fallen recently and filled the water-holes, but fourteen of my eighteen camels died of starvation before we reached Tajura.

from *Arabian Sands*

I chartered a dhow to take us to Jibuti and we left in the evening of May 23rd. A storm was threatening but luckily passed over the land, for we were on an open deck without shelter. Tajura vanished into the distance and the sun set behind Guda. As night fell, the moon lit the sea. With small waves breaking against the bows the boat rolled slightly, her long raking yard dipping and rising against the stars above the much-patched lateen sail. I was very content, travelling like this across a sea which de Monfreid had made his own.

In Jibuti I spent three days waiting for a boat to Marseilles, and I did not find a congenial soul in the town. Chapon Baisac, the Governor, summoned me for an interview. After I had been kept waiting a long time I was shown into his office, where I had hardly sat down before he asked me abruptly why I had brought Abyssinian soldiers into French territory, and why I had not handed over my weapons before leaving Dikil for Tajura. He barely listened to my explanations, which I should have thought self-evident, and during the half-hour I spent with him never spoke a gracious word. This corpulent, pompous and short-tempered little man was certainly not one I would have wished to serve under.

I had bought *Secrets de la Mer Rouge* and *Aventures de Mer* written by Henri de Monfreid while I was in Addis Ababa and I had been fascinated by de Monfreid's account of his adventurous and lawless life. He had come to Jibuti in 1910 as a clerk in a commercial firm, but he had found himself frustrated and bored by the life he was leading, having no interests in common with his fellow Frenchmen among whom he was living. The Danakil however appealed to his romantic nature and he spent all his spare time associating with them and learning their language. The French community was scandalized by his behaviour and he was sent for by the Governor and reprimanded. He resigned from his job, abandoned his association with the French, and joined the local Danakil. He became a Muslim. He bought a dhow, enlisted a Danakil crew and made a living by fishing for pearls off the Farsan isles and smuggling guns into Abyssinia through Tajura.

I had just finished reading de Monfreid's books when I reached the French outpost at Aseila, commanded by Sergeant Antoniali. He made me very welcome and I stayed with him for days before going on to Dikil. I was interested to find that his cook, Fara, had been one of de Monfreid's crew and was evidently devoted to him.

I had hoped when I got to Jibuti to meet de Monfreid. He had however gone on a visit, I think it was to France, but his dhow, the *Altair*, was anchored in the bay. I went on board her and met his crew. From his books I already knew their names. I heard he was selling the *Altair*. I thought fleetingly of buying her and leading a life resembling his, but reality took charge.

My men were anxious to return to their homes and families, and on the evening of our second day at Jibuti all but Omar and his servant left on the train. I went to the station to see them off, and the parting with them deepened my depression. Kassimi and Goutama, Birru and Said, Abdullahi, Said Munge,

Abdi, Bedi and his fellow camelmen, and the rest: they were twenty-two in all, and some had been with me since I left Addis Ababa with Haig-Thomas for the Arussi mountains eight months before. All had proved utterly reliable, often under conditions of hardship and danger. None had ever questioned my decisions, however seemingly risky, and I had never doubted their loyalty. Despite their fundamental religious and racial differences as Amhara, Galla and Somali, they had never quarrelled or intrigued among themselves, but had worked side by side throughout.

I was glad to leave Jibuti next day, even third-class in a Messageries Maritimes boat returning from French Indo-China to Marseilles. Omar accompanied me on board and there we parted. As I watched him descend the gangway I was more conscious than ever how much of my success was due to him. He had ensured the loyalty of my men, accurate information, and the successful outcome of negotiations with tribal chiefs and with the Sultan himself, and his imperturbability had given me the assurance that I had sometimes needed.

I had come far, overcome many difficulties and risked much, but I had achieved what I had set out to do.

In the summer of 1934, after my return from Abyssinia, I was instructed to appear before a Selection Board for the Sudan Political Service. There was no written examination for this service; a number of previously selected applicants were interviewed by six senior officials from the Sudan and were assessed on their academic record and athletic prowess at the university, the recommendations of their schoolmasters, university tutors and heads of colleges, and by the impression they made at the interview.

My own selection may have been partly due to four turn-over

articles, just published in *The Times*, in which I had described my exploration in the Danakil country.

When I reported to the Civil Secretary's Office, the day after my arrival in Khartoum, I was delighted to learn that I had been posted to Kutum in Northern Darfur, generally regarded as one of the three most coveted districts in the Northern Sudan. I learnt later that I owed this posting to Charles Dupuis, Governor of Darfur, whom I had met at a friend's house in Wales shortly after I had been selected for the Service. Dupuis was a lean, weathered man of forty-nine, attentive, courteous and unassuming. We had had a long and, for me, enthralling talk, mostly about Darfur. I sensed at once that his heart was in that remote province. Apparently, on getting back to Khartoum from leave he had enquired and been told I was being sent to Wad Medani, a sophisticated cotton-growing area on the Blue Nile, with the intention of breaking me in to routine office work. Dupuis told Gillan he was certain I would resign if I was posted there, and persuaded him to send me to Darfur instead.

Northern Darfur was the largest district in the Sudan, covering some sixty thousand square miles. It bordered the French Sahara, extended northwards into the Libyan Desert, and was inhabited by various tribes of Berber, negroid and Arab origin.

The District Commissioner was Guy Moore; he and I would be the only two British officials in the district. Kutum, the District Headquarters, had no wireless station, and mail arrived fortnightly by runner from Fasher, the Provincial Headquarters. Well-meaning people warned me that Moore travelled incessantly about his district, covered extraordinary distances with his camels, never bothered about meal times, and ate – when

75

he did eat – at the oddest hours, and would expect me to do the same. I welcomed the prospect of serving under such a man.

In early August 1935 Guy Moore went on leave; before going he told me to go to the Bani Husain country to meet the neighbouring Assistant District Commissioner, and settle a boundary dispute. Knowing lion were plentiful in that region, I hoped I should have the chance on this journey to shoot one.

I got my chance on the way, near Kebkabia. After hearing lion roaring in the night I went out to look for them at dawn with three Bani Husain; they soon found tracks of five lion, which they followed for two hours. I was amazed at the skill with which, even over stony ground, they followed the tracks with seeming ease, noting here a shifted pebble, there a crushed grass stem, before picking up yet another slight indication a few yards further on. Only occasionally did they halt and stoop to check that they were right.

Suddenly one of them pointed. I looked and saw, lying under an acacia bush about forty yards away, a nearly full-grown lion. It saw us too, and sat up, but I was hoping for a fully adult lion and did not shoot. However, the next instant a lioness sprang up and I fired and heard the bullet strike. Then the scrub erupted with lions. I counted one, two, three, as if marking birds at a pheasant drive, and killed one lioness and wounded another, firing my Rigby .350 almost as fast as I could work the bolt. Then the first lioness charged and I broke her shoulder and killed her with the next shot.

Meanwhile, the other wounded lioness had disappeared into a patch of bushes and long grass, leaving a trail of blood. Before going in to look for her we skinned the two I had killed, hoping she would die in the meantime. It was an uninviting place to have to follow a wounded lion, and when we did so we noticed she had lain down frequently and bitten everything in reach. Then she came at us from under a bush and I killed her as she charged.

At our next camp we again heard lion in the night, and soon after sunrise some Fur from a nearby village found the tracks of a very large male. About fifteen Fur, armed with spears, went with me, following the tracks at a loping pace that was hard on my wind. One would hold the spoor and the rest would fan out on either side and pick it up as soon as he lost it, attracting each other's attention with a few clicks. After about an hour and a half we came to where the lion had lain up, but he had evidently seen us and moved off again.

The country here was fairly open, with only scattered bushes and occasional gullies. Lion dislike going faster than a walk and this one only broke into a trot when we got close: by pushing him along we hoped to provoke him into facing us. We seemed to have been following him for hours before I got a brief glimpse of him among some scrub, and a little further on two dogs that were with us brought him to bay. I approached to within forty yards. He looked enormous as he stood there, flicking his tail from side to side and growling, a vibrant, hair-raising noise. I had read that when a lion flings his tail out straight behind him he invariably charges. I shot him in the chest as he did so. He staggered and the next shot killed him.

As we were loading the camels a man arrived from one of the Bani Husain villages, reporting that a lion had killed a horse in the night and imploring me to come and shoot it. Needing no persuasion, I followed the man to his village. Nearby they showed me the horse's half-eaten carcass. I selected three men to come with me, and insisted that the others, most of them mounted, should remain behind. It did not occur to me to ride the lion down, which was what they would have done.

The country hereabouts was intersected by numerous dry watercourses bordered by thick bush and tall grass, green after recent rain. It had poured in the night and even I could follow the tracks without difficulty; they were those of a very big male. We disturbed him where he was lying up; we did not see him but heard him growl as he made off.

At first he stuck to thick cover, then took to more open country where some vultures wheeling above him indicated where he was. An hour or so later he descended into a large wadi. I shall never forget those enormous pug marks slowly filling with water where he had gone down the sandy wadi-bed before us, the drops from his coat still glistening on the pebbles where he had crossed a pool. Every now and then he took to the bank and left a track through the reeds like a buffalo's. Once he sprang with a snarl from a nearby thicket, but I was on the opposite side. After a pause to collect ourselves we again took up his trail, which now twisted and turned. I realized he was only just ahead. Then I heard the sound of panting. It was long past noon and we had been going for hours under a blazing sun and I was exhausted. Confusedly, I thought the sound must be from a dog that had followed us unobserved. A second later, the others whispered, 'Ahu! Ahu!' ('That's him! That's him!') and I realized it was the lion. I just hoped he would not make off again.

The grass was long and he was half-concealed under some bushes: I peered for some seconds before vaguely making out his shape six or eight yards away. He had started to growl threateningly, and I was sure he was about to charge. I fired at what I thought was his head. Then he came straight at us. He kept low, only at the last moment rearing up. My rifle went off again as I was knocked over backwards; I think the lion's shoulder must have caught me. The man beside me thrust his spear like a pike into the lion's jaw; as I went down I saw him collapse with the lion on top, and his brothers close in to help him. Before I could get back on my feet one man had been pulled down and the lion had hooked the other in the shoulder. I pushed my gun into the lion's ear and pulled the trigger.

The first man had deep claw-marks in his chest; one of his brothers had been clawed across the thigh, the other across the back of the shoulder. It had all been over in seconds, too quickly for the lion to do more damage. The three of them stood there inspecting their wounds and one said: 'God be praised, that brute won't kill any more of our cattle.' None showed any sign of pain. For them it was all in the day's work; if a lion killed their stock they hunted it down and speared it, regardless of casualties.

I wondered what the hell I was going to do, with three wounded men on my hands, no transport and no idea where I was. Fortunately, the others from the village had followed us, and hearing the shots and the lion's snarls galloped to our assistance.

On my return to Kutum, while I was inspecting the prison, I noticed a fifteen-year-old boy among the prisoners. He was called Idris Daud and came from Sultan Dosa's village of Tini but he had unusually negroid features for a Zaghawi. Idris was charged with homicide. The *mamur*, who had made a preliminary enquiry, told me that in a scuffle over the ownership of a horse Idris had inadvertently knifed a boy: it was obviously a case to be settled by payment of blood money. I disliked seeing a boy of his age locked up indefinitely with a crowd of men, so after one of his elders had guaranteed that he would not run away I released him, and told him to go and help in my house. Not long afterwards I had to sack my *sufragi* for pilfering my stores and drinking the whisky I kept for my guests, and a little later I sent the cook back to Khartoum because I wanted local tribesmen with me, not professional servants from the Nile valley. I found in the village a Furawi called Adam, who could cook, took on a boy to help him, and put Idris in charge of the house. He proved reliable and intelligent, and was always cheerful, a relief after the gloomy *sufragi*.

From now on Idris identified himself with me. I soon discovered he was a skilful tracker and utterly fearless. Once, after lion, we found some barely discernible tracks which the Zaghawa with me declared were fresh. Idris maintained they were from the previous day, and was told by his elders not to talk out of turn. However, he was right, as we discovered on following the spoor to where the lion had lain up the night before.

I now began to receive constant appeals to come and shoot lion that were killing stock. The Fur at Ain Qura, a village some forty miles from Kutum, complained bitterly that they were losing a cow every few days, so I went there in the box-car with Idris. In the evening we walked down to a nearby spring, returning at dusk to the village. Next morning we found we had been followed by three lion which had then killed a horse in an Arab encampment close by. I sent out men to locate them; they did so and one came back in the afternoon with news.

Idris and I immediately set off with a party from the village, all of them quiet and tense like a raiding party. Some figures waved to us from the top of a steep ridge and we scrambled up to join them. Here the lions had lain up that morning, looking down on the village and the grazing cattle. There were three of them; their tracks followed the ridge and we needed only an occasional indication to keep us right. As we rounded some rocks we were greeted by rumbling growls, not unduly loud but continuous and menacing. I could see no sign of lion but standing there with every sense alert I knew they were near, and was very conscious that the last lion I had shot had knocked me down.

After what seemed hours, one of them stood up behind a rock forty yards away. He was facing me, growling and lashing his tail. I fired and he staggered out of sight. The other two growled more loudly and threateningly. I got occasional glimpses of them among the rocks and bushes, but never long enough to risk a shot, especially as there was dead ground between us. Then I saw them for a second as they topped a rise and disappeared. I went forward cautiously to where I had shot one lion, and as I did so one of the others broke back across the plateau, no doubt turned by herdsboys from below who had appeared waving sticks and spears. The lion was moving fast, a hundred yards away. I knocked him over and as he got to his feet hit him again, but it took yet another shot to kill him. Once wounded, a lion will sometimes temporarily survive a second bullet which had it been the first would have killed him dead; it is this that makes the charge of a wounded lion particularly dangerous. I found the first lion dead within twenty yards of where I had shot him.

Celebrations in the village lasted till dawn: at midnight I was fetched out of bed to watch the women dancing. I was also expected to mark the occasion with gifts of money all round, and was happy to do so . . .

I keenly looked forward to seeing Tibesti. This unbroken mass of mountains, situated near Chad's frontier with Libya, extends some two hundred miles north to south and two hundred and fifty east to west, and includes what are by far the highest summits in the Sahara.

The first European to reach Tibesti was Gustav Nachtigal in 1863, during his extensive travels in the Western Sahara. However, he had only penetrated as far as Bardai, and he had barely escaped with his life. The French, during their expansion eastwards across the Sahara, had established a military post at Bardai and another at Zouar. In 1916 during the Tuareg revolt in Aïr they had evacuated both, and not till 1930 did they again occupy Tibesti, though various military expeditions, of which Colonel Tilho's in 1925 was the most important, explored and mapped the Tibesti mountains. When I went there in 1938, Nachtigal was still the only European to have been to Tibesti, other than the French officers who now served there.

From the Tedda, who inhabited Tibesti, the French had never met with serious opposition such as they encountered from the Tuareg and Senussi: being essentially individualists whom no chief had effectively controlled, the Tedda had always been divided by blood feuds. However, with incredible powers of endurance and unrivalled knowledge of the desert, they had been famous raiders. They had raided the Tuareg, their age-old enemies, as far away as Aïr in the west; they had also raided northwards deep into the Fezzan and east as far as the Nile valley; and they had harried the rich lands beyond the desert to the south.

The Tedda can perhaps be identified with the ancient Garamantes referred to by Herodotus and Ptolemy. The Garamantes hunted the troglodyte 'Ethiopians', rode in four-horsed chariots and lived somewhere between Tripolitania and the Fezzan; eventually they may well have withdrawn into the inaccessible mountains of Tibesti, which may be looked on as the cradle of the modern Tedda race. These are certainly related to the Badayat and Zaghawa, though their language is different: all three tribes are generally held to be of Libyan origin, with a mixture of negro blood that is especially pronounced among the Zaghawa.

When the French assumed control they confiscated the rifles of the Tedda; their camel-mounted desert patrols of Groupes Nomades effectively prevented further raiding. Armed now only with their barbed throwing-spears, crudely forged swords, long knives carried above the elbow, and throwing-knives, the Tedda could still carry on their blood feuds but posed no threat to the French.

On our way north from the Western Nuer Idris and I arrived at Kutum on 30 July 1938. Guy Moore had gone on leave, but his assistant, Miles Stubbs, sent us by car to Tini where Moore had arranged for Kathir and five Zaghawa to meet us with camels. Kathir gave us a warm welcome and greetings from his Badayat kinsmen in the Wadi Hawar. The five Zaghawa were from Muhammadain's people; the only one I knew was a tough, thickset, middle-aged man called Ali Bakhit whom I had seen several times at Muhammadain's house. Muhammadain had now given him orders to remain with me all the time and ensure my safety. At Tini I stayed with Sultan Dosa, very content to be back here, if only for a night. The old man urged me to stay longer but I explained that we had a long journey ahead of us and only three months in which to make it. That evening Idris had many stories to tell of his adventures among the Nuer, and he presented his father with the tusks of a hippo he had shot.

Next morning we crossed the Wadi Hawar into French territory. I had my .275 rifle and field glasses, and in my saddle bags my camera, films, two or three books, some medicine and spare clothes. For rations we carried flour for *assida*, dried meat, onions, ladies' fingers, and ghee for the *mullah*. We took our blankets and a small tent. There had been heavy rain this year and it poured during that night, but by crowding into the tent we all kept dry.

From Tini our route was northwards to Fada, the head-quarters of the Ennedi *circonscription*, and then westwards across the desert to Faya in Borkou, where the French had their main headquarters. Tibesti was a hundred miles north of Faya. For the first day or two we travelled among the Kobe Zaghawa, Idris's kinsmen, but beyond the Wadi Hauash we found ourselves among the Badayat. They owned fair-sized herds of cattle as well as camels but, though nomadic, did not range far afield. Their encampments consisted of mat huts or crude shelters of grass and branches woven through a framework of sticks. They spoke a dialect similar to the Zaghawa, whom they resembled in appearance and in many of their customs, but they were a wilder, hardier race who retained many pre-Islamic practices. North of the Badayat, the Goran inhabited the desert as far as Erdi; they had camels and goats but no cattle, and were entirely nomadic.

Beyond the Wadi Hauash we followed the western edge of the Ennedi massif, where a series of plateaux, weathered peaks and pinnacles rising to five thousand feet were intersected by sheer-sided gorges. In their rock faces were many caves, in some of which I found paintings in different colours, depicting hunting scenes, horsemen, camels, long-horned cattle, and human figures clothed and naked. I copied some, and they later proved similar to paintings from Uwainat and the Hoggar mountains. The Badayat said there were many such drawings in the Basso, the heart of the Ennedi mountains, which I hoped to visit on my way back from Tibesti.

On 10 August we arrived at Fada where I was welcomed by the French officers stationed in the large, well-designed fort.

From Fada we crossed the desert to Borkou with a Gorani, Isa Adam, as our guide; we were following the main caravan route from Borkou to Wadai and Darfur, and we watered at the three small oases of Oueita, Oudai and Moussou.

On the last stage to Moussou we halted at sunset for a meal among the dunes, intending to go on as soon as the moon rose. Then, without warning, a sandstorm swept down, and lasted for three hours. Swathed in my *tobe* and sheltering against the side of my camel from the driving sand, I felt utterly isolated. When the storm had finally blown over, all our things were more or less buried. Digging them out, we found that the weight of sand had squeezed our water out of the goatskins. Isa Adam assured me we could reach Moussou in the morning if we started at once, and I was relieved to hear it; I did not fancy travelling all day in this heat without water.

The sky being overcast, no stars were visible, and though the moon had risen it gave only a dim light. After we had been going an hour or so, Isa Adam confessed he had lost all sense of direction and insisted we must wait till dawn. However, since Moussou was marked on my map, I knew the general direction, so I took over as guide, using my compass. We passed some scattered rocks, which became more numerous as we went, but I began to have a horrid feeling that since they were volcanic they were interfering with my compass. Still, we could but hope for the best and carry on. At daybreak, to my relief, Isa Adam saw some hills he recognized, and said Moussou lay just beyond.

On 21 August I left Faya on my way to Tibesti, with Idris, Kathir and Ali Bakhit, leaving the other four Zaghawa to look after our camels until we returned. The captain at Faya had engaged two Tedda with eight camels to take us as far as Gouro. At first we passed through a waste of volcanic rocks half-buried

85

in sand, and did long marches to put it behind us, though this did not meet with the approval of the two Tedda. One of them, a young man called Ibrahim, soon earned the nickname of 'Abu Shakwa', or 'Father of Complaints'; yet his grumbles hid a ready laugh and his endurance was our envy. On the third day, starting in early afternoon, we made a forced march of twenty hours across the worst of this shadeless, scorching desert to the Kada wells near Gouro. When dawn broke, I saw, like a cloud on the desert's edge, the faint outline of Emi Koussi, at 11,200 feet the highest mountain in Tibesti.

At Gouro was a grove of palms and small fresh-water marshes, ringed by a black wall of rock against which the sand had drifted deep. This was the territory of the Arnah, a Tedda tribe whose chief, Adam Nater-Mi, before finally surrendering to the French, had acquired great fame as a raider and outlaw.

Since neither of the Tedda with us knew the tracks on Emi Koussi, I engaged an elderly Arnah named Kuri as our guide; thirteen years before he had been to the crater on Emi Koussi. With him we travelled north to the wells of Modiunga, dominated even at a distance by the great hump-backed mass of Emi Koussi. On our way there I shot two gazelle; Kuri said it was the first meat he had eaten since the feast at his fifteen-year-old son's circumcision more than a year before.

We now climbed with difficulty on to a sun-scorched tableland of volcanic rocks riven by great gorges descending from the mountain range to which this tableland formed a base. All life was absent here; even the camel flies seemed to have left us. At the foot of the mountains we separated. Idris, Kathir, Kuri and I, with the two best camels, turned south to work back along the mountains and then up to the summit of Emi Koussi, while Ali Bakhit, the two Tedda and the rest of the

Portraits of Wilfred Thesiger's father and mother, taken in 1909, the year they were married.

The thatched *tukul*, or mud-walled hut - one of the original British Legation buildings at Addis Ababa - where Thesiger was born in June 1910.

Above Thesiger photographed by Umar, his Somali headman, when the Danakil expedition had reached the coast.
Right Wilfred Thesiger with lion cubs, outside his house at Kutum in northern Darfur, Sudan. He wrote: 'I reared them successfully and they made the most delightful pets.'
Far right Sudan: Thesiger's Nuer porters in conversation. 'Some wore their hair long, dyed a golden colour with cows' urine, and this enhanced their good looks.'

Right Wilfred Thesiger in Arab dress, photographed by Salim bin Kabina, in the Empty Quarter. 'I wore their clothes – they would never have gone with me otherwise – and went bare-footed as they did.' *Below* Shibam, Hadhramaut. 'The town is surrounded by a high wall, but this is dwarfed by the close-packed houses, which rise inside it to seven or eight storeys.'

Left Salim bin Ghabaisha during the second crossing of the Empty Quarter, from Manwakh to Sulaiyil. Alert, brooding, defiant, like a resting bird of prey, he embodies Thesiger's attraction to nomadic, desert Arab tribes and the Arabian desert and everything connected with it.
Below Wilfred Thesiger during his second crossing of the Empty Quarter, in 1947–8.

Right Salim bin Kabina in the western Sands, 1948. This photograph was used for the dustjacket and frontispiece of the first edition of *Arabian Sands,* in 1959.

Below A Kuwaiti *boom* returning from Zanzibar. 'It was thrilling to watch these great *dhows* surging along beside us through the breaking seas. They were the last trading vessels in the world that made long voyages entirely by sail.'

Left Bin Kabina and bin Ghabaisha in Oman, 1950. Thesiger has disengaged his young companions from their surroundings and photographed them, posed on rocks, from a low angle, with the sky as a neutral background.

Below left Salim bin Kabina riding a camel. 'The Bedu either sit with a leg on either side of the hump, or kneel in the saddle, sitting on the upturned sides of their feet, in which case they are riding entirely by balance.'

Below Bin Ghabaisha in 1950, aged about twenty, on the Trucial Coast. By then he had a reputation as an outlaw.

A typical mud-roofed village in the mountains of Iraqi Kurdistan. 'Nasser [Thesiger's companion] and I stayed in villages of flat-roofed houses rising in tiers up the hillsides, and slept in rooms furnished only with rugs and pillows.'

The Qandil Range, Thesiger's first sight of the Kurdish mountains from the Persian border. In the foreground, Nasser Hussain, a young Kurd, accompanied Thesiger throughout two journeys in Kurdistan, 1950–1.

camels crossed directly by an easier pass into the Miski valley, where we arranged to meet them.

We struggled along, climbing and descending but slowly working upwards, until we came to the great gorge of the Mashakazy, a thousand feet deep or more, and so sheer that a stone tossed from the top fell clear. A faint track marked with donkey droppings disappeared over the edge. Somehow the camels went, protesting, down that winding track, while we hung back on their tails and saddle-ropes, and loosened boulders crashed down ahead of us. We reached the bottom at last, but I could not imagine how even these small, agile camels would get up the far side: it looked too steep and difficult even for a loaded donkey. Yet somehow they did it, slowly and with many pauses, often dropping on to their knees to heave themselves up the worst places.

At sunset we reached the farther side of the gorge, the two camels trembling and exhausted, and camped among some prehistoric stone circles. We had been going for eleven hours. A light shower had recently fallen and pools were still lying among the rocks. I was astonished to find in one such pool, perhaps two feet across and six inches deep, a few tiny fish, half an inch long, silvery in colour, with crimson tails and dorsal fins. During the night we were troubled by mosquitoes.

Next morning Kuri found fresh camel-tracks which led to a Tedda encampment nearby, where a woman and a little boy herded two camels and a small flock of goats. She lent us her two camels to take us to Emi Koussi, and brought us a bowl of milk, which must have been about all she had; we left our camels with her and gave her some dried meat and flour. These mountain Tedda lived in caves or in unroofed stone circles, eking out a livelihood with small herds of goats and an occasional camel, and enduring extreme hardship of hunger and cold. No proper rain had fallen here for two years, and this was not exceptional. During the worst times they kept their goats alive on crushed date stones, and the camels on a handful of dates, fetched in season from the oases in the Miski, the Modra and other large valleys. Beyond the woman's encampment we passed other stone circles, some of them extensive, with great boulders aligned upon a level space. They had been built by giants of old, my companions declared; for who could shift such stones today?

We reached the mountain-top and camped. To the north an awe-inspiring view across range after range of mountains, rising to jagged peaks above shadow-filled gorges. To the north-west, beyond the yellow streak of the Miski far below us, were more mountains, while to the east was a limitless expanse of sand. Southwards, the shoulder of Emi Koussi shut out the view. Towards evening the air turned bitterly cold, and the mountains stood out in the sunset, dark purple and sharp-cut under massed banks of molten cloud.

Next day, after several failures, for Kuri's knowledge of the route proved understandably vague, we found a track down into the great crater of Emi Koussi. This crater, eight miles long and five across, looked to us like an extensive plain ringed by mountains, for the crater wall rose as much as thirteen hundred feet. On the north side it fell in two steps to the floor, which was stony and sparsely covered with a heath-like plant, useless as camel fodder but welcome as fuel. When we camped for the night under a small hill, close to the great vent of Kohor near the crater's southern edge, once again it was bitterly cold.

Next morning we climbed down into Kohor, a huge hole perhaps a mile across at its widest and a thousand feet deep, with almost sheer sides except to the north, where steep screes lay below a small cliff; the bottom was covered with a deposit of sodium salt and ash. Idris and I then climbed the crater's southern wall, thereby attaining the highest point in Tibesti. It was hard work, and as I scrambled up behind him a ridiculous jingle kept running through my head. Even at noon it was very cold, and unfortunately hazy even with a strong wind, but despite the haze the view was tremendous.

While we had been away Ibrahim had found two more Tedda, who, with six camels, were prepared to take us to the French fort at Bardai. They belonged to the Tikah section and one of them, a lad called Dadi, distinguished by his great mop of hair, was a nephew of the Tikah chief; he had been born in Kufrah and brought up by the Senussi, so he spoke good Fezzani Arabic. The six camels were fine beasts in splendid condition, for the Miski was renowned for its grazing, mainly a variety of salt bush called *siwak*. To eat their fill of it, camels need to be watered daily.

Three days later, with Idris, Kathir and the two Tedda, I arrived at the Modra valley and camped in a village on the mountainside. Tieroko, the most magnificent of the Tibesti mountains, loomed above the precipices that confined the valley at our feet, where a small, swift stream, bordered by bullrushes, ran past palms and gardens. The village headman was away but his two sons, small, handsome boys, brought us food: sweet, stoneless dates and *assida* seasoned with curdled milk. That night the moon was full; it lit Tieroko and filled the misty valley with shifting lights and shades, while the music of running water rose to us in the stillness. In the morning we climbed the pass and crossed a desolate, stony table-land where the wind blew in tearing gusts. Then, after skirting Tarso Toon, we descended into the Zoumorie at the small oasis of Edimpi.

Next day we arrived at Bardai. The square mud-built Turkish

fort had been reconstructed by the French and was garrisoned by forty Tirailleurs commanded by a lieutenant and two sergeants. Like all the French I met during this journey, they were hospitable and helpful. The lieutenant was convinced that the desiccation of the whole region was increasing yearly. Apparently the failure of the rains had been especially pronounced since 1914, and valleys on the northern slopes that had once had good pasturage and been populated were now barren and deserted. In the past the Tedda had been nomads, herdsmen and raiders by inclination; it remained to be seen if they would become settled, under force of circumstances.

Kathir seemed worn out, so I left him in Bardai to recuperate while I went next day to Aouzou with Idris and Dadi.

Aouzou, which we reached in the evening of the second day after an unexpected descent off a bare, black plateau, came as a complete surprise, its tranquil loveliness in striking contrast to the wild beauty of Bardai. In the morning we visited a small village called Erbi. The miniature valley, with crystal-clear water gushing from a cleft in the rocks, the green grass, the palms, the small gardens and clusters of houses shaded by tall acacias, symbolized for me the paradise for which desert-dwellers have always yearned. Three boys, bringing us a tray of dates, climbed the small cliff to join us where we sat; their grace and simple courtesy were touching.

The sergeant who commanded the small fort in Aouzou had served in French Somaliland from 1932 to 1935, and remembered hearing of my journeys among the Danakil. Wine, which I never wanted, was seldom in short supply in these forts, and the sergeant was embarrassingly hospitable.

When we returned to Bardai, we found Kathir had benefited from his rest. On 22 September we regretfully bade the lieutenant and his two sergeants farewell and left for the hot springs of Sobouroun, passing through spectacular mountain scenery on the way. The springs lay in a small valley among jumbled rocks fantastically streaked with varying shades of purple, red, orange, green, yellow and white. The many jets of boiling water were surrounded by basins of bubbling mud; clouds of steam escaped noisily among the rocks and the air stank of sulphur. It was an astonishing but pestilential place which we were glad to leave.

Beyond Sobouroun we travelled through the wildest country I had seen in Tibesti, to the gorge of Forchi. This gorge was twenty-two miles long and its walls, thirty to ninety feet apart, were never less than two hundred and more often five or seven hundred feet high, falling not in tiers but in clean, unclimbable faces of hard rock. A clear stream fringed with rushes, among a tangle of tamarisk and acacia, ran through much of the gorge. Then, passing through groves of dom palms in the wadis Tehegam and Moussou we reached Zouar, headquarters of the Tibesti *circonscription*. There were no palms or villages here, just the fort dominating the wells on a plain surrounded by rocky foothills. It was a desolate place made worse by the news I heard: I had arrived on 27 September 1938, in the middle of the Munich crisis. War with Germany, the captain told me as soon as I arrived, now seemed inevitable. That evening, I drank to the Anglo-French *entente* with him and his lieutenant.

Next day we trekked south as fast as possible towards Faya on my way back to the Sudan. At first our route lay along the edge of the Tibesti foothills, all of which were utterly barren. Then we left Tibesti behind and were once again in Borkou. In this country even the best camels were never trotted, and to spare ours, which were showing signs of exhaustion, we walked on foot for long hours: indeed I found, especially at night, it was the only way to stay awake.

I was now on my way back to Fada and the Sudan, but the colonel insisted that on my way I should visit the strange lakes at Ounianga Kebir. My leave was running out, but by sending the Zaghawa direct to Fada and taking only Idris, Kathir and a guide, I reckoned I could do it in the time.

I was sorry to part with Dadi. He had been always light-hearted and indefatigable, swinging along beside his camel and singing interminable, lilting camel songs. I had never known him grumble, however long the march, and the hours passed quickly in his company. His hair was even longer now than when he had joined me in the Miski, but he told me he would never cut it until he had settled a blood feud. At present his enemy was a military guide at Zouar, but Dadi assured me that one day he would kill him. The four new camels, hired from the sedentary Doza, turned out to be clumsy, slow-plodding brutes, and soft-footed, so they limped among the rocks. There was water on this route but little grazing among the volcanic rocks and sand. However, by doing as much as fourteen hours on the longest day, we reached the fort at Ounianga in four days, arriving at dawn on 10 October.

The lakes lie in a deep depression and our first view of Yoa, the largest of them, was lovely. The sands were golden in the early light and the dense palm groves along the water's edge cast heavy shadows; the water was a deep Mediterranean blue and the cliffs were of rose-coloured rock. This lake was two miles long and three-quarters of a mile wide; nearby were the smaller lakes of Ouma, Midji and Forodone. The water of Ouma and Midji was deep red, of Forodone vivid green. All four lakes were impregnated with salt, though warm springs of fresh water flowed into Yoa and Ouma; in Midji the salt formed crusts which were thrust up throughout the lake, and collected by the Ounia. The Fezzan have legends of great lakes covering most of the Ounianga, Gouro and Tekro areas, and it was evident that these present ones were but remnants from the past: on the plateau two hundred feet above Yoa, and five miles from its present shores, I found some fossilized bones of a hippo.

The Ounia, who lived round the lakes, were a small tribe. In the past they had been entirely settled, owning palms and small gardens; when raided by the Tedda they escaped by swimming out into the lakes. Recently they had acquired camels, and now they neglected their palms and had abandoned their gardens, and were making money by transporting salt. Only the old men still spoke their own language, which was being superseded by Goran.

I stayed for two interesting days with the French officer who commanded the fort here, and then, with camels hired from the Ounia, left for Fada. Thirty miles from Ounianga Kebir we passed the dozen small lakes of Ounianga Saghir, only one of which was salt; the others were half-hidden in thick reedbeds. Colonel D'Ornano had told me that as many as ten thousand camels visited the saltworks at Dimi every year; being anxious to see these, we left the direct route from Ounianga to Fada and continued eastwards towards Erdi, joining up with a large caravan of Mourdia Goran. Their long line of camels was an impressive sight, silently wending its way by moonlight among the soft, steep-sided dunes.

In the Wadi Nkaula we passed the grave of Nkaula, reputed ancestor of the Gaida Goran, a rough stone wall around a tattered mat shelter before which offerings were left. Then, crossing the north-west edge of Ennedi, where the wadis seemed very green after the harsh mountains of Tibesti and the deserts to the north, we entered Fada on 19 October.

We were now back in the territory of the Warrah, a section of the Kobe Zaghawa. Hamid, Idris's grandfather, had been their *malik* until the French, during the reign of Ali Dinar, had destroyed the Kobe forces at Tini and killed their aged Sultan. Hamid, with a shattered thigh, had been carried from the field by Daud, Idris's father. Idris's uncle was sheikh of the village where we camped on 24 October, and here we saw at sunset the new moon that marked the beginning of Ramadan. That night we feasted well; then, sitting among our camels, I listened to stories of bygone fights, of successful raids and also of crippling losses, until far into the night.

Like many young Zaghawa, Idris fretted at security and craved at heart for those wild, lawless days, when the *nahas* beat for war and young men could prove their manhood and win the approval of the girls. He had once said to me, 'The only excitement I have had in my life has been riding down lions with you.' Listening to him, old men shook their heads, saying that the young these days were suffering from *sakar al laban*, were drunk on too much milk.

For me, this journey in the heat of summer served as an apprenticeship to the five years I would later spend in Arabia. It so conditioned me that even under the worst conditions there, with thirst and hunger my daily lot, I would never wish I were elsewhere. On this Tibesti journey, I had in fact suffered neither thirst nor hunger, but I was never again to ride for such long hours, day after day, for weeks on end. In Arabia we would spare our camels as much as possible, for our lives depended on their survival, whereas in Tibesti, where I was always pressed for time, when they were exhausted we could change them for others.

Looking back on my attitude to the commonly accepted pleasures of life, I can say that I have never set much store by them. I hardly care what I eat, provided it suffices, and I care not at all for wine or spirits. When I was fourteen someone gave me a glass of beer, and I thought it so unpleasant I have never touched beer again. As for cigarettes, I dislike even being in a room where people are smoking. Sex has been of no great consequence to me, and the celibacy of desert life left me untroubled. Marriage would certainly have been a crippling handicap. I have therefore been able to lead the life of my choice with no sense of deprivation. Existence in the desert had a simplicity that I found wholly satisfying; there, everything not a necessity was an encumbrance. It was those three months in the Sahara in 1938 that taught me to appreciate things that most Europeans are able to take for granted: clean water to drink; meat to eat; a warm fire on a cold night; shelter from rain; above all, tired surrender to sleep.

The Danakil country in 1934 had afforded me the challenge of the unknown, the excitement of travelling among dangerous tribes, but throughout that journey I had remained apart from my followers. Tibesti, on the other hand, had been explored and was effectively administered, but during those three months there I had lived on equal terms with my companions, and the hardship of our journeying had drawn us close together. That closeness had been my reward.

On my return to Malakal I was given a letter from the Civil Secretary's Office offering me a six-week course in Khartoum leading to a commission in the Sudan Defence Force as one of thirty new combatant officers. I accepted as it sounded promising: when Britain had gone to war with Germany, I assumed that Italy would shortly be involved and that back in the Sudan

I should be despatched to Abyssinia; but the weeks had passed and to my frustration Italy remained neutral.

I went to Khartoum for the course. It was with the Cheshire Regiment, and twelve of us were on it, one from the Gezira Cotton Scheme, the others contemporaries of mine in the Sudan Service, among them two very agreeable companions, Paul Daniel and J. E. Kennett. It was a well-run and essentially practical course, and I enjoyed and profited from it. Now that I was destined for the Sudan Defence Force I was to go back as an administrative supernumerary at provincial headquarters in Malakal until I was commissioned in the Army. Newbold approved my returning there by way of the Nuba mountains, to enable me to see more of these remarkable people, and I spent four days touring the western jabals.

One day I went to watch Nuba wrestling at the funeral games of a man who had died some months earlier. The contenders were massively built, and conspicuously coated with ash; each individual group was distinctively adorned. They challenged their opponents by swaggering up to them, bending at the knees and thrusting a shoulder forward. Each pair then feinted and sparred while they tried to get a grip. A fall was usually achieved by heaving up an opponent's leg and throwing him off balance. The contests were watched by umpires who if there was a foul at once separated the wrestlers. A score or more contests went on at the same time, each surrounded by the wrestlers' partisans, who shouted encouragement and surged forward the moment there was a fall. Half an hour before sunset the wrestling ended. Then a bull was driven up, and the Nuba swarmed over it and hacked it to pieces; almost in minutes every vestige of meat, entrails, bones and skin had vanished from the blood-soaked earth. It seemed a brutal but fitting conclusion to an impressively African spectacle.

Six weeks later I was ordered to Khartoum, this time for an attachment with the Essex Regiment, which had replaced the Cheshires. This lasted till the end of April 1940, after which I was given a Governor-General's commission as a Bimbashi in the Sudan Defence Force. Though I wore an Egyptian crown and star, the insignia of a Bimbashi, my Governor-General's commission did not rate me in British Army terms as even a second lieutenant.

On arrival in Khartoum, I was told to report to Major Wingate. Although Wingate had served from 1928 to 1933 in the Eastern Arab Corps, I had not yet heard of him. In Khartoum I was to hear plenty about him. As I came into his office he was studying a map on the wall. He swung round, said, 'I've been expecting you,' and immediately launched into his plans to invade Gojjam, destroy the Italian forces stationed there, reach Addis Ababa before the South African Army from Kenya could do so, and restore Haile Selassie to his throne. While expounding his seemingly impossible plans, he strode about his office, his disproportionately large head thrust forward above his ungainly body; in his pale blue eyes, set close together in a bony angular face, was more than a hint of fanaticism.

I asked him what forces the Italians had in Gojjam: Intelligence estimated them at forty thousand, he said. Having seen Metemma, I could visualize the strength of their forts. I then asked how many troops he would have: he said he would have the Frontier Battalion of the Sudan Defence Force raised and commanded by Colonel Hugh Boustead; a newly raised battalion of Abyssinian refugees; and half a dozen Operational Centres, each comprising one British officer, four British sergeants and fifty Abyssinians. It was obvious as he talked that Wingate never doubted he would be given command of the forthcoming campaign in Gojjam, even though Colonel Sandford, who was organizing Patriot resistance there, and Colonel Boustead, had both served with distinction in the First World War and were a rank senior to him.

Wingate, who was now thirty-seven, had served before the war under Wavell in Palestine. There he had organized and led Jewish night squads against Arab guerrillas with outstanding success and had won a DSO. So far this was the only active service he had seen. Although not himself a Jew, Wingate was a passionate believer in the Zionist cause, with which he identified himself completely. In Palestine he had been justifiably suspected by the military authorities of revealing information to the Jewish leaders, and of being involved in their intrigues.

His personal service file described him as a good soldier but a security risk, who as far as Palestine was concerned could not be trusted, since he put Jewish interests before British. It recommended that he should not be allowed into Palestine again, and he was sent back to England. There, as a Gunner, he served for two years in an anti-aircraft battery. However, he bitterly resented his expulsion from Palestine and continued to consort with Zionist leaders in England and openly to support their demands for a Jewish state. Always an arrogant and ill-disciplined officer, he now became increasingly aggressive and resentful of authority. He was an ambitious soldier, but had apparently wrecked his army career by the time war broke out.

Wavell, who had been appointed Commander-in-Chief, Middle East, had known Wingate in Palestine and recognized his potential as a guerrilla leader. He therefore sent for him. When Wingate reached Cairo in summer 1940 he soon made himself cordially disliked at GHQ, but in October Wavell sent him to Khartoum to organize the Abyssinian forces.

Soon after his arrival he met Haile Selassie. The Emperor was despondent, feeling that time was passing and nothing was being done. Wingate assured him he would raise a force that would take him back to Addis Ababa. This was a strange and eventful meeting, between the diminutive but indomitable Emperor and the uncouth, inspired soldier who was going to liberate Gojjam for him. Haile Selassie's legendary descent from Solomon and Sheba may have given him special standing in Wingate's eyes: certainly Wingate emerged from this encounter dedicated to the liberation and independence of Abyssinia.

Wingate took me round various offices at Headquarters. As he shambled from one to another, in his creased, ill-fitting uniform and out-of-date Wolseley helmet, carrying an alarm clock instead of wearing a watch, and a fly-whisk instead of a cane, I could sense the irritation and resentment he left in his wake. His behaviour certainly exasperated Platt, who anyway had little sympathy with irregular operations. I once heard Platt remark, even before Wingate's appointment, 'The curse of this war is Lawrence in the last.'

Wingate seemed to take pleasure in provoking people, and was often deliberately rude and aggressive. Once, breakfasting at the hotel with Dodds Parker, his staff captain, he gratuitously accused two young officers at a nearby table of cowardice, for taking staff jobs. He would make appointments with officers at his hotel, and then receive them lying naked on his bed; one of them described to me how Wingate had been brushing his body-hair with a tooth-brush as he gave him his instructions. Behaviour such as this made him disliked wherever he went.

Some weeks after he had arrived in Khartoum, Wingate was summoned by Wavell to a conference in Cairo on the forthcoming invasion of Abyssinia. Wingate was a major, whereas the other participants were generals and brigadiers. A story soon went the rounds of Khartoum that when a general questioned the feasibility of Wingate's plans for conquering Gojjam, which he had expounded for twice the time allotted him, Wingate said to him, 'You are an ignorant fool, General. It is men like you who lose us wars.' Wingate, who constantly referred to his superiors as military apes, was quite capable of saying this, but I suspect that if he had done so at this stage in his career he would not have got away with it.

Orde Wingate has often been compared with T. E. Lawrence, but in nothing did they differ more than in their personal relationship with others. Lawrence, despite his Arab dress and unconventional behaviour, won the confidence and friendship of Allenby and his staff; he consequently received all the help he asked for, in money, weapons and camels. Wingate, on the other hand, never received the support he could have expected during the Gojjam campaign, and when it was over received virtually no recognition of his achievements.

I myself found Wingate inspiring, realizing as soon as I met him that he did not regard the Gojjam campaign as just another step towards winning the war. For both of us the liberation of Abyssinia and the restoration of Haile Selassie were in the nature of a crusade. He had always appreciated my passionate involvement with the Abyssinian cause. Months later I heard that he had recommended me for a DSO. In due course I received this award which, for a subaltern, was far beyond my expectations.

In the Western Desert we must have killed and wounded many people, but as I never saw the casualties we inflicted my feelings remained impersonal. I did, however, begin to feel that our luck could not last much longer. It seemed inevitable that sooner or later a sentry would identify us and fire a burst into our car. Even if he missed Lieutenant Gordon Alston and myself the land mines in the car would probably go up.

Several times while lying up at El Fascia, we heard the sound of engines and suspected that patrols were hunting for us.

One morning Alston took the two signallers in our jeep to fetch water. Shortly after he had left I noticed a small reconnaissance plane flying towards the cistern; it circled and went off. A little later I heard the sound of several heavy vehicles coming along the wadi towards me. We had carefully hidden the wireless jeep under a camouflage net among some bushes. I took a blanket, went some distance away into the open, where there was no apparent cover, and lay down in a small hollow, covering myself with the blanket on which I scattered earth and bits of vegetation. Peeping out from under it, I saw two armoured cars; I thought I heard others on the far side of the wadi.

The cars nosed about but failed to find the jeep. One of them passed within a couple of hundred yards of where I lay. I heard it stop; my head was under the blanket and I wondered if they had seen me and were about to open fire; then it went on. It seemed ages before they finally drove off. Soon after they had gone I heard several bursts of machine-gun fire. I felt certain they had either killed or captured the others, and that I was now on my own.

Thinking things over under my blanket, I decided the best thing would be to remain at El Fascia and hope the Eighth Army would eventually turn up; there was water in the cistern, food in the wireless jeep and some petrol, but I had no idea how to work the wireless. I felt that the Germans, having searched the place once, would probably not come back another day; meanwhile I stayed under the blanket in case they came back now. I had Doughty's *Arabia Deserta* in my haversack but felt little inclination to read.

Some hours later I spotted Alston moving about cautiously among the bushes and startled him by calling from cover, 'Hello, Gordon. I thought they'd got you.'

'I thought they'd got *you* when I heard the firing. I just hoped they hadn't found the wireless jeep. I came back to look for it. The plane came right over our heads. Luckily our jeep was in some bushes and they didn't spot it. The armoured cars never came very close.'

'Well, they came damned close to me!'

Alston went off and fetched the jeep and the other two. Later that afternoon Lieutenant Martin and his driver, both of them Free French, turned up in their jeep. They had been with one of the patrols in 'B' Squadron and had been surprised by the Germans, but had managed to escape. When they got near El Fascia they had again been chased and shot at by armoured cars. This accounted for the firing we had heard.

We now decided that after dark we would move to another wadi some distance from the well, and lie up there to await the arrival of the Eighth Army. Our petrol was very low; we had not enough left to go on raiding the road. Martin was also short of petrol and decided to remain with us. In the late evening several armoured cars arrived and laagered nearby. They must have heard us when we eventually motored off; it looked as if, having found our tracks, they intended to deny us the cistern, and go on searching for us.

Our new hiding place was in a delightful wadi full of trees and carpeted with green grass and flowers. Some Arabs turned up in the morning. Like all these tribal Arabs, they wore white blankets wrapped round their clothes. They were very friendly and I found their Arabic comparatively easy to understand. We made them tea and later they fetched us a goat and spent the night with us. They hated the Italians, who during the pacification of Libya had treated the inhabitants with incredible brutality. I was confident that as the Germans were helping the Italians these Arabs would not betray us. On Christmas Day, two days after we had left El Fascia, we again heard armoured cars; they sounded fairly close but did not enter our wadi. I was certain that they would not be able to follow our tracks over the rocky ground we had crossed to get there.

Stirling had given El Fascia as the rendezvous for 'B' Squadron, and we expected some of the other patrols to arrive shortly in our neighbourhood. We had no idea that all the others had actually been killed or captured; but we were aware that our combined raids had brought night traffic more or less to a halt during the critical days of Montgomery's offensive.

Rommel had been very concerned by these SAS raids on his communications. He wrote in his diary, which was later edited in English by B. H. Liddell Hart:

They succeeded again and again in shooting up supply lorries behind our lines, laying mines, cutting down telegraph poles and similar nefarious activities . . .

On 23 December we set off on a beautiful sunny morning to inspect the country south of our front. First we drove along the Via Balbia and then, with two Italian armoured cars as escort, through the fantastically fissured Wadi Zem-Zem towards El Fascia. Soon we began to find tracks of British vehicles, probably made by some of Stirling's people who had been round here on the job of harassing our supply lines. The tracks were comparatively new and we kept a sharp look out to see if we could catch a 'Tommy'. Near to El Fascia I suddenly spotted a lone vehicle. We gave chase but found its crew were Italian. Troops from my Kampfstaffel were also in the area. They had surprised some British commandos the day before and captured maps marked with British store dumps and strong points. Now they were combing the district, also hoping to stumble on a 'Tommy'.

When I read this after the war I realized that Rommel himself must have been with the armoured cars that I had seen searching for us at El Fascia.

In October 1943 Haile Selassie asked for me to be sent to Dessie as advisor to his eldest son, Asfa Wossen, whom he had appointed ruler of the province of Wollo. This was a request which, despite my reluctance to leave the SAS at this juncture of the war, I felt unable to refuse.

Dessie was an attractive place, consisting largely of thatched *tukuls* among groves of eucalyptus. Here I often watched lammergeyers at the town rubbish tip; half a dozen of these great bearded vultures, with their nine-foot wing span, might sail past, sometimes close by my head.

After I had been at Dessie a fortnight, the Crown Prince arrived and the following evening gave a dinner party. During the Italian occupation he had been educated in England, so he spoke fluent English. To me he was invariably welcoming and friendly, and was well aware that twenty-seven years earlier, during the critical days of the Revolution, my parents had sheltered him in the Legation.

Dessie was his first administrative appointment. Unfortunately, his relationship with his father was strained. The Emperor, who preferred the younger Prince Makonnen of Harar, kept Asfa Wossen in the background; this had undermined his self-confidence so that he consulted his retainers unduly and made no important decision without reference to the Minister of the Pen, who was also Minister of the Interior.

Abyssinia had a real need both for outside advisors to help organize the financial, legal, educational and administrative departments, and for technicians to maintain the services which the Italians had installed in the larger towns. In the capital, some officials recognized the necessity for such specialized assistance; but in the provinces few could see any need for political or administrative advice. They were conservative by nature, holding instinctively to the methods of the past and mistrusting innovation. The Abyssinian officials at Dessie certainly did not want an Englishman interfering in their administration, suggesting land reforms or new methods of taxation: they felt there was too much of this going on in Addis Ababa. Since I had been appointed by the emperor himself they tolerated my presence, but they were determined to limit my influence with the Crown Prince. Consequently, I only saw him about once a week: our meetings tended to be purely social; rarely did we have any serious discussion.

Here in Dessie I had my own house and servants, and I found I was never invited out, except by Asfa Wossen himself. Actually, this was normal behaviour towards Europeans on the part of Abyssinians in the larger towns: even the Sandfords in Addis Ababa were seldom invited to a meal. I inevitably contrasted this treatment with my experience of the Druze and Arabs in Syria. They had welcomed me to their homes, overwhelmed me with hospitality; even strangers, whom I just chanced to meet, had insisted on entertaining me.

After my arrival Asfa Wossen had presented me with a splendid Arab stallion, and almost every day I rode out into the country; sometimes I went shooting for snipe or duck. I was in Dessie throughout the 'big rains', which normally start in June and are expected to end in mid-September, in time for Mascal, the Feast of the Cross. During the rainy season the mornings were usually fine, but by midday the clouds had banked up and then the rain deluged down, often continuing late into the night. When the rains were over the landscape was yellow with Mascal daisies. In Abyssinia individual flowers are of course beautiful, but only these daisies provide an overall effect comparable with the massed colour of the anemones, poppies and tulips in Iraq and Persia.

That year at Dessie was the most frustrating of my life. Elsewhere tremendous events were taking place. In Europe and the Far East, great battles were being fought. The SAS were engaged in the Mediterranean, Wingate was leading his Chindits into Burma, while here was I, stuck in Dessie, achieving nothing. Yet, such is the fortuitous nature of events, had I been anywhere else I should never have been offered the chance of exploring the Empty Quarter of Arabia, which was to prove the most important experience of my life.

Though my appointment at Dessie had been for two years, I resigned at the end of the first. Then, in Addis Ababa, at dinner in a friend's house, while I was waiting to leave the country, I happened to meet O. B. Lean of the Desert Locust Research Organization. During dinner he offered me a job, to look for locust outbreak centres in the deserts of Southern Arabia. I accepted at once, without asking about pay or anything else. Lean assured me that his organization could get me the Sultan of Muscat's permission to travel into the desert from the south coast of Arabia. That meant Dhaufar: and Dhaufar was the threshold of the Empty Quarter.

from *The Life of My Choice*

PART TWO
1945–60

I shall always remember the first camp at the foot of the Qarra mountains. We had stopped in a shallow watercourse which ran out into the plain, and we had dumped our kit wherever there was room for it among thorn bushes and boulders. The others were soon busy, greasing water-skins, twisting rope, mending saddles, and looking to their camels. I sat near them, very conscious of their scrutiny. I longed to go over and join them in their tasks, but I was kept awkwardly apart by my reserve. For the first and last time I felt lonely in Arabia. Eventually old Tamtaim hobbled over and invited me to drink coffee with them, and Sultan fetched my blankets and saddlebags and put them down beside the fire. Later Musallim cooked rice and six of us fed together.

I asked them about the Rub al Khali, or the Empty Quarter, the goal of my ambitions. No one had heard of it. 'What is he talking about? What does he want?' 'God alone knows. I cannot understand his talk.' At last Sultan exclaimed 'Oh! he means the Sands', and I realized that this was their name for the great desert of southern Arabia.

Larks were singing round our camping place. Butterflies flitted from plant to plant. Lizards scuttled about, and small black beetles walked laboriously across the sand. We had seen a hare that morning, and the tracks of gazelle. The sand around us was still marked where jerboas and other small rodents had scampered about during the night. I wondered how they got here, how they had located this small green island, in the enormous emptiness which surrounded it.

Sultan, Musallim, and several others had gone off with the herdsboy to the Bait Musan encampment. Al Auf was herding the camels. Several people were sleeping, their faces covered with their head-cloths. I climbed a slope above our camp and bin Kabina joined me. I was hungry; I had eaten only half my portion of ash-encrusted bread the night before. The brackish water which I had drunk at sunset had done little to lessen my nagging thirst. Yet the sky seemed bluer than it had been for days. The sand was a glowing carpet set about my feet. A raven croaked, circling round us, and bin Kabina shouted, 'Raven seek thy brother.' Then another raven flew over the shoulder of a nearby dune and he laughed, and explained to me that a single raven is unlucky, a bearer of ill-tidings. We sat there happily together.

He talked about his mother and his young brother Said, whom I had not met, and about his cousin whom he hoped to marry. The distant camels drifted in greedy haste from bush to bush. Then we saw Sultan and the others returning. As they drew near, bin Kabina said, 'Sultan will make trouble. He is frightened and does not wish to go on', and I knew that bin Kabina was right. They brought a bag of sour milk with them. We drank it thirstily and it was very good. Then Sultan called the others and they went off and sat in a circle apart from me. I told bin Kabina to fetch al Auf. Later Sultan asked me to join them. He said that they had discussed the situation and agreed that the Bait Musan camels were all in poor condition, that neither they nor our camels were capable of getting to Dhafara, that we must therefore return to the others on the southern coast, where if I wished we could hunt oryx in the Jaddat al Harasis. He added that our food was insufficient and that we had not enough water to go on, even if the camels had been in good condition. I then suggested that six of us should go on with the best of the camels, and that the other six should go back. But Sultan said that six would be too small a party, since the country on the other side of the Sands would be full of raiders as a result of the fighting between the rulers of Abu Dhabi and Dibai; to discourage me he said that the Bait Musan had told him that a party of Arabs, well mounted and with plenty of water, had tried to cross to Dhafara two years before, when the grazing was good, and that all of them had died in the Sands. He declared that we must either all go on or all go back. We argued for a long time but I knew that it was useless. His nerve had gone. He had always been the undisputed leader, with a reputation for daring. It was a reputation not easily acquired among the Bedu; but he had lived all his life in the mountains and on the steppes. In the Sands he was confused and bewildered, no longer self-reliant. He looked an old and broken man and I was sorry. He had helped me so often and I liked him. I asked al Auf if he would come with me, and he said: 'I thought we came here to go to Dhafara. If you wish to go on I will guide you.' I asked bin Kabina, and he answered that where I went he would go. I wondered if Musallim would come with us. The camel which I rode belonged to him; without it I did not see how I could go on. I knew that he was jealous of Sultan. I asked him, and he answered, 'I will come.' The others said nothing.

Once again we divided up the food. We took as our share fifty pounds of flour, some of the butter and coffee, what remained of the tea and sugar, and a few dried onions. We also took four skins of water, choosing the best skins that did not leak. Musallim told me that the Bait Musan possessed a bull camel in good condition, and suggested that we should buy it and take it with us as a spare. He also said that Mabkhaut bin Arbain was his friend and would come with us if he asked him to. I thought that Mabkhaut's camel looked thin, but al Auf replied that they knew about camels and that this one would stand much hard work. He was anxious for Mabkhaut to accompany us, for he said that it would be better if we had one more person with us and that Mabkhaut was the most reliable of the Bait Kathir. Musallim went off to see about this. Later Mabkhaut came over, carrying his saddlery, and joined us. In the evening bin Turkia asked if he too might come with us. He was a relation of Mabkhaut's and wished to share with him the dangers that were ahead of us. Unfortunately his camel was one of the worst, so reluctantly we refused. I promised him instead that I would take him and his young son bin Anauf with me to Mukalla, when I travelled there from Salala on my return from my present journey. We bought the bull, a large and very powerful black animal, after much haggling and for a fantastic price, paying the equivalent of fifty pounds, more than twice what it was worth. I felt more confident than I had felt for days. I had with me chosen companions all mounted on good camels. We had a spare camel with us which was used to the Sands. If our food ran out we could kill one of our animals and eat it. Water was short. We should have to be careful with this, and ration ourselves to a pint a day. Bin Kabina, Musallim, and Mabkhaut each carried one of the service rifles which belonged to me. Al Auf had a long-barrelled .303 Martini, a weapon favoured by the Bedu. I carried a sporting model .303. We divided the spare ammunition between us. There was more than a hundred rounds for each of us. Next day after we had left the others, I told my companions that they could have these weapons as presents, and promised al Auf that he could take the pick of my remaining rifles as soon as we returned to Salala. Nothing that I could have given them could have delighted them more. Service rifles in good condition were unprocurable among these tribes. Even ammunition was scarce. All tribesmen like to wear a dagger or carry a rifle, even in peaceful surroundings, as a mark of their manhood, as a sign of their independence, but in southern Arabia the safety of their herds, even their lives, may at any moment depend upon their rifles. Bin Kabina had already confided to me that he hoped to buy a rifle with the money I gave him. He no doubt had visualized himself as the proud owner of some ancient weapon, such as he had borrowed when he accompanied me to the Hadhramaut, a fighting-man at last, envied by his young brother. Now he owned the finest rifle in his tribe. I watched the disbelief slowly fading from his eyes.

The Bait Musan came to us at dusk, carrying bowls of camel's milk. The milk was soothing and cool after the bitter water, which rasped our throats. I sat with the Bait Kathir but there was constraint among us so I went and joined al Auf and bin Kabina who were mending a saddle. If they had not come to Shisur I should be turning back as Thomas had once turned back from Mughshin.

The Bait Kathir helped us to load our camels. The Rashid took the lead, their faded brown clothes harmonizing with the sands: al Auf, a lean, neat figure, very upright; bin Kabina, more loosely built, striding beside him. The two Bait Kathir followed close behind, with the spare camel tied to Musallim's saddle. Their clothes, which had once been white, had become neutral-coloured from long usage. Mabkhaut was the same build as al Auf, whom he resembled in many ways, though he was a less forceful character. In the distance he was distinguishable from him only by the colour of his shirt. Musallim, compactly built, slightly bow-legged, and physically tough, was of a different, coarser breed. The least likeable of my companions, his personality had suffered from too frequent sojourns in Salala and he tended to be ingratiating.

After a short distance al Auf suggested that, as he did not know what we should find to the north, it would be wise to halt near by, with the Bait Imani, to allow our camels a further day's grazing. The Arabs, he added, would give us milk so that we need not touch our food and water. I answered that he was our guide and that from now on such decisions must rest with him.

Two hours later we saw a small boy, dressed in the remnants of a loin-cloth and with long hair falling down his back, herding camels. He led us to the Bait Imani camp, where three men sat round the embers of a fire. They rose as we approached. 'Salam alaikum', 'Alaikum as salam', and then, after we had exchanged the news, they handed us a bowl of milk, its surface crusted with brown sand. These Bait Imani belonged to the same section of the Rashid as al Auf and bin Kabina and were from three different families. Only one of them, a grizzled elderly man called Khuatim, wore a shirt over his loin-cloth, and all were bareheaded. They had no tent; their only possessions were saddles, ropes, bowls, empty goat-skins, and their rifles and daggers. The camping ground was churned and furrowed where the camels slept, and littered with camel droppings, hard and clean on the sand like dried dates. These men were cheerful and full of talk. The grazing was good; their camels, several in milk, would soon be fat. Life by their standards would be easy this year, but I thought of other years when the exhausted scouts rode back to the wells to speak through blackened, bleeding lips of desolation in the Sands, of emptiness such as I myself had seen on the way here from Ghanim; when the last withered plants were gone and walking skeletons of men and beasts sank down to die. Even tonight, when they considered themselves well off, these men would sleep naked on the freezing sand, covered only with their flimsy loin-cloths. I thought, too, of the bitter wells in the furnace heat of summer, when, hour by reeling hour, they watered thirsty, thrusting camels, until at last the wells ran dry and importunate camels moaned for water which was not there. I thought how desperately hard were the lives of the Bedu in this weary land, and how gallant and how enduring was their spirit. Now, listening to their talk and watching the little acts of courtesy which they instinctively performed, I knew by comparison how sadly I must fail, how selfish I must prove.

After milking, the Bait Imani couched their camels for the night, tying their knees to prevent them from rising. Al Auf told us to leave ours out to graze, adding that he would keep an eye on them. Our hosts brought us milk. We blew the froth aside and drank deep; they urged us to drink more, saying, 'You will find no milk in the sands ahead of you. Drink – drink. You are our guests. God brought you here – drink.' I drank again, knowing even as I did so that they would go hungry and thirsty that night, for they had nothing else, no other food and no water. Then while we crouched over the fire bin Kabina made coffee. The chill wind whispered among the shadowy dunes, and fingered us through our clothes and through the blankets which we wrapped about us. They talked till long after the moon had set, of camels and grazing, of journeys across the Sands, of raids and blood feuds and of the strange places and people they had seen when they had visited the Hadhramaut and Oman.

In the morning bin Kabina went with one of the Bait Imani to collect our camels, and when he came back I noticed he was no longer wearing a loin-cloth under his shirt. I asked him where it was and he said that he had given it away. I protested that he could not travel without one through the inhabited country beyond the Sands and in Oman, and that I had no other to give him. I said he must recover it and gave him some

115

money for the man instead. He argued that he could not do this. 'What use will money be to him in the Sands. He wants a loin-cloth,' he grumbled, but at length he went off to do as I had told him.

Meanwhile the other Bait Imani had brought us bowls of milk which al Auf poured into a small goatskin. He said we could mix a little every day with our drinking water and that this would improve its taste, a custom which enables Arabs who live in the Sands to drink from wells which would otherwise be undrinkable. They call this mixture of sour milk and water *shanin*. When we had finished this milk a week later we found in the bottom of the skin a lump of butter, the size of a walnut and colourless as lard. Al Auf also poured a little milk into another skin which was sweating, explaining that this would make it waterproof.

Then, wishing our hosts the safe keeping of God, we turned away across the Sands. As he walked along, al Auf held out his hands, palms upwards, and recited verses from the Koran. The sand was still very cold beneath our feet. Usually, when they are in the Sands during the winter or summer, Arabs wear socks knitted from coarse black hair. None of us owned these socks and our heels were already cracking from the cold. Later these cracks became deeper and very painful. We walked for a couple of hours, and then rode till nearly sunset, encouraging our camels to snatch mouthfuls from any plants they passed. They would hasten towards each one with their lower lips flapping wildly.

At first the dunes were brick-red in colour, separate mountains of sand, rising above ash-white gypsum flats ringed with vivid green salt-bushes; those we passed in the afternoon were even higher – 500 to 550 feet in height and honey-coloured. There was little vegetation here.

116

Musallim rode the black bull and led his own camel, which carried the two largest water-skins. Going down a steep slope the female hesitated. The head-rope attached to the back of Musallim's saddle tightened and slowly pulled her over on to her side. I was some way behind and could see what was going to happen but there was no time to do anything. I shouted frantically at Musallim but he could not halt his mount on the slope. I prayed that the rope would break, and as I watched the camel collapse on top of the water-skins I thought, 'Now we will never get across the Sands'. Al Auf was already on the ground slashing at the taut rope with his dagger. As I jumped from my saddle I wondered if we should have even enough water left to get back to Ghanim. The fallen camel kicked out, and as the rope parted heaved herself to her knees. The water-skins which had fallen from her back still seemed to be full. Hardly daring to hope I bent over them, as al Auf said 'Praise be to God. They are all right,' and the others reiterated 'The praise be to God, the praise be to God!' We reloaded them on to the bull, which, bred in the sands, was accustomed to these slithering descents.

Later we came on some grazing and stopped for the night. We chose a hollow sheltered from the wind, unloaded the water-skins and saddle-bags, hobbled the camels, loosened the saddles on their backs and drove them off to graze.

At sunset al Auf doled out a pint of water mixed with milk to each person, our first drink of the day. As always, I had watched the sun getting lower, thinking 'Only one more hour till I can drink', while I tried to find a little saliva to moisten a mouth that felt like leather. Now I took my share of water without the milk and made it into tea, adding crushed cinnamon, cardamom, ginger, and cloves to the brew to disguise the taste.

Firewood could always be found, for there was no place in the Sands where rain had not fallen in the past, even if it was twenty or thirty years before. We could always uncover the long trailing roots of some dead shrub. These Arabs will not burn tribulus if they can find any other fuel, for *zahra*, 'the flower' as they call it, is venerated as the best of all food for their camels and has almost the sanctity of the date palm. I remember how I once threw a date-stone into the fire and old Tamtaim leant forward and picked it out.

Bin Kabina brewed coffee. He had stripped off his shirt and head-cloth, and I said, 'You couldn't take your shirt off if I had not rescued your loin-cloth for you.' He grinned, and said, 'What could I do? He asked for it,' and went over to help Musallim scoop flour out of a goatskin: four level mugfuls measured in a pint mug. This, about three pounds of flour, was our ration for the day and I reflected that there must be very few calories or vitamins in our diet. Yet no scratch festered or turned septic during the years I lived in the desert. Nor did I ever take precautions before drinking what water we found. Indeed, I have drunk unboiled water from wells, ditches, and drains all over the Middle East for twenty-five years without ill-effect. Given a chance, the human body – mine at any rate – seems to create its own resistance to infection.

When Musallim had made bread, he called to al Auf and Mabkhaut, who were herding the camels. It was getting dark. Though a faint memory of the vanished day still lingered in the west, the stars were showing, and the moon cast shadows on the colourless sand. We sat in a circle round a small dish, muttered 'In the name of God', and in turn dipped fragments of bread into the melted butter. When we had fed, bin Kabina took the small brass coffee-pot from the fire and served us with coffee, a few drops each. Then we crouched round the fire and talked.

I was happy in the company of these men who had chosen to come with me. I felt affection for them personally, and sympathy with their way of life. But though the easy equality of our relationship satisfied me, I did not delude myself that I could be one of them. They were Bedu and I was not; they were Muslims and I was a Christian. Nevertheless, I was their companion and an inviolable bond united us, as sacred as the bond between host and guest, transcending tribal and family loyalties. Because I was their companion on the road, they would fight in my defence even against their brothers and they would expect me to do the same.

But I knew that for me the hardest test would be to live with them in harmony and not to let my impatience master me; neither to withdraw into myself, nor to become critical of standards and ways of life different from my own. I knew from experience that the conditions under which we lived would slowly wear me down, mentally if not physically, and that I should be often provoked and irritated by my companions. I also knew with equal certainty that when this happened the fault would be mine, not theirs.

During the night a fox barked somewhere on the slopes above us. At dawn al Auf untied the camels, which he had brought in for the night, and turned them loose to graze. There would be no food till sunset, but bin Kabina heated what was left of the coffee. After we had travelled for an hour we came upon a patch of grazing freshened by a recent shower. Faced with the choice of pushing on or of feeding the camels al Auf decided to stop, and as we unloaded them he told us to collect bundles of tribulus to carry with us. I watched him scoop a hole in the sand to find out how deeply the rain had penetrated, in this case about three feet; he invariably did this wherever rain had fallen – if no plants had yet come up on which to graze the camels while we waited, we went on, leaving him behind to carry out his investigations. It was difficult to see what practical use this information about future grazing in the heart of the Empty Quarter could possibly be to him or to anyone else, and yet I realized that it was this sort of knowledge which made him such an exceptional guide. Later I lay on the sand and watched an eagle circling overhead. It was hot. I took the temperature in the shade of my body and found it was 84 degrees. It was difficult to believe that it had been down to 43 degrees at dawn. Already the sun had warmed the sand so that it burnt the soft skin round the sides of my feet.

At midday we went on, passing high, pale-coloured dunes, and others that were golden, and in the evening we wasted an hour skirting a great mountain of red sand, probably 650 feet in height. Beyond it we travelled along a salt-flat, which formed a corridor through the Sands. Looking back I fancied the great, red dune was a door which was slowly, silently closing behind us. I watched the narrowing gap between it and the dune on the other side of the corridor, and imagined that once it was shut we could never go back, whatever happened. The gap vanished and now I could see only a wall of sand.

We stopped at sunset for the evening meal, and fed to our camels the tribulus we had brought with us. All the skins were sweating and we were worried about our water. There had been a regular and ominous drip from them throughout the day, a drop falling on to the sand every few yards as we rode along, like blood dripping from a wound that could not be staunched. There was nothing to do but to press on, and yet to push the camels too hard would be to founder them. They were already showing signs of thirst. Al Auf had decided to go on again after we had fed, and while Musallim and bin Kabina baked bread I asked him about his former journeys through these Sands. 'I have crossed them twice,' he said. 'The last time I came this way was two years ago. I was coming from Abu Dhabi.' I asked, 'Who was with you?' and he answered, 'I was alone.' Thinking that I must have misunderstood him, I repeated, 'Who were your companions?' 'God was my companion.' To have ridden alone through this appalling desolation was an incredible achievement. We were travelling through it now, but we carried our own world with us: a small world of five people, which yet provided each of us with companionship, with talk and laughter and the knowledge that others were there to share the hardship and the danger. I knew that if I travelled here alone the weight of this vast solitude would crush me utterly.

I also knew that al Auf had used no figure of speech when he said that God was his companion. To these Bedu, God is a reality, and the conviction of his presence gives them the courage to endure. For them to doubt his existence would be as inconceivable as for them to blaspheme. Most of them pray regularly, and many keep the fast of Ramadhan, which lasts for a whole month, during which time a man may not eat or drink from dawn till sunset. When this fast falls in summer – and the Arab months being lunar it is eleven days earlier each year – they make use of the exemption which allows travellers to observe the fast when they have finished their journey, and keep it in the winter. Several of the Arabs whom we had left at Mughshin were fasting to compensate for not having done so earlier in the year. I have heard townsmen and villagers in the Hadhramaut and the Hajaz disparage the Bedu, as being without religion. When I have protested, they have said, 'Even if they pray, their prayers are not acceptable to God, since they do not first perform the proper ablutions.'

These Bedu are not fanatical. Once I was travelling with a large party of Rashid, one of whom said to me, 'Why don't you become a Muslim and then you would really be one of us?' I answered, 'God protect me from the Devil!' They laughed. This invocation is one which Arabs invariably use in rejecting something shameful or indecent. I would not have dared to make it if other Arabs had asked me this question, but the man who had spoken would certainly have used it if I had suggested that he should become a Christian.

After the meal we rode for two hours along a salt-flat. The dunes on either side, colourless in the moonlight, seemed higher by night than by day. The lighted slopes looked very smooth, the shadows in their folds inky black. Soon I was shivering uncontrollably from the cold. The others roared out their songs into a silence, broken otherwise only by the crunch of salt beneath the camels' feet. The words were the words of the south, but the rhythm and intonation were the same as in the songs which I had heard other Bedu singing in the Syrian desert. At first sight the Bedu of southern Arabia had appeared to be very different from those of the north, but I now realized that his difference was largely superficial and due to the clothes which they wore. My companions would not have felt out of place in an encampment of the Rualla, whereas a townsman from Aden or Muscat would be conspicuous in Damascus.

Eventually we halted and I dismounted numbly. I would have given much for a hot drink but I knew that I must wait eighteen hours for that. We lit a small fire and warmed ourselves before we slept, though I slept little. I was tired; for days I had ridden long hours on a rough camel, my body racked by its uneven gait. I suppose I was weak from hunger, for the food which we ate was a starvation ration, even by Bedu standards. But my thirst troubled me most; it was not bad enough really to distress me but I was always conscious of it. Even when I was asleep I dreamt of racing streams of ice-cold water, but it was difficult to get to sleep. Now I lay there trying to estimate the distance we had covered and the distance that still lay ahead. When I had asked al Auf how far it was to the well, he had answered, 'It is not the distance but the great dunes of the Uruq al Shaiba that may destroy us.' I worried about the water which I had watched dripping away on to the sand, and about the state of our camels. They were there, close beside me in the dark. I sat up and looked at them. Mabkhaut stirred and called out, 'What is it, Umbarak?' I mumbled an answer and lay down again. Then I worried whether we had tied the mouth of the skin properly when we had last drawn water and wondered what would happen if one of us was sick or had an accident. It was easy to banish these thoughts in daylight, less easy in the lonely darkness. Then I thought of al Auf travelling here alone and felt ashamed.

The others were awake at the first light, anxious to push on while it was still cold. The camels sniffed at the withered tribulus but were too thirsty to eat it. In a few minutes we were ready. We plodded along in silence. My eyes watered with the cold; the jagged salt-crusts cut and stung my feet. The world was grey and dreary. Then gradually the peaks ahead of us stood out against a paling sky; almost imperceptibly they began to glow, borrowing the colours of the sunrise which touched their crests.

A high unbroken dune-chain stretched across our front. It was not of uniform height, but, like a mountain range, consisted of peaks and connecting passes. Several of the summits appeared to be seven hundred feet above the salt-flat on which we stood. The southern face confronting us was very steep, which meant that this was the lee side to the prevailing winds. I wished we had to climb it from the opposite direction, for it is easy to take a camel down these precipices of sand but always difficult to find a way up them.

Al Auf told us to wait while he went to reconnoitre. I watched him walking away across the glistening salt-flat, his rifle on his shoulder and his head thrown back as he scanned the slopes above. He looked superbly confident, but as I viewed this wall of sand I despaired that we would ever get the camels up it. Mabkhaut evidently thought the same, for he said to Musallim, 'We will have to find a way round. No camel will ever climb that.' Musallim answered, 'It is al Auf's doing. He brought us here. We should have gone much farther to the west, nearer to Dakaka.' He had caught a cold and was snuffling, and his rather high-pitched voice was hoarse and edged with grievance. I knew that he was jealous of al Auf and always ready to disparage him, so unwisely I gibed, 'We should have got a long way if you had been our guide!' He swung round and answered angrily, 'You don't like the Bait Kathir. I know that you only like the Rashid. I defied my tribe to bring you here and you never recognize what I have done for you.'

For the past few days he had taken every opportunity of reminding me that I could not have come on from Ramlat al Ghafa without him. It was done in the hope of currying favour and of increasing his reward, but it only irritated me. Now I was tempted to seek relief in angry words, to welcome the silly, bitter squabble which would result. I kept silent with an effort and moved apart on the excuse of taking a photograph. I knew how easily, under conditions such as these, I could take a violent dislike to one member of the party and use him as my private scapegoat. I thought, 'I must not let myself dislike him. After all, I do owe him a great deal; but I wish to God he would not go on reminding me of it.'

I went over to a bank and sat down to wait for al Auf's return. The ground was still cold, although the sun was now well up, throwing a hard, clear light on the barrier of sand ahead of us. It seemed fantastic that this great rampart which shut out half the sky could be made of wind-blown sand. Now I could see al Auf, about half a mile away, moving along the salt-flat at the bottom of the dune. While I watched him he started to climb a ridge, like a mountaineer struggling upward through soft snow towards a pass over a high mountain. I even saw the tracks which he left behind him. He was the only moving thing in all that empty, silent landscape.

What were we going to do if we could not get the camels over it? I knew that we could not go any farther to the east, for al Auf had told me that the quicksands of Umm al Samim were in that direction. To the west the easier sands of Dakaka, where Thomas had crossed, were more than two hundred miles away. We had no margin, and could not afford to lengthen our journey. Our water was already dangerously short, and even more urgent than our own needs were those of the camels, which would collapse unless they were watered soon. We *must* get them over this monstrous dune, if necessary by unloading them and carrying the loads to the top. But what was on the other side? How many more of these dunes were there ahead of us? If we turned back now we might reach Mughshin, but I knew that once we crossed this dune the camels would be too tired and thirsty to get back even to Ghanim. Then I thought of Sultan and the others who had deserted us, and of their triumph if we gave up and returned defeated. Looking again at the dune ahead I noticed that al Auf was coming back. A shadow fell across the sand beside me. I glanced up and bin

Kabina stood there. He smiled, said 'Salam alaikum', and sat down. Urgently I turned to him and asked, 'Will we ever get the camels over that?' He pushed the hair back from his forehead, looked thoughtfully at the slopes above us, and answered, 'It is very steep but al Auf will find a way. He is a Rashid; he is not like these Bait Kathir.' Unconcernedly he then took the bolt out of his rifle and began to clean it with the hem of his shirt, while he asked me if all the English used the same kind of rifle.

When al Auf approached we went over to the others. Mabkhaut's camel had lain down; the rest of them stood where we had left them, which was a bad sign. Ordinarily they would have roamed off at once to look for food. Al Auf smiled at me as he came up but said nothing, and no one questioned him. Noticing that my camel's load was unbalanced he heaved up the saddle-bag from one side, and then picking up with his toes the camel-stick which he had dropped, he went over to his own camel, caught hold of its head-rope, said 'Come on', and led us forward.

It was now that he really showed his skill. He picked his way unerringly, choosing the inclines up which the camels could climb. Here on the lee side of this range a succession of great faces flowed down in unruffled sheets of sand, from the top to the very bottom of the dune. They were unscalable, for the sand was poised always on the verge of avalanching, but they were flanked by ridges where the sand was firmer and the inclines easier. It was possible to force a circuitous way up these slopes, but not all were practicable for camels, and from below it was difficult to judge their steepness. Very slowly, a foot at a time, we coaxed the unwilling beasts upward. Each time we stopped I looked up at the crests where the rising wind was blowing streamers of sand into the void, and wondered how we should ever reach the top. Suddenly we were there. Before slumping down on the sand I looked anxiously ahead of us. To my relief I saw that we were on the edge of rolling downs, where the going would be easy among shallow valleys and low, rounded hills. 'We have made it. We are on top of Uruq al Shaiba', I thought triumphantly. The fear of this great obstacle had lain like a shadow on my mind ever since al Auf had first warned me of it, the night we spoke together in the sands of Ghanim. Now the shadow had lifted and I was confident of success.

We rested for a while on the sand, not troubling to talk, until al Auf rose to his feet and said 'Come on'. Some small dunes built up by cross-winds ran in curves parallel with the main face across the back of these downs. Their steep faces were to the north and the camels slithered down them without difficulty. These downs were brick-red, splashed with deeper shades of colour; the underlying sand, exposed where it had been churned up by our feet, showing red of a paler shade. But the most curious feature was a number of deep craters resembling giant hoof-prints. These were unlike normal crescent-dunes, since they did not rise above their surroundings, but formed hollows in the floor of hard undulating sand. The salt-flats far below us looked very white.

We mounted our camels. My companions had muffled their faces in their head-cloths and rode in silence, swaying to the camels' stride. The shadows on the sand were very blue, of the same tone as the sky; two ravens flew northward, croaking as they passed. I struggled to keep awake. The only sound was made by the slap of the camels' feet, like wavelets lapping on a beach.

To rest the camels we stopped for four hours in the late afternoon on a long gentle slope which stretched down to another salt-flat. There was no vegetation on it and no salt-bushes bordered the plain below us. Al Auf announced that we would go on again at sunset. While we were feeding I said to him cheerfully, 'Anyway, the worst should be over now that we are across the Uruq al Shaiba.' He looked at me for a moment and then answered, 'If we go well tonight we should reach them tomorrow.' I said, 'Reach what?' and he replied, 'The Uruq al Shaiba', adding, 'Did you think what we crossed today was the Uruq al Shaiba? That was only a dune. You will see them tomorrow.' For a moment, I thought he was joking, and then I realized that he was serious, that the worst of the journey which I had thought was behind us was still ahead.

It was midnight when at last al Auf said, 'Let's stop here. We will get some sleep and give the camels a rest. The Uruq al Shaiba are not far away now.' In my dreams that night they towered above us higher than the Himalayas.

Al Auf woke us again while it was still dark. As usual bin Kabina made coffee, and the sharp-tasting drops which he poured out stimulated but did not warm. The morning star had risen above the dunes. Formless things regained their shape in the first dim light of dawn. The grunting camels heaved themselves erect. We lingered for a moment more beside the fire; then al Auf said 'Come', and we moved forward. Beneath my feet the gritty sand was cold as frozen snow.

We were faced by a range as high as, perhaps even higher than, the range we had crossed the day before, but here the peaks were steeper and more pronounced, rising in many cases to great pinnacles, down which the flowing ridges swept like draperies. These sands, paler coloured than those we had crossed, were very soft, cascading round our feet as the camels struggled up the slopes. Remembering how little warning of imminent collapse the dying camels had given me twelve years before in the Danakil country, I wondered how much more these camels would stand, for they were trembling violently whenever they halted. When one refused to go on we heaved on her head-rope, pushed her from behind, and lifted the loads on either side as we manhandled the roaring animal upward. Sometimes one of them lay down and refused to rise, and then we had to unload her, and carry the water-skins and the saddle-bags ourselves. Not that the loads were heavy. We had only a few gallons of water left and some handfuls of flour.

We led the trembling, hesitating animals upward along great sweeping ridges where the knife-edged crests crumbled beneath our feet. Although it was killing work, my companions were always gentle and infinitely patient. The sun was scorching hot and I felt empty, sick, and dizzy. As I struggled up the slope, knee-deep in shifting sand, my heart thumped wildly and my thirst grew worse. I found it difficult to swallow; even my ears felt blocked, and yet I knew that it would be many intolerable hours before I could drink. I would stop to rest, dropping down on the scorching sand, and immediately it seemed I would hear the others shouting, 'Umbarak, Umbarak'; their voices sounded strained and hoarse.

It took us three hours to cross this range.

On the summit were no gently undulating downs such as we had met the day before. Instead, three smaller dune-chains rode upon its back, and beyond them the sand fell away to a salt-flat in another great empty trough between the mountains. The range on the far side seemed even higher than the one on which we stood, and behind it were others. I looked round, seeking instinctively for some escape. There was no limit to my vision. Somewhere in the ultimate distance the sands merged into the sky, but in that infinity of space I could see no living thing, not even a withered plant to give me hope. 'There is nowhere to go', I thought. 'We cannot go back and our camels will never get up another of these awful dunes. We really are finished.' The silence flowed over me, drowning the voices of my companions and the fidgeting of their camels.

We went down into the valley, and somehow – and I shall never know how the camels did it – we got up the other side. There, utterly exhausted, we collapsed. Al Auf gave us each a little water, enough to wet our months. He said, 'We need this if we are to go on.' The midday sun had drained the colour from the sands. Scattered banks of cumulus cloud threw shadows across the dunes and salt-flats, and added an illusion that we were high among Alpine peaks, with frozen lakes of blue and green in the valley, far below. Half asleep, I turned over, but the sand burnt through my shirt and woke me from my dreams.

Two hours later al Auf roused us. As he helped me load my camel, he said, 'Cheer up, Umbarak. This time we really are across the Uruq al Shaiba', and when I pointed to the ranges ahead of us, he answered, 'I can find a way through those; we need not cross them.' We went on till sunset, but we were going with the grain of the country, following the valleys and no longer trying to climb the dunes. We should not have been able to cross another. There was a little fresh *qassis* on the slope where we halted. I hoped that this lucky find would give us an excuse to stop here for the night, but, after we had fed, al Auf went to fetch the camels, saying, 'We must go on again while it is cool if we are ever to reach Dhafara.'

We stopped long after midnight and started again at dawn, still exhausted from the strain and long hours of yesterday, but al Auf encouraged us by saying that the worst was over. The dunes were certainly lower than they had been, more uniform in height and more rounded, with fewer peaks. Four hours after we had started we came to rolling uplands of gold and silver sand, but still there was nothing for the camels to eat.

A hare jumped out from under a bush, and al Auf knocked it over with his stick. The others shouted 'God has given us meat.' For days we had talked of food; every conversation seemed to lead back to it. Since we had left Ghanim I had been always conscious of the dull ache of hunger, yet in the evening my throat was dry even after my drink, so that I found it difficult to swallow the dry bread Musallim set before us. All day we thought and talked about that hare, and by three o'clock in the afternoon could no longer resist stopping to cook it. Mabkhaut suggested, 'Let's roast it in its skin in the embers of a fire. That will save our water – we haven't got much left.' Bin Kabina led the chorus of protest. 'No, by God! Don't even suggest such a thing'; and turning to me he said, 'We don't want Mabkhaut's charred meat. Soup. We want soup and extra bread. We will feed well today even if we go hungry and thirsty later. By God, I am hungry!' We agreed to make soup. We were across the Uruq al Shaiba and intended to celebrate our achievement with this gift from God. Unless our camels foundered we were safe; even if our water ran out we should live to reach a well.

Musallim made nearly double our usual quantity of bread while bin Kabina cooked the hare. He looked across at me and said, 'The smell of this meat makes me faint.' When it was ready he divided it into five portions. They were very small, for an Arabian hare is no larger than an English rabbit, and this one was not even fully grown. Al Auf named the lots and Mabkhaut drew them. Each of us took the small pile of meat which had fallen to him. Then bin Kabina said, 'God! I have forgotten to divide the liver', and the others said, 'Give it to Umbarak.' I protested, saying that they should divide it, but they swore by God that they would not eat it and that I was to have it. Eventually I took it, knowing that I ought not, but too greedy for this extra scrap of meat to care.

Our water was nearly finished and there was only enough flour for about another week. The starving camels were so thirsty that they had refused to eat some half-dried herbage which we had passed. We must water them in the next day or two or they would collapse. Al Auf said that it would take us three more days to reach Khaba well in Dhafara, but that there was a very brackish well not far away. He thought that the camels might drink its water.

That night after we had ridden for a little over an hour it grew suddenly dark. Thinking that a cloud must be covering the full moon, I looked over my shoulder and saw that there was an eclipse and that half the moon was already obscured. Bin Kabina noticed it at the same moment and broke into a chant which the others took up.

> God endures for ever.
> The life of man is short.
> The Pleiades are overhead.
> The moon's among the stars.

Otherwise they paid no attention to the eclipse (which was total), but looked around for a place to camp.

We started very early the next morning and rode without a stop for seven hours across easy rolling downs. The colour of these sands was vivid, varied, and unexpected: in places the colour of ground coffee, elsewhere brick-red, or purple, or a curious golden-green. There were small white gypsum-flats, fringed with *shanan*, a grey-green salt-bush, lying in hollows

132

in the downs. We rested for two hours on sands the colour of dried blood and then led our camels on again.

Suddenly we were challenged by an Arab lying behind a bush on the crest of a dune. Our rifles were on our camels, for we had not expected to meet anyone here. Musallim was hidden behind mine. I watched him draw his rifle clear. But al Auf said, 'It is the voice of a Rashid', and walked forward. He spoke to the concealed Arab, who rose and came to meet him. They embraced and stood talking until we joined them. We greeted the man, and al Auf said, 'This is Hamad bin Hanna, a sheikh of the Rashid.' He was a heavily-built bearded man of middle age. His eyes were set close together and he had a long nose with a blunt end. He fetched his camel from behind the dune while we unloaded.

We made coffee for him and listened to his news. He told us that he had been looking for a stray camel when he crossed our tracks and had taken us for a raiding party from the south. Ibn Saud's tax-collectors were in Dhafara and the Rabadh, collecting tribute from the tribes; and there were Rashid, Awamir, Murra, and some Manahil to the north of us.

We had to avoid all contact with Arabs other than the Rashid, and if possible even with them, so that news of my presence would not get about among the tribes, for I had no desire to be arrested by Ibn Saud's tax-collectors and taken off to explain my presence here to Ibn Jalawi, the formidable Governor of the Hasa. Karab from the Hadhramaut had raided these sands the year before, so there was also a serious risk of our being mistaken for raiders, since the tracks of our camels would show that we had come from the southern steppes. This risk would be increased if it appeared that we were avoiding the Arabs, for honest travellers never pass an encampment without seeking news and food. It was going to be very difficult to escape detection. First we must water our camels and draw water for ourselves. Then we must lie up as close as possible to Liwa and send a party to the villages to buy us enough food for at least another month. Hamad told me that Liwa belonged to the Al bu Falah of Abu Dhabi. He said that they were still fighting Said bin Maktum of Dibai, and that, as there was a lot of raiding going on, the Arabs would be very much on the alert.

We started again in the late afternoon and travelled till sunset. Hamad came with us and said he would stay with us until we had got food from Liwa. Knowing where the Arabs were encamped he could help us to avoid them. Next day, after seven hours' travelling, we reached Khaur Sabakha on the edge of the Dhafara sands. We cleaned out the well and found brackish water at seven feet, so bitter that even the camels only drank a little before refusing it. They sniffed thirstily at the water with which al Auf tried to coax them from a leather bucket, but only dipped their lips into it. We covered their noses but still they would not drink. Yet al Auf said that Arabs themselves drank this water mixed with milk, and when I expressed my disbelief he added that if an Arab was really thirsty he would even kill a camel and drink the liquid in its stomach, or ram a stick down its throat and drink the vomit. We went on again till nearly sunset.

The next day when we halted in the afternoon al Auf told us we had reached Dhafara and that Khaba well was close. He said that he would fetch water in the morning. We finished what little was left in one of our skins. Next day we remained where we were. Hamad said that he would go for news and return the following day. Al Auf, who went with him, came back in the afternoon with two skins full of water which, although slightly brackish, was delicious after the filthy evil-smelling dregs we had drunk the night before.

The start of Thesiger's journey from Swat towards the Kachi Kuni Pass, in Chitral. 'The mountainsides were steep, covered with holly-oak and deodars; the river here was milky-coloured and fast flowing.'

Above Thesiger's party on the Baroghil Pass, northern Chitral, in 1952. 'There on the top of the pass it was very still; only the shadow of an occasional cloud drifted across the vast land.'

Right Two days after leaving Gilgit, in September 1953, Thesiger had his first sight of Rakaposhi (25,550 ft), the great mountain which dominates the valley route from Gilgit to Baltit, in Hunza. 'I remembered Eric Shipton describing Rakaposhi to me in the Travellers Club [in London] and how this had fired me with the desire to see it.'

Under the Chilinji Pass, near Biatar, looking down on the glacier far below. 'Ploughing upwards, knee-deep, through the snow [towards the pass], I was worried about crevasses, but the porters appeared unconcerned.'

On the Karumbar glacier, looking down the Ishkoman Valley. The glacier, a chaos of tumbled rock, stones, earth and ice, rises from the 25,000-foot Batura mountains, northwest of Baltit.

In the heart of the Karakorams, north of Baltit, capital of Hunza, 1953.

Floodwater, six feet deep, roughened by a gale, covers the desert on the western edge of the Marshes. In 1954, the year of the great floods, life in the Marshes 'went on much as usual, inconvenienced but not seriously affected by the disaster that overwhelmed much of Iraq.'

Marsh Arabs in a *tarada*, or high-prowed canoe, going home from market in the evening.

The eastern Marshes. 'During nearly every year, from 1951 to 1958, I spent months in this remote world, and came to regard it as home.'

Right A Suaid herdboy wearing the tribe's distinctive, ochre-colour headcloth: the frontispiece of the first edition of *The Marsh Arabs*. 'These Suaid were not cultivators but lived in the Marshes with their herds.' *Below* A *mudhif* on the Shatt al Gharraf. This river leaves the Tigris at Kut and flows south-west in the direction of Nasiriya, the capital of Muntifiq Province.

A group of Samburu women and children at South Horr, in the former Northern Frontier District of Kenya. On his first journey in northern Kenya, 1960–1, Thesiger and his companion, Frank Steele, camped at South Horr, 'in a beautiful grove of tall, slender acacias with a clear stream of running water nearby'. Thesiger found the Samburu 'a tall, strikingly handsome people'.

Rendille warriors, northern Kenya. At a Rendille encampment, Thesiger watched a dance which started at midnight. 'It was spectacularly effective, with camels couched all around and the dancers' spears stuck upright in the ground. The songs were rousing and the dancing very energetic in short bursts, men and women together.'

It was 12 December, fourteen days since we had left Khaur bin Atarit in Ghanim.

In the evening, now that we needed no longer measure out each cup of water, bin Kabina made extra coffee, while Musallim increased our rations of flour by a mugful. This was wild extravagance, but we felt that the occasion called for celebration. Even so, the loaves he handed us were woefully inadequate to stay our hunger, now that our thirst was gone.

The moon was high above us when I lay down to sleep. The others still talked round the fire, but I closed my mind to the meaning of their words, content to hear only the murmur of their voices, to watch their outlines sharp against the sky, happily conscious that they were there and beyond them the camels to which we owed our lives.

For years the Empty Quarter had represented to me the final, unattainable challenge which the desert offered. Suddenly it had come within my reach. I remembered my excitement when Lean had casually offered me the chance to go there, the immediate determination to cross it, and then the doubts and fears, the frustrations, and the moments of despair. Now I had crossed it. To others my journey would have little importance. It would produce nothing except a rather inaccurate map which no one was ever likely to use. It was a personal experience, and the reward had been a drink of clean, nearly tasteless water. I was content with that.

Once more we rode across an empty land, but now it was not only empty, it was dead. Shallow depressions in the limestone floor held sloughs of glutinous black mud, crusted with scabs of salt and sand, like putrescent patches on a carcase rotting in the sun. We rode for seven and eight and nine hours a day, without a stop, and it was dreary work. Conversation died with the passing hours and boredom mounted within me like a dull ache of pain. We muffled our faces against the parching wind, screwed up our eyes against the glare which stabbed into our heads. The flies we had brought with us from our butchers' work at Haushi clustered black upon our backs and heads. If I made a sudden movement they were thick about my face in a noisy questing cloud. I rode along, my body swaying backwards and forwards, backwards and forwards, to the camel's stride, a ceaseless strain upon my back which from long practice I no longer felt. I watched the sun's slow progress and longed for evening. As the sun sank into the haze it became an orange disc without heat or brilliance. I looked at it through my field-glasses and saw the sun-spots like black holes in its surface. It disappeared while still a span above the horizon, vanishing in a yellow sky that was without a cloud.

We rode across the flatness of the Jaddat al Harasis, long marches of eight and even ten hours a day. We were like a small army, for many Harasis and Mahra travelled with us, going to Salala to visit the Sultan of Muscat, who had recently arrived there. I was as glad now to be back in this friendly crowd as I had been to escape from it at Mughshin. I delighted in the surging rhythm of this mass of camels, the slapping shuffle of their feet, the shouted talk, and the songs which stirred the blood of men and beasts so that they drove forward with quickened pace. And there was life here. Gazelle grazed among the flat-topped acacia bushes, and once I saw a distant herd of oryx looking very white against the dark gravel of the plain. There were lizards, about eighteen inches in length, which scuttled across the ground. They had disc-shaped tails, and in consequence the Arabs called them 'The Father of the Dollar'. I asked if they ate them, but they declared that they were unlaw-ful; I knew that they would eat other lizards which resembled them except for their tails. But, anyway, there was no need now for us to eat lizard-meat. Every day we fed on gazelles, and twice Musallim shot an oryx.

We watered at Khaur Wir: I wondered how much more foul water could taste and still be considered drinkable. We watered again six days later at Yisbub, where the water was fresh and maidenhair fern grew in the damp rock above the pool. We went on again and reached Andhur, where I had been the previous year, and camped near the palm grove. Then we climbed up on to the Qarra mountains and looked upon the sea.

More than a hundred tribesmen from the Rashid, Bait Kathir, Mahra, and Manahil were camped around us that night, and soon they were all collected round our fire. They belonged to tribes which had suffered from Dahm raids. The moon was nearly full, so that I could see them clearly as they sat there, crowded together with their rifles in their hands. Behind them the cliffs were white in the moonlight, and above were the wooded slopes of the Qarra mountains. All around us were the couched camels and the dying light of many fires. Bin Kabina and bin Anauf moved round pouring out coffee for each man in turn. I could sense the expectancy which is always present when Bedu contemplate a raid. I knew that many of them were already picturing the looted camels which would make them rich.

Bin al Kamam argued that the Dahm were tribesmen and would be bound to return camels taken during a truce. He spoke slowly, poking at the ground with his camel-stick. There were mutters of 'Yes, by God!' and 'True! True!' Someone interrupted him, saying that the Dahm were faithless, worse even than the Saar. Another man spoke, trying by raising his voice to hold the attention of the crowd, but his words were lost in the growing din. Suddenly an excited Rashid, whose

137

name I did not know, sprang to his feet, hurled his head-cloth on the ground, and shouted, '*Ba Rashud*, if twenty men will come with me I will go and fetch the two camels they have taken from me. What is more, by God, I will bring back a hundred Dahm camels as well!' He turned on bin al Kamam and asked furiously, 'What is the good of your negotiations? You made a truce for the Rashid, and the Dahm immediately broke it. The only result of your truce was that we were caught unprepared. How many camels have the Rashid lost? The Dahm are utterly faithless. God's curse on them! Our rifles should be our answer to this raid. Let the rifles speak. Listen to me, you people. Get together and raid. God almighty, are the Rashid women thus to be harried by the Dahm? It would be a disgrace to negotiate now.'

Everyone was shouting, and I could hardly make out a word. Old one-eyed Abdullah was arguing furiously with a group of Mahra, while he hammered the ground with his stick. Bin Mautlauq was shouting for war, abetted by a handsome boy in a blue loin-cloth. Bin Kabina had stopped pouring out coffee and was gesticulating with the pot. Occasionally one man commanded attention for a while, and then the strained silence was broken only by a single urgent voice, but inevitably someone else joined in and the two voices rose, the one against the other, until both were lost in the returning noise. I noticed a little man sitting opposite me who was insistent that the tribes should unite and inflict a really crushing defeat on the Dahm. His clothes were stained and torn, but he wore a large silver-hilted dagger set with cornelians and a belt filled with cartridges, and he held a brass-bound Martini rifle between his knees. He had very bright eyes, and all his movements were jerky. He looked rather like an assertive sparrow, but I noticed that the others listened carefully to everything he said. I asked bin Kabina who he was, and he answered, 'Don't you know him? He is bin Duailan, "The Cat".' I looked at him again with interest, for bin Duailan was the most famous raider in southern Arabia. Eight months later he was to die on the Yemen border, surrounded by the men he had killed in his last and most desperate fight, which plunged the desert into war. Bin al Kamam made a joke which I could not catch, and everyone nearby laughed; and then bin Kalut, who had been sitting silent and unmoved, spoke in his deep voice. 'Let bin al Kamam go to the Dahm and demand the return of the Rashid camels. If they hand them over the Rashid will keep the truce. If they refuse we will collect a force and raid them after we have taken Umbarak to Mukalla.' The decision seemed to have been made as far as the Rashid were concerned.

Next day we crossed the Kismim pass and camped once more by the pool of Aiyun. Bin Kabina was accompanied by the boy I had noticed the night before. They were about the same age. This boy was dressed only in a length of blue cloth, which he wore wrapped round his waist with one tasselled end thrown over his right shoulder, and his dark hair fell like a mane about his shoulders. He had a face of classic beauty, pensive and rather sad in repose, but which lit up when he smiled, like a pool touched by the sun. Antinous must have looked like this, I thought, when Hadrian first saw him in the Phrygian woods. The boy moved with effortless grace, walking as women walk who have carried vessels on their heads since childhood. A stranger might have thought that his smooth, pliant body would never bear the rigours of desert life, but I knew how deceptively enduring were these Bedu boys who looked like girls. He told me that his name was Salim bin Ghabaisha and he asked me to take him with us. Bin Kabina urged me to let him join us, saying that he was the best shot in the tribe and that he was as good a hunter as Musallim, so that if he was with us we should feed every day on meat, for there were many ibex and gazelle in the country ahead of us. He added, 'He is my friend. Let him come with us for my sake. The two of us will go with you wherever you want. We will always be your men.'

After dinner bin Kabina got up from beside me, saying that he was going to fetch his camel. Suddenly someone called out, 'Bin Kabina has fallen down.' I looked round and saw him lying on the sand. He was unconscious when I reached him. His pulse was very feeble and his body cold; he was breathing hoarsely. I carried him to the fire and piled blankets on him to warm him. I then tried to pour a little brandy down his throat but he could not swallow. Gradually his breathing became easier and his body a little warmer, but he did not recover consciousness. I sat beside him hour after hour wondering miserably if he was going to die. I remembered how I had first met him in the Wadi Mitan, how he had come to Shisur to join me, how he had unhesitatingly remained with me at Ramlat al Ghafa when the Bait Kathir had deserted me. I remembered his happiness when I gave him his rifle, and I knew that whenever I thought of the past months I should be thinking of him, for he had shared everything with me, even my doubts and difficulties. I remembered with bitter regret how I had sometimes vented my ill-temper on him to ease the strain under which I lived, and how he had always been good-tempered and very patient. The others crowded round and discussed the chances of his dying, until I could scarcely bear it; and then someone asked where we were going tomorrow and I said that there would be no tomorrow if bin Kabina died. Hours later as I lay beside him I felt him relax and knew that he was sleeping and was no longer unconscious. He woke at dawn and at first could hear but could not speak, and signed to me that his chest was hurting. By midday he could speak and in the evening he was all right again. The Rashid gathered round him, chanting incantations and firing off their rifles; and then sprinkled flour, coffee, and sugar in the stream-bed to appease the spirits which they had exorcized. Later they slaughtered a goat, sprinkled him with its blood, and declared him cured. I have often wondered what was wrong with him and can only think it was some kind of fit.

I have often been asked, 'Why do the Bedu live in the desert where they have to put up with the appalling conditions which you describe? Why don't they leave it and find an easier life elsewhere?' and few people have believed me when I have said, 'They live there from choice.' Yet obviously the great Bedu tribes of Syria could at any time have dispossessed the weaker cultivators along the desert's edge and settled on their land. They continued instead to dwell as nomads in the desert because that was the life they cherished. When I was in Damascus I often visited the Rualla while they were camped in summer on the wells outside the city. They urged me to accompany them on their annual migration, which would start southward for the Najd as soon as grazing had come up after the autumn rains. Only in the desert, they declared, could a man find freedom. It must have been this same craving for freedom which induced tribes that entered Egypt at the time of the Arab conquest to pass on through the Nile valley into the interminable desert beyond, leaving behind them the green fields, the palm groves, the shade and running water, and all the luxury which they found in the towns they had conquered.

Knowing that I should not come back, I advised bin Kabina and bin Ghabaisha to return to their homelands in the south as soon as the weather got cool. Already they had many blood-feuds on their hands, and I feared that they would inevitably be killed if they remained in these parts. The following year I heard that bin Kabina had collected his camels and gone back to Habarut; bin Ghabaisha, however, remained on the Trucial Coast, where his reputation became increasingly notorious. Henderson wrote and told me how he was woken in the early hours to find bin Ghabaisha on his doorstep seeking sanctuary with a badly-wounded man in his arms. They had been raiding camels on the outskirts of the town. Henderson sent the wounded man to hospital in Bahrain, and bin Ghabaisha went there with him. Two years later I saw a report by the Political Resident which stated that the Sheikh of Sharja had succeeded at last in capturing 'the notorious brigand bin Ghabaisha who had been Thesiger's companion' and that he was determined to make an example of him. I was relieved when I heard soon afterwards that the Sheikh had released him after receiving an ultimatum from the Rashid and Awamir.

One evening the Political Officer who had taken over from Noel Jackson came to dinner. He led me aside and said, 'I am afraid, Thesiger, that I have a rather embarrassing duty to perform. The Sultan of Muscat, His Highness Sayid Saiyid Bin Taimur, has demanded that we should cancel your Muscat visa. I have been instructed to do so by the Political Resident. I am afraid I must therefore have your passport.' I replied, 'All right, I'll get it; but you realize I've never had a Muscat visa.'

Although we joked during dinner about a 'visa for Nazwa,' I realized that it would not be long before visas really were required, even for travel in the Empty Quarter. Even now I was probably barred from going back there. To reach the Sands, I had to start from somewhere on the coast, and I could no longer land in Oman or in Dhaufar; even if I returned to the Trucial Coast my presence would probably be regarded as an embarrassment by the Political Resident. I recalled that the previous year the Aden Government, hearing that I was planning another journey, had sent me a telegram advising me for my own sake not to enter Saudi territory. Although I had no political or economic interest in the country few people accepted the fact that I travelled there for my own pleasure, certainly not the American oil companies nor the Saudi Government. I knew that I had made my last journey in the Empty Quarter and that a phase in my life was ended. Here in the desert I had found all that I asked; I knew that I should never find it again. But it was not only this personal sorrow that distressed me. I realized that the Bedu with whom I had lived and travelled, and in whose company I had found contentment, were doomed. Some people maintain that they will be better off when they have exchanged the hardship and poverty of the desert for the security of a materialistic world. This I do not believe. I shall always remember how often I was humbled by those illiterate herdsmen who possessed, in so much greater measure than I, generosity and courage, endurance, patience, and lighthearted gallantry. Among no other people have I ever felt the same sense of personal inadequacy.

On the last evening, as bin Kabina and bin Ghabaisha were tying up the few things they had bought, Codrai said, looking at the two small bundles, 'It is rather pathetic that this is all they have.' I understood what he meant; I had often felt the same. Yet I knew that for them the danger lay, not in the hardship of their lives, but in the boredom and frustration they would feel when they renounced it. The tragedy was that the choice would not be theirs; economic forces beyond their control would eventually drive them into the towns to hang about street-corners as 'unskilled labour'.

The lorry arrived after breakfast. We embraced for the last

time. I said, 'Go in peace,' and they answered together, 'Remain in the safe keeping of God, Umbarak.' Then they scrambled up on to a pile of petrol drums beside a Palestinian refugee in oil-stained dungarees. A few minutes later they were out of sight round a corner. I was glad when Codrai took me to the aerodrome at Sharja. As the plane climbed over the town and swung out above the sea I knew how it felt to go into exile.

from *Arabian Sands*

After my drive across Persia in 1949 into Iraq, I returned to Iraqi Kurdistan for three months in August 1950 and for another five the following May. I suspect that no foreigner ever saw as much of this country as I did during those eight months; there can have been few villages I did not visit, few mountains I did not climb.

I was accompanied by a cheerful, good-natured and indefatigable young Kurd called Nasser, who spoke Arabic. I knew no Kurdish: only a few of the chiefs, or Aghas, spoke Arabic. Sometimes we hired a mule or a horse to carry our saddle-bags, while we walked; at other times our hosts lent us horses to our next destination, and then we rode. I took little with me: some spare clothes, a few medicines, a book or two – *Lord Jim* and *Kim* have been stand-bys on many of my journeys – a camera, a Rigby .275, cartridges and a couple of blankets in case we camped out. We relied on our hosts for food and bedding. More welcoming and hospitable than Persian villagers, they would have felt insulted if we had fed ourselves. Mostly we ate flaps of unleavened bread with curds, or boiled wheat, sometimes meat and vegetable stews with rice. In season there was fruit: mulberries, apricots, peaches, melons, sometimes grapes.

Never had I seen such country: the great rock-girt bastion of Hendren, above the gorge of Rowunduz; Helgord's twelve thousand feet; the snow-capped range of Qandil, with sheer-faced precipices of five thousand feet; and, higher still, across the Turkish frontier, Kara Dagh, the 'Black Mountain', and beyond that the other Hakari peaks. Everywhere one range was superimposed upon another. The knees of the mountains, and the valley sides up to six thousand feet, were wooded with holly-oaks interspersed with a few ash, hawthorn and wild pear, and rare stands of juniper. In the valley bottoms the Zab, the Little Zab and other smaller rivers and torrents flowed down to join the far-off Tigris, foaming ice-cold through narrow gorges of polished rock, and swirling among great boulders tumbled from the cliffs above; or calm in deep green pools under grassy banks and overhanging willows.

In spring there were the wild flowers: red and white anemones on the lower slopes, covering whole hillsides with carpets of colour; and among them red ranunculus like poppies, yellow marigolds, gladioli, stocks, dark blue squills and irises. High up on the mountains scarlet tulips grew in profusion, scattered tiger-lilies flowered in hollows among the rocks, dark blue gentians bordered drifts of snow.

In such a setting the Kurds in tasselled turbans were fittingly colourful. The Jaf, who lived in the south round Halabja and had been nomadic till Persia closed the frontier, wore long robes like the Arabs, with short jackets over elaborately-wound cummerbunds, and baggy trousers drawn in at the ankle. The northern Kurds, the nomadic Herki in particular, wore loose wide-bottomed trousers and tucked their jackets under their cummerbunds. Whereas the Jaf wore dark uniform colours, the clothes of the northern tribes were dyed with blues, greens and browns of varying shades, woven with wide, light-coloured stripes and patterns. Most men were hung about with bandoliers, wore formidable daggers in their cummerbunds and carried revolvers in holsters at their sides.

The Kurds, generally regarded as the descendants of the Medes, have inhabited at least since Parthian times the mountains where they now live. Today their land is divided between Turkey, Persia and Iraq, while a few live in northern Syria. Formidable fighters and turbulent by nature, their unquenchable craving for independence has led them time and again to revolt against their alien rulers. The Turks, with characteristic brutality, have suppressed them, denied them their identity and the use of their language, and would have them known as Mountain Turks. Reza Shah tried to do the same with the Kurds in Persia: equally harsh, he was less effective. Indeed after the Second World War the Kurds, with Russian encouragement, set up a short-lived Independent Kurdish Republic at Mahabad. The Iraqi Government allowed the Kurds to carry arms, to wear their tribal dress, to learn Kurdish in their schools, and employed Kurdish officials to administer them: yet even these concessions could not satisfy Kurdish aspirations.

The most interesting character I met in Kurdistan was Sheikh Mahmud. Intensely ambitious and aspiring to rule an independent Kurdistan, he had led his tribesmen in insurrection after insurrection from 1919 to 1930 against the British who then controlled Iraq. Defeated each time after fierce fighting, he would be exiled, pardoned and allowed to return, only to rebel once more. His last uprising was against the Iraqis in 1941. I had known him well by repute: some of my older friends, including Guy Moore, who had often spoken of him as we sat beside the fire at Kutum, had fought against him. A stout, jovial figure, Sheikh Mahmud entertained me in his house: in the evening, after we had fed, he would recall ancient battles, and

British officers he had known. A few years later he died. I am glad I met him.

Nasser and I stayed in villages of flat-roofed houses rising in tiers up the hillsides, and slept in rooms furnished only with rugs and pillows; we shared the black tents, and cabins built from branches, in which the tribes lived in spring after they had moved with their herds to the mountainsides. I remember coming down from Helgord, tired and thirsty, to the tents of the Baliki pitched on green turf where yellow buttercups and pink primulas flowered among the moss, bordering threads of water and shallow pools. How good the yoghurt they gave me tasted.

When I was travelling near Sulaymaniyah the Administrative Officer insisted on sending three policemen with me for a two-day journey through the area of a notorious outlaw, Kula Piza. Once a law-abiding man, he had originally been arrested for some minor offence, but after brutal treatment from the police-man, had killed him and taken to the hills. More police were sent after him: he killed them too. Actively supported only by his brothers and a few friends, he made war on the police, killing any he met. He was reported to have accounted for a hundred. He and his band also killed the District Judge from Sulaymaniyah. I should have felt safer without my escort. Kula Piza was eventually killed by the army while I was in northern Kurdistan. The day news of his death arrived official flags were at half-mast for King Abdullah's assassination. Many Kurds, including Nasser, presumed this was a mark of respect for Kula Piza: in their eyes he was a national hero who for years almost single-handedly fought the police, local representatives of an Arab Government in Baghdad.

That autumn Nasser and I joined the Herki, as they moved down from the high mountains along the Turkish border towards the plains round Mosul. Though the flocks were travelling separately the passes and tracks were choked with loaded mules and ponies. On some of the loads were partridges in wicker-work cages. The women, who wore turbans round soft red caps like fezzes, often carried rifles, which looked incongruous but left the men freer to struggle with wedged animals and slipping loads. The migration covered six or seven miles a day. In the afternoons the tents went up and food was cooked; we stayed with the Agha, Sidi Khan, and fed well. All night there was bedlam as packs of dogs rushed barking from one end of the camp to the other. Great savage brutes, these dogs could be very dangerous to a stranger who approached tents where there were no men to beat them off.

I climbed innumerable mountain faces looking for bear and ibex while in Kurdistan. On one occasion I slipped crossing a tongue of frozen snow and slid for thirty yards or more down the icy slope towards a precipice. Luckily the gradient eased and I clawed to a stop. After that I always wore felt-soled Kurdish slippers, the best footwear on such mountains. Without the urge to hunt I should never have seen half the country that I did, nor looked on many a stupendous view. But in all my months in Kurdistan I only shot one bear and one ibex, and as I looked on the dead bear I resolved I would never shoot another animal unless for food or because of the destruction it caused. On several of those hunts I was accompanied by a tireless Assyrian, a former officer of the Iraq Levies. He was well-informed about the wildlife of the mountains. During our hunts we sometimes camped in the woods or slept in caves. One night we were woken by the 'woof' of a bear which found us in possession of its home. Bears were not uncommon, especially in the north, but I saw only four. Sometimes we spotted ibex, threading their way across the face of a sheer precipice without apparent footholds – we would sit and watch them while griffon vultures circled above us or a lammergeyer sailed past on motionless wings, so close that I could see the bristles that gave it its other name, bearded vulture; and always there were choughs, swooping and tumbling shrill-voiced around the crags. Not infrequently we disturbed wild boar in the woods, and once I saw a roe deer. Wolves were fairly common and took a toll from the flocks, and in the remoter areas there were said to be some leopard.

The Assyrians, who were Nestorian Christians, were an ill-fated people. Their homelands had been in the Hakari mountains, but in the First World War they rose unsuccessfully against the Turks. Some twenty thousand escaped retribution and after a nightmare journey reached Persia. From there they were moved by the British to Iraq, where many were enlisted in the Levies. After Iraq became independent the Assyrians provoked trouble, fought against the army and were defeated. Their defeat was followed by a shameful massacre of their women and children at Simel. Staying near the Hakari mountains in villages which had always belonged to them, I saw what a splendid people they once had been.

Another oppressed people whom I met were the Yazidis. Of Kurdish stock, they lived in villages round Jebel Sinjar, a mountain in the desert west of Mosul, and among the Kurdish foothills north-east of Mosul, near the shrine of Sheikh Adi, founder of their community. Reputed to worship the Devil, they were abhorred in consequence by their neighbours and by the Government. I met a senior Kurdish official who was administering them. I had known and liked him when he was in Halabja; now he horrified me by bursting out, 'These filthy people should be exterminated!' In fact the Yazidis do not worship the Devil but seek to placate him, believing that the

Supreme Being delegated power to him over the world after he was cast forth from Heaven. They will never say his name, 'Shaitan', nor use any word that begins with 'Sh'. They have various other curious prohibitions: they will never wear blue, nor a shirt opening down the front, nor eat lettuces, nor defecate into water. Their religion, in origin an Islamic dervish brotherhood, now apparently contains elements of nature worship, Zoroastrianism and Christianity, in which Malek Taus, the Peacock King, has an important place. Once a year, early in October, they assemble at Sheikh Adi and sacrifice a bull to the sun. On the doorway of the shrine is an embossed black serpent, symbol of Shaitan, which the pilgrims kiss. I attended this festival but did not see the sacrifice. Booths had been set up among the trees, near the shrine with its two fluted, pointed white cones, and the scene resembled a fair, crowded with happy, relaxed people. There was much dancing and singing, in which the women joined.

The Yazidis round Sheikh Adi affected Kurdish dress; those who lived round Jebel Sinjar wore their own distinctive and becoming garb. The young men and boys, many of whom were remarkably good-looking, dressed in long white shirts and coats, and their braided hair fell in plaits to their shoulders from beneath round felt caps. The older men, of the ascetic order of *Faqirs*, wore short coarse black shirts next to their skin, black turbans round their felt caps, short white jackets and baggy trousers. Most had distinguished faces, enhanced by their long beards. I was captivated by these much maligned people; I had visited most of their villages on the lower slopes of Jebel Sinjar before attending the festival at Sheikh Adi. I would willingly have stayed longer among them, but time pressed.

Nasser and I went south again, travelling hither and thither for some four hundred miles throughout the length of Kurdistan, passing once more through the territories of the Baradost, Mungur, Pizdhar, Jaf and other tribes whom we had already met. Then, far to the south, we left the mountains and reached the plains where Kurd merged into Arab, and here we found ourselves among the Bani Lam, one of the great shepherd tribes of southern Iraq. Escorted by our hosts and riding on their horses, we travelled from one encampment to the next until we came at last to the town of Amara, and beyond it to the strange remote world of the Marshes.

from *Desert, Marsh and Mountain*

Memories of that first visit to the Marshes have never left me: firelight on a half-turned face, the crying of geese, duck flighting in to feed, a boy's voice singing somewhere in the dark, canoes moving in procession down a waterway, the setting sun seen crimson through the smoke of burning reedbeds, narrow waterways that wound still deeper into the Marshes. A naked man in a canoe with a trident in his hand, reed houses built upon water, black, dripping buffaloes that looked as if they had calved from the swamp with the first dry land. Stars reflected in dark water, the croaking of frogs, canoes coming home at evening, peace and continuity, the stillness of a world that never knew an engine. Once again I experienced the longing to share this life, and to be more than a mere spectator.

Six months later I was travelling down a branch of the Tigris towards the Marshes in a leaky bitumen-coated canoe paddled by two Arabs. One of them was a gaunt old man, dressed in a patched shirt of indeterminate colour, that reached half-way to his calves. The other, a stocky boy of fifteen with a squint, wore the remains of a European jacket over a new white shirt hitched up through his belt to prevent it trailing on the ground. Both wore headcloths of the kind generally used by the Shia tribesmen of Southern Iraq, a three-foot square with a black net pattern on a once-white base. Not having head-ropes, they had twisted the cloths, folded into a triangle, round their heads. The old man sat on the raised stern. I sat on the bottom of the canoe at his feet, cross-legged on a piece of matting with my luggage in front of me. It consisted of two black tin boxes, one filled with medicine, the other with books, films, cartridges and odds and ends. On top of the boxes a Kurdish saddle-bag, woven in rich colours, was stuffed with blankets and spare clothes. Propped against it were my shotgun and a .275 Rigby rifle in a canvas cover.

The river was thirty yards wide, fast-flowing and obviously deep. The tips of my fingers were in the water as I grasped the sides. A stiff breeze blew upstream, raising small waves that splashed on to me and my luggage. I sat very still, convinced that the smallest move on my part would capsize us. The two Arabs, however, shifted about with complete unconcern, never disturbing the balance of the canoe.

The boy stopped paddling, turned and crouched down to shelter while he lit a cigarette. The old man stood up, looking for a friend working in the fields. From the bottom of the canoe I could see nothing but the steep-sided banks three or four feet high. They were intersected at intervals by irrigation channels of various sizes draining out of the main stream, and were crowned with thorn scrub, two or three feet tall and a dusty bluish-green. Terrapins slithered back off shelves on the banks and flopped into the opaque brownish water. Some of them were flat in shape, with soft shells as much as two feet across which undulated at the edges as they moved; others, smaller, resembled more conventional tortoises. Pied kingfishers darted past or hung in the air with rapidly beating wings before diving, kites circled above us, and the occasional flock of rooks rose noisily from the cultivation behind the banks. A dusty haze toned down the sky and everything was a drab earth colour.

We passed a small settlement of reed huts, grey like weathered ricks, where dark-clothed women washed dishes at the water's edge among a fleet of black canoes drawn up on a mud bank. A man came out of a hut and the elder of my Arabs called out a greeting, '*Salam alaikum*' (Peace be on you). The man replied, '*Alaikum as salam*' (On you be peace), and added, '*Filbu*' (Stop and feed). We answered, '*Kafu, Allah yahafadhak*' (We have fed, God protect you). Half a dozen dogs raced along the bank beside us, barking and snarling hysterically until stopped by a ditch too wide for them to jump.

Abd ar Ridha, the coffee-maker, appeared in the grey dawn and lit the fire, which soon filled the room with smoke. The boy had gone. The two old men got up hawking and spitting. After performing their ritual ablutions, they said their prayers and then crouched over the fire. It seemed cold, so I stayed where I was until two servants came to remove the bedding, when I joined the others and was handed a cup of coffee. A servant brought breakfast – thin pancakes of rice flour on a grass platter and hot sweetened milk in a kettle. He laid our portions on the carpet in front of us as the sun rose gilding the entrance pillars.

An hour or two later, Falih, accompanied by a throng of armed retainers, came in to fetch me for the promised pig shoot. After they had all drunk coffee, I got into the same canoe as Falih and his son.

She was a beautiful craft that could carry as many as twelve people. Thirty-six feet long but only three and a half feet at her widest beam, she was carvel-built, flat-bottomed and covered outside with a smooth coating of bitumen over the wooden planks. The front swept forwards and upwards in a perfect curve to form a long, thin, tapering stem; the stern too rose in a graceful sweep. Two feet of the stern and of the bows were decked; there was a thwart a third of the way forward, and a strengthening beam across the boat two thirds of the way forward. Movable boards covered the floor. The top part of the ribs was planked along the inside and studded with five rows of flat, round nail-heads two inches across. These decorative nails were the distinguishing mark of a *tarada* which only a sheikh may own. Years later, in Oslo, I saw the Viking ships preserved there and was at once reminded of the *taradas* in the Marshes. Both types of craft have the same beautiful simplicity of line.

Four men punted the canoe, two in the stern and two in the bows, moving rhythmically in time as they drove their poles into the water on the same side and changing over as one man when necessary. They had laid their rifles in the canoe beside them and had taken off their cloaks. Each wore a bandolier filled with cartridges and a curved, narrow-bladed dagger in the front of his belt.

Their bitumen-covered canoes were mostly small. The generic term for all canoes was *mashuf*, though each type and size had a special name. A few, low in the water and called *mataur*, would carry only one man and were used for wildfowling. Others, slightly larger, would seat two, while some were the same size as the canoe in which I had travelled from Majar al Kabir. Many of the men punted these canoes with fish-spears, the butt end in the water. These spears were formidable-looking weapons with bamboo shafts as long as twelve feet, and five-pronged heads like giant toasting forks, but with each prong barbed.

Falih had suggested that I should arm myself with my shotgun, as it would be dangerous to use a rifle with so many people about.

I climbed into a small canoe which had been drawn up at my feet. Falih and his son each got into another, and we started towards the reedbeds, followed by the rest. When the water deepened, each man laid down the pole or fishing spear with which he had been punting, settled himself in the canoe and started to paddle with short quick strokes. When more than one person was in a boat, they dipped in time together on the same side.

The haze of the previous day had disappeared and the sky was a pale luminous blue, touched here and there with semi-transparent wisps of cirrus cloud. The paddles dug a succession of tiny whirlpools and the sparkling drops fell back into the clear water, which looked very cold. We had left the muddy flow from the stream's mouth behind us, among the beds of grey, battered bulrushes that grew in the shallows. Now we were among the *qasab* (*Phragmites communis*) which covered most of the permanent marsh. This giant grass, which looked like a bamboo, grew in the dense reedbeds to a height of more than twenty-five feet. The stems, each terminating in a tasselled head of palest buff, were so thick that the Marshmen used them as punt-poles. At this season the reedbeds bordering the narrow waterways were light and airy. Relics of the past year, they were pale gold and silvery grey, except at their base where the new growth, as yet only a few feet high, was very green. Small parties of coot scuttered along the water ahead of us to the shelter of the reedbeds; pigmy cormorants and darters, sitting

155

with their dark wings spread out to dry on reed stumps, white with droppings, took fright and dived into the water or flew off low above it; herons rose with a noisy disturbance of dry reeds to flap away with their long legs trailing behind.

The canoes, of which there must have been at least forty, jostled and bumped as they crowded down the narrow lanes, or spread out on the more open stretches, the crews racing each other with shouts and laughter.

Soon I could not tell whether we were travelling deeper into the Marshes or parallel with the shore, for the reedbeds closed in on us and the waterways became narrower and more tortuous. Suddenly we were out of the reeds and on to a small sheltered lagoon. Mallard rose quacking and flew back high over our heads. Many small islands, some only a few yards across, others covering an acre or more, enclosed the far end of the lagoon. The Marshmen called such islands *tubul*. Some were anchored, others were loose and drifted about. All were smothered under a mass of *qasab*, here only eight to ten feet high, tall clumps of sedge, the leaves sharp-cutting as razors, brambles, a few small willow bushes, and several different kinds of creeper. Underneath all this was a carpet of mint, sow thistle, willow herb, pondweed and other plants.

The ground looked solid but felt very soggy. Actually it consisted of a layer of roots and decomposed vegetation floating on the surface. Some years later I shot a large boar feeding on a similar island that had been burnt not long before. He stood there as if on firm ground, but when we passed the place an hour later the corpse was gone. 'I can't have killed him. He must have recovered and gone off.'

'No, no,' my companion answered. 'He was dead enough. He has sunk.'

At one of these islands Falih's canoe drew alongside mine.

'This is the place,' he said and shouted to the others: 'Come on, get into it and see if there is anything there.' Several men stepped ashore holding their spears in front of them. They drew blank, so they tried another island and then a third. I was watching two warblers, hopping about among the reeds, when I was startled by several loud crashes, followed by shouts. 'There he is! Quick! Look out! By God! Four of them.' Then a splash and silence.

'Where have they gone?' asked another voice.

'They have taken to the water. One got up right under my feet, by God! As big as a donkey, by Abbas!'

Someone else cried: 'I threw my spear and just missed; a sow with three young.'

More shouts, 'They have gone in here. Get round quick and cut them off.'

We were wedged in a narrow passage between two islands, but my canoeman backed out hurriedly into the open water where several more canoes joined us. The hunt had moved on to another island and, as we hastened towards it, there was more excitement. Then a piercing squeal cut off short, a laugh and a man shouting: 'I've got it; one of the small ones; I have speared it. It was in the water; I am drowning it.'

Falih's canoe went past. He had taken off his cloak and was himself paddling. 'Where has the big one gone, Manati?' he asked a vigorous old man who had led the hunt so far.

'Into the large island over there I think, *Ya Muhafadh* . . . Yes, here are its tracks. Come on. Let's get it out!'

Manati plunged out of sight into the jungle of reeds followed by two others. I could hear them moving about. One of them called, 'It has not gone this way,' and a little later Manati shouted, 'Here are its tracks.'

Nothing happened, however, and I thought they must have

lost it when a series of splintering crashes came from the far side and a voice screamed, 'It is killing me! It is killing me!'

Someone shouted, 'It has got Manati. Come on lads. Quick! Where are the warriors?'

Many people answered his call, splashing through the reeds.

Falih, I and some others paddled frantically to the far side of the island where we found Manati being helped into one of the larger canoes. His shirt, covered with blood, was torn half off and he lay with his eyes closed. There was a hole in his right buttock I could have put my fist in. Falih leant over him and asked anxiously, 'How are you, Manati?' The old man opened his eyes and whispered, 'I am all right, *Ya Muhafadh.*' Falih gave orders to go back at once to the mouth of the Khirr, which luckily was not far.

As we paddled back, a boy said, 'It was a sow that bit him. A boar would have slashed him with its tushes and killed him.'

We arrived at the stream's mouth. Falih's *tarada* with a small crowd was waiting for us where the embankment was high and fairly wide. We landed and drew up the canoe with Manati in it. He was lying on his side, a man supporting his head and shoulders. He seemed to have bled very little for the water in the bottom of the boat was only tinged with pink, but the wound was a ghastly-looking mess, the torn ends of muscles sticking out from the oozing flesh. Manati moved slightly to look at his injury but said nothing.

In my boxes at Falih's village was a large supply of drugs. I was not qualified as a doctor, but after twenty years in wild places, where everyone assumed, as a matter of course, that I would treat their sick and injured, I had acquired some experience of medicine. Furthermore, I had always taken every opportunity to go round wards of hospitals and to watch operations and in that way had picked up quite a bit of surgical knowledge.

I was to acquire a great deal more during the years I spent in the Marshes.

Now I said to Falih: 'We had better get him back as quickly as we can to your *mudhif*, where I can give him morphia and try to patch him up, not that there is much I can do for him. We must send him to hospital in Amara.'

'Don't send me to hospital,' Manati pleaded, 'not hospital. Let me stay in my village. Ask the Englishman to doctor me.'

I said, 'Let's get him back anyway to your village,' but Falih insisted that the meal was ready. 'Let us first eat and then go.'

I was getting angry when Manati smiled at me and said, 'Eat, Sahib, eat; I am all right,' and added, 'Anyway I am hungry. I want some food myself before I go any farther.'

I gave in and walked over to where the food was spread out on a reed mat. There was a great dish of rice and joints of mutton, as well as roast chickens and dishes of stew. I found it impossible to eat and rose quickly, hoping that now we could be off, but the others sat down in turn until everyone had fed; after that there was coffee and tea. Unable any longer to conceal my irritation and impatience, I walked over to Manati. He was holding a mutton bone. I wondered whether he had really eaten anything. He looked ghastly.

Back at Falih's village Manati begged again not to be sent to hospital, but Falih eventually persuaded him to go. The pig appeared to have bitten a great lump out of his buttock. I gave him an injection of morphia, washed his wound and sprinkled it thickly with sulphonamide powder. Then we made him as comfortable as we could in a canoe and sent him off to Majar al Kabir on his way to Amara.

I met him again a year later when I lunched in his village and was horrified to find him permanently crippled, unable to move unless he supported himself on a pole. I asked how long he had been in hospital and he answered, 'When I got there they wouldn't let me in, so I came back. Thanks be to God, your medicine cured me. It was all I had.'

I suspected, however, that he had never been near the hospital but had returned to his village from Falih's *mudhif*.

from *The Marsh Arabs*

On another occasion we were hunting pig in our *tarada*. The others were dragging it through shallow water when we saw two big boars about two hundred yards away across the mud flat. The boys turned the canoe sideways and stood behind it. Sitting in it I fired, and hit the larger boar. He spun round and came straight for us, the other close behind. I fired again and heard the bullet smack, but he never faltered. Then again, and still he came on. Now he was very close. I fired a fourth time and he dropped. I had one shot left. I worked the bolt and swung to face the other boar which would be on me in two more bounds. I fired my last shot and down he went, skidding right up to the boat. I reloaded. Neither boar moved. I could touch the nearer. The other was a foot or so out of reach. I had been too busy to be afraid, but the double charge and the seeming ineffectiveness of my shooting must have been very alarming to my companions, who were unarmed, my shotgun and pistol being beside me in the boat. I turned to find them half-crouched, their daggers in their hands. 'What would you have done if it had got into the boat?' 'We would have jumped on it and killed it with our daggers', Amara answered.

from *Desert, Marsh and Mountain*

Like many Englishmen of my generation and upbringing I had an instinctive sympathy with the traditional life of others. My childhood was spent in Abyssinia, which at that time was without cars or roads, and then, after leaving Oxford, I lived for the next eighteen years in remote parts of Africa and the Middle East. All this made it easy for me to consort with tribal people, to adapt myself to their ways and to find an interest in their lives, but difficult for me to feel at home with those who had discarded their own customs and were trying to adapt themselves to Western civilization.

My own tastes went, perhaps, too far to the other extreme. I loathed cars, aeroplanes, wireless and television, in fact most of our civilization's manifestations in the past fifty years, and was always happy, in Iraq or elsewhere, to share a smoke-filled hovel with a shepherd, his family and beasts. In such a household, everything was strange and different, their self-reliance put me at ease, and I was fascinated by the feeling of continuity with the past. I envied them a contentment rare in the world today and a mastery of skills, however simple, that I myself could never hope to attain.

I had spent many years in exploration, but now there were no untouched places left to explore, at least in the countries that attracted me. I therefore felt inclined to settle down among a people of my choosing. In Arabia I had been very close to my companions, but constant journeying had prevented me from getting to know any particular community as well as I could have wished. What little I had seen so far of the Marshmen appealed to me. They were cheerful and friendly and I liked the look of them. Their way of life, as yet little affected by the outside world, was unique and the Marshes themselves were beautiful. Here, thank God, was no sign of that drab modernity which, in its uniform of second-hand

European clothes, was spreading like a blight across the rest of Iraq.

Among the Madan some old men, mostly *Zairs*, prayed regularly. A few others, like Sahain, compromised by saying the dawn and sunset prayers. Most of them, however, did not pray at all. When they did pray, they first placed in front of them a small rectangular tablet of sacred earth from Karbala, which they touched with their foreheads as they prostrated themselves. The tablets were always kept in a little basket hanging on the wall.

Having finished his prayer, Sahain returned the sacred tablet to the basket, built up the fire with dung cakes and told me to come and get warm. A boy brought a lamp, a bottle half-filled with paraffin with a wick of shredded cloth held in its neck by a lump of squashed dates. Two men talked quietly together next door. I could hear every word they said. The walls of the two houses, each a single thickness of matting, were not more than two feet apart. I soon found that these people had no privacy in their lives and never expected any. They accepted the fact that whatever concerned one of them concerned them all. If a family had a row among themselves their neighbours at once turned up, offering advice and taking sides, and thereby adding more raised voices to the original din. The only way to have a private conversation was to go out in a canoe with someone. Even so, the subject of conversation would soon become generally known, for they were both extremely inquisitive and quite incapable of keeping a secret.

After dinner, the visitors started to arrive. When there seemed no room even for another child, two or three more would push in, step with difficulty between us and sink down into the crowd. The mat walls bulged outwards a little farther and they were accommodated. There was only a space left by the fire. While our canoeman sang, everyone else talked, raising their voices to make themselves heard. Our host handed round cigarettes, and even tiny children smoked if they could pick up a stub. More tea was brewed, more fuel was stacked on the glowing fire from which columns of blue smoke rose and drifted against the matting overhead. It was all very primitive and uncomfortable, but I felt content.

When we reached Ramla at last, we were across the Marshes. Although reeds and bulrushes grew close to the village and men came and went in canoes, there were palms among the houses and beyond the village an open plain. We stopped at a *mudhif*. Our host took me for a stroll round the village, which was intersected by deep ditches full of water and bridged with palm logs.

We walked out across the open plain. The fact that the ground was covered with fallen sedge, like straw from an abandoned harvest, showed that it had been flooded. Now it was iron hard, with hoof-prints like plaster casts. Plovers rose crying into the wind, wheeled and settled again; herons and white cattle egrets took off as we approached and a pallid harrier drifted, banking and turning, a few feet above the ground. In the distance dark clumps of palms marked the villages along the Euphrates. My companion pointed to a far-off mound and said, 'The Turks had a cannon there when they fought us; they shelled our village and killed many people.' Probably this had happened during some punitive expedition that went up from Basra, for the Turks were always having trouble with these tribes.

We went back to the *mudhif* at sunset. The guests left early, saying we must be tired after our journey, and we settled down to sleep. Somewhere in the village a woman lamented for her dead child. Without a pause, hour after hour, she repeated the words 'Oh my son, my son,' an agony of grief that poured out into the night and found no comfort.

The next day the others would return and leave me on my own.

The desert Arabs who immigrated into Iraq were few compared with the original inhabitants, but theirs were the customs and standards that prevailed. The people of Iraq might proudly have claimed descent from Sumerians or Babylonians, from the Assyrians, whose armies had overrun Egypt, from the Persians who had followed Cyrus or fought under Darius or Xerxes, or from the Parthians who had wiped out the legions of Rome. Instead, they boasted they were of Bedu stock. Alexander too had passed this way, and in Central Asia the magic of his name still lingers in mountain valleys where men swear they are descended from his soldiers. In Iraq, however, he was forgotten. When I heard old men round the fire telling legendary tales of courage and generosity, it was never of two-horned Alexander that they spoke, nor of Caliphs who had ruled in splendour in Baghdad, but of tattered herdsmen in the deserts of Arabia.

The desert Arabs had always been a people born to hardship. For them there was no ease or comfort, only the weariness of long marches and toil at well-heads. 'We are Bedu,' they boasted, and asked only the freedom that was theirs. Stoical in pain, and often very brave, they lived for the raid and counter-raid, which were conducted according to set rules and usually with great chivalry. They took a fierce pride in danger and suffering, and never doubted their superiority over villager and townsman. Thoroughbreds, they called themselves, using the same word '*asil*' as they used to describe their bloodstock. They came indeed of the purest race in the world, and for centuries had interbred, cousin marrying cousin as was their custom. They were saved from degeneracy by their environment, where only the best survived and all else was ruthlessly weeded out. Accustomed since childhood to the incessant nag of hunger, they starved when the rains failed, which was often, and discounted thirst as a trivial everyday discomfort. Sometimes, however, they miscalculated and then they died. All through the long months of summer they endured heat that struck like the blast from a furnace door. Then was a grim time for herdsboys; but in winter it was as bad, for icy winds swept across the naked sands, and driving rain soaked them to the skin. During the long winter nights they lay on the ground wrapped only in their rags, and woke too stiff to move. For food they had a bowl of camel's milk morning and evening, if they were lucky. And always there was the threat of raiders, fear of the blood feud and of sudden death.

Their nomad life allowed the Bedu few possessions; everything not a necessity was an encumbrance. The clothes in which they stood, their weapons and saddlery, a few pots and waterskins and goat-hair shelters, were all they owned; those and the animals whose welfare regulated their every move and for whose sake they cheerfully suffered every hardship. Arrogant, individualistic and intensely proud, they never willingly accepted any man as their master, and would rather die than be shamed. The most democratic of people, they yet valued lineage highly, and for centuries had guarded the purity of their blood with the dagger. To their sheikhs they accorded a measure of respect due to their descent, but gave them no more unless they earned it. The head of a tribe was the first among equals. He had no servants and paid retainers to enforce his will, or to effect his judgements. His tribesmen followed him only so long as he commanded their respect, and he ruled them only so long as they obeyed him; if he displeased them they followed another of his family, and his guest tent was left empty. Living crowded together in the open desert, no concealment was possible, every act was noted and every word was overheard. Inveterate gossips, they knew all that passed, and the question, 'What is the news?' succeeded every greeting. If a man distinguished himself, his fellows paraded him through the encampment on a camel shouting, 'God whiten the face of so-and-so!' If he had disgraced himself, they drove him forth with cries of, 'God blacken the face of so-and-so!', and he became an outcast. Avid for acclaim, they went to great lengths to win it, and many of their acts were theatrical in consequence. Though jealous of others, they were staunchly loyal to their fellow tribesmen; to betray a companion was the blackest sin, far worse than murder to people whose disregard for human life enabled them in settlement of a blood feud to knife an unarmed herdsboy with a jest. But while they were callous about their own sufferings, and the sufferings of others, they were never deliberately cruel. Their honour was easily touched and they were quick to repay an insult, real or imagined, but usually they were humorous and light-hearted.

Theirs was a character of opposites. Garrulous by nature, they were always careful of their dignity, and would sit in silence for hours on formal occasions. Indifferent to natural beauty, they had a passionate love for poetry. Often impractically generous, they would give away their only shirt to someone who asked for it. Their hospitality was legendary – a man would think nothing of killing one of his precious camels to feed a stranger who had chanced on his tent; but at heart they were avaricious, with all the Semite's love of money. They were deeply religious and saw the hands of God in everything. It

would have been as inconceivable for them to doubt his existence as to blaspheme. Yet they were not naturally fanatical,
nor were they passively fatalistic. In their hard lives they fought
to the bitter end, and then accepted their fate with dignity, as
the will of God.

At Kubaish I visited the *Mudir*, who invited me to dine with
him at the Club. This proved to be the sort of cheap brick
building that, in this climate, was bound to be hot in summer,
cold and dank in winter. It stood behind a mat fence, under
which some zinnias wilted for lack of water. Iron chairs painted
green and a few circular iron tables were set on a patch of worn
grass. Two or three officials were there already, others arrived
later. I had met most of them that morning. We sat round the
tables and were served with tea by a harassed old man, in a
pair of torn khaki trousers that were too large for him and a
jacket that was too tight. One of the schoolteachers fetched
a wireless from the building, fixed up the aerial and spent the
next four or five hours fiddling with the knobs. Against a background of music, song and recitation from all over the world,
and the incidental sounds of atmospherics, the others discussed
their allowances, Arab politics and a scandal that had taken
place recently in official circles in Nasiriya. Not caring for *araq*,
I took endless glasses of sweet black tea, the only other drink
available. My hosts, who did not share my prejudice, drank
araq steadily, argued more heatedly, and seemed to forget
that they had invited me to dinner. Behind the mat fence a
generator thumped asthmatically, supplying a single naked
bulb suspended over our heads; an unpleasant selection of
insects, attracted by the light, rained down on the tables. The
iron chair on which I sat added physical discomfort to boredom.
It was after midnight when the *Mudir* remembered to order

dinner, and the *kabab* and rice had not been improved by waiting.

Most of these officials had been born within a hundred miles of Kubaish, but their education had taught them to feel at home only in the towns. Exiled in this uncongenial tribal atmosphere, they dreamed of a transfer and spent much time scheming to bring one about. Meanwhile they confined themselves, for as long as they were here, to the few hundred yards which contained their houses, their offices and the Club. During the years that I was in Iraq, I do not remember meeting an official who had any real interest in, or affection for, the tribal people whom he administered. More than one asked how I could bear to live among the Madan, adding that they were no better than wild beasts.

Nor were they interested in the countryside. In Kurdistan, the previous summer, I had spent a day with a young Iraqi police officer in one of the most beautiful places I had seen. He had been posted there for two months while a large nomad tribe was in the area. Mountains of eight and nine thousand feet rose from the oak woods to the bare green slopes above, and a glittering stream of ice-cold water tumbled down the valley towards further ranges of purple mountains. There were bears in the woods and ibex on the peaks. The weather was perfect. When I called on the young man in his tent, he was sitting beside the wireless and an ashtray full of stubs. 'You are a lucky chap to be living here,' I said enthusiastically, and he burst out, 'Lucky! By God, if it wasn't for my wireless I should go mad. What is there for a civilized person to do in this awful spot? The man who was here before me left after a week. He paid and they moved him. I am poor and can't afford to do that so I just sit and listen to Radio Baghdad.'

*   *   *

In spite of the social stigma of being uncircumcised, some boys not unnaturally refused. In other cases the fathers would not allow their sons to be operated on, because there was no one else to look after the buffaloes. A few maintained that they had been circumcised by an angel at birth, a superstition that is also current in Egypt. Later I visited villages, among the Suaid and Kaulaba in particular, where I heard that hardly anyone was circumcised – almost incredible among Moslems.

In the morning, Abid suggested I should do the operation out of doors, in order not to defile the house with blood. A small crowd waited among the buffaloes in the yard, which was not the ideal surgery. A number of Kharaibid's contemporaries had turned up, to give him moral support as I presumed. I selected an intelligent-looking boy as my assistant. Kharaibid produced a large wooden mortar, turned it upside down and sat on it.

I could have wished for a simpler first operation. Examination showed that he had an 'attached foreskin'. I prepared a syringe with local anaesthetic, but Kharaibid said immediately, 'What is that for?' I explained that an injection would stop him feeling any pain. 'No, no, I don't want any needles stuck into me; just cut it off,' and nothing I could say would change his mind. By then I was wondering if he was as nervous as I was, though he showed no signs of it. While I operated, which in this case took some time, he sat absolutely motionless, and after I had finished said, 'Thank you,' and stood up. My assistant, who had been holding the various forceps, dropped them in the manure and pushing another boy aside, sat down on the mortar and said, 'Now it's my turn.' I realized with a shock that Kharaibid's nine friends had all come to be circumcised. The youngest was about fifteen, the eldest twenty-four, and I learnt later that they all recovered in a few days. Evidently sulphonamide powder and penicillin were more efficacious than powdered foreskins. The news had reached the next village by the time I got there and I found a score of boys waiting for me.

The Madan were never visited by a doctor, and if they went to the local dispensary at Kubaish would be made to pay for drugs which, they maintained, did them no good. Wherever I happened to be, my surgery grew daily in numbers, and from now on I spent hardly a day in the Marshes without treating someone. Sometimes half a dozen turned up, sometimes a hundred or more. Often I was still asleep when the first patients arrived, and I would be shaken awake, perhaps by an old man who would lean over me and explain wheezingly that he had a cough. Many of them suffered from nothing worse than colds, headaches, constipation, or minor cuts and bruises. These were easily dealt with, although even they took time. Others, however, were seriously, and perhaps fatally, ill. Some I could help; others I could do nothing for. On such occasions I would have given much for a proper medical training.

They suffered from trachoma, and other eye troubles, from scabies and piles, from stones, from intestinal worms of many varieties, from dysentery, both amoebic and bacillary, from bilharzia and from bajal, to name only a few of their complaints. Bajal was one of the commonest diseases and perhaps the most unpleasant. Resembling syphilis, but non-venereal, it is a form of yaws and highly contagious. The sores, which might occur anywhere on the body, were often extensive and sometimes stank horribly. I usually felt sick when there were several such patients in the room. No doubt some of the cases which I thought were bajal were really syphilis, but penicillin injections were effective for both. Gonorrhoea was almost unknown; in seven years, I only treated three cases, all infected in Amara. I could do nothing about the bilharzia from which everyone suffered. The course of injections lasted a month and I was never that long in one place. I treated my own canoeboys, but they always got reinfected. There were also epidemics of measles, chickenpox, mumps and whooping cough, and there was the 1958 epidemic of Asiatic 'flu which most of the Madan caught. My drugs saved many who developed pneumonia as a consequence of the 'flu. Although we were surrounded day after day by the sufferers demanding medicines, my canoeboys and I somehow escaped; to my relief, for I dreaded catching it in summer under these conditions.

Surprisingly, I met few typical cases of malaria, and most of those were probably contracted outside the Marshes. On the other hand, many of the Madan suffered from recurrent low fevers, and a large number of children had enlarged spleens. The dominant mosquito there, *Anopheles pulcherrimus*, was a poor carrier of malaria. The more malignant variety, *Anopheles stephensi*, was comparatively rare in the Marshes themselves.

But there was much that I could not even attempt to do and I had many failures. I am still haunted by the face of a small boy dying of dysentery. Often, too, it was very difficult to convince them that I could do nothing. They would bring me, perhaps from a great distance, an old man dying in agony of cancer, or a girl coughing up her lungs from tuberculosis, confident that I could cure them, and would go on begging pathetically, 'Just give us medicine, Sahib, give us medicine.' Others could have been cured if only they would have gone to hospital in Amara or Nasiriya, but they were terrified of hospitals and would seldom consent.

The doctors in Majar, Kubaish and Amara might well have resented my lack of qualifications, but they never appeared to. On the contrary, several helped me with advice and medicines.

The Minister of the Interior in Baghdad agreed to my doing medical work in the Marshes, but warned me that if anyone died as a result of my ministrations, and the family made trouble, nothing could save me from criminal prosecution. This was a risk I was willing to take. I treated many people who were already dying; no one afterwards suggested that I had killed them.

'That's a good lad,' said Falih, pointing to one of two boys who were helping Zair Mahaisin to serve lunch. 'Thuqub, his old father, can't work now and Amara keeps the family; they are very poor.' He asked the boy: 'It is true, isn't it, that you're called Amara because your mother gave birth to you there in the market?' Amara smiled and answered: 'Yes, it is true, but I've never been there since.' Slightly built and remarkably handsome, he was deft and self-possessed, a natural aristocrat. In contrast, the other boy was rather clumsy and far from handsome, but obviously good-natured. Falih called him Sabaiti and told me that his father kept the village shop, adding that they were well off and very hospitable. Sabaiti looked pleased. Next morning I found both boys, and several others from their village which was about five miles away, waiting outside Falih's *mudhif* for me to circumcise them. When I asked Amara how they proposed to get home afterwards, he said, 'We will stay here until the pain wears off a bit and the bleeding has stopped, then we will walk back,' which they did.

In his own *mudhif*, Falih kept up the state becoming to a sheikh of his importance, but in the villages he was friendly and informal. The warmth with which all the villagers greeted him was rather moving. Children would scamper ahead of us, shouting 'Falih is coming!' and when we arrived their parents would press round urging him to honour their house. On occasion he could be hard, even merciless, but they respected him the more for it and I never heard his judgement called other than just. He fulfilled their ideal of a sheikh; nobly born, he was a leader whom they admired, trusted and feared. All envied him his skill with a gun and on a horse and were pleased that, unlike so many sheikhs, he could handle a canoe with ease. Of the other sheikhs, Majid and Muhammad al Araibi were still impressive in their old age, survivors from harder and more vigorous times. Most of the rest, and especially the younger ones, were fat, slack-bodied and indolent; they worried perpetually about their health and were for ever experimenting with patent medicines. Jasim, Muhammad al Araibi's son, was alone reputed to have been Falih's equal, but he had died and men now said, 'There is only Falih left.'

When I got back to Qabab a week later, I bought myself a canoe, a roomy craft more stable than most, for which I paid ten pounds. It was nearly new and in good condition. Yasin said, 'Now you are one of us: in this boat we will take you wherever you wish to go, to Suq ash Shuyukh, to Kut, to Basra, anywhere.' We returned in it to Falih's village after a further six weeks, and as we landed I asked him with pride, 'What do you think of my new boat?'

'Not bad, but wait until you see what I have waiting for you.'

He gave an order to one of his servants who went off and came back poling a brand-new *tarada*. Dark and glistening, slim and high-prowed, she glided towards us through the water.

'She arrived yesterday from Huwair. She is yours; I had her built for you,' Falih said. 'You may like to think that you are one of the Madan, but in fact you are a sheikh. This *tarada* is worthy of you.'

Yasin exclaimed, 'God, she is beautiful! One of Haji Hamaid's and the best he ever built. There is not another like her.'

Much moved, I tried to express my thanks, but Falih put his hand on my shoulder, saying, '*Sahib inta sahibi*' (Friend, you are my friend).

That evening Falih suggested that I needed two more lads like Yasin and Hasan to complete my crew. Anyone older and married would not wish to leave his family for months on end. Amara and Sabaiti, having heard of this, turned up next morning to offer their services. I asked them how long they had taken to recover and Amara said, 'As done by you, there was nothing to it. I was cutting reeds three days later, and the others were the same.'

Amara had a quiet charm that was very engaging, but I doubted if he was strong enough to paddle a *tarada* on long journeys. However, Hasan, who was also from the Feraigat, assured me that he was stronger than he looked. Yasin belonged to the Shaghanba, and Sabaiti to an obscure tribe I had never heard of. I told Amara and Sabaiti they could join us, and both remained with me until I left Iraq. Although considerably younger than the others Amara had the strongest character. Sabaiti followed him without question and Hasan seldom demurred from his decisions. Only Yasin was sometimes resentful of his leadership and apt to find himself the odd man out in consequence. Amara and Sabaiti soon learnt to assist me with my medicines, and Amara generally gave the injections. I never paid my canoeboys a regular wage, saying that I wanted companions not hired servants. I clothed them and in fact gave them more money than they could have hoped to earn. Later, when they married, I helped them with their bride price. When asked what the Englishman paid them they took a pride in answering, 'We have no wages, we accompany our friend for our pleasure. He is generous and takes care of us.'

Unlike most of the sheikhs, Falih disliked town life and seldom visited Baghdad or Amara. Sometimes he stayed away for a night or two with relations near Majar, most often with his uncle Muhammad, Majid's youngest brother, who, though poor, was the most open-handed of his family and one of the most likeable. Muhammad's ill-fated son Abbas, a thick-set youth of twenty, was Falih's favourite cousin. Accompanying Falih, I spent several amusing evenings with Muhammad. After dinner in the *mudhif* we would retire to a private room in his house. His retainers included several boys exceptionally gifted at singing and dancing. One lad in particular used to mime, with what, I hope, was startling exaggeration, local officials enjoying themselves in their leisure hours.

The air was crisp and clear, a gentle breeze blew from the north, the sun was pleasantly warm, and cirrus cloud marbled the pale-blue sky. We worked the *tarada* along a succession of narrow channels that twisted across an open plain covered with fallen sedge. In the Central Marshes, except on the occasional lagoons, the reedbeds always restricted visibility, sometimes to a few yards. Here we could see for miles. The ground had been dry throughout the winter and now, where still uncovered, it was as hard as baked clay and grey in colour. In other places the rising water covered it to a depth of several inches and the resulting mud was the colour and consistency of melted chocolate.

We disturbed many kinds of wader; some rose singly with shrill cries, others in dense flocks that wheeled and turned above the sheets of water and the bleached sedge. I recognized curlews and whimbrel, redshank, godwit, ruffs, avocet, stilts and various kinds of plover. There were duck, too, that took off long before we could get within range, and herons and ibises and egrets and spoonbills. Once, in the far distance, we saw a flock of cranes. Hasan made constant sorties after any bird that he considered edible, but never got close enough to shoot. He returned each time to be greeted with ribald comments on his inadequacy as a wildfowler. Meanwhile Yasin and Sabaiti walked along the banks on either side pushing the *tarada*, their poles wedged in the bows. The watercourse was barely wide enough in places for the canoe, and sometimes made a right-angle bend. Then I thought we should have to go back, for our *tarada* was thirty-six feet long, but in the end the boys always managed to ease her round.

I was wearing a long Arab shirt and if I had to get into the water to help them, I tucked it round my waist. I have always suspected of exhibitionism travellers who adopt the local dress without good reason. Arab clothes, in particular, are not easily managed by anyone unaccustomed to them. I had worn them for five years in Southern Arabia because I would have been unacceptable to my companions otherwise. In Iraq the tribes-men were well used to the sight of European clothes – all Government officials were careful to wear nothing else in public – and I wore them when I first visited the Marshes. Later, when I felt accepted, I wore a headcloth and long Arab shirt for their obvious convenience – with a jacket on top, a fashion that was increasingly popular with the Madan themselves. Sitting in a canoe or in a house, the shirt protected my legs and feet from flies and mosquitoes. But I always changed into European clothes before visiting officials or going to a town.

My companions were skilled at remembering the way, and dur-ing the years they were with me acquired a knowledge of the

Marshes that must have been unrivalled. But even in places where they had never been before, their instinct seemed to guide them. I noticed this especially when they were searching among reeds and islets, along the edge of a lagoon, for the entrance to some small estuary that was indistinguishable from a hundred others leading nowhere. The same kind of skill, acquired since childhood, enabled them to track a swimming pig, tell one kind of fish from another by its wake, or recognize at a single glance a canoe they had only once seen. Curiously, however, they were hopeless at remembering names. Suffering myself from the same disability, I was always exasperated when not one of the four could recall the name of our last host.

As we paddled along one or other of my companions would sometimes call out to us to stop, and would then reach into the water and pull up a young shoot of *birdi*, their name for a bulrush. They would eat the crisp etiolated stem near the roots, but apparently only certain shoots of *birdi* were fit to eat. They would also occasionally chew the stems of selected pieces of *qasab* as if they were chewing sugar cane. In the spring, the Madan women gathered the heads of bulrushes and from the pollen made a hard yellow cake, much esteemed as a sweetmeat, though personally I found what little taste it had unpleasant.

We spent several nights at Dibin, setting off each morning to explore the Hawaiza Marshes. We found lakes as extensive as Zikri, hidden behind vast reedbeds, but never ventured far out on them for fear of sudden storms. As we pushed along ill-defined waterways, that seemed always to end against a solid wall of reeds, our guide kept urging me to have my rifle ready, saying repeatedly, 'Brigands could kill us here and no one would ever know.' These lakes were a natural sanctuary for wild-fowl; nowhere else did I see such numbers. They darkened acres of water and there was a roar when even a small part of this enormous gathering took wing. Apart from occasional smugglers or raiders heading for Persia, few men disturbed them.

But throughout the Marshes duck and geese were becoming fewer year by year. In 1951 I had seen duck flighting in at sunset to feed on harvested rice-fields near Saigal, in such numbers that they reminded me of swarms of locusts. When I left the Marshes in 1958 there were nothing like as many. A million cartridges were imported annually at that time into Iraq, and most of the people who used them counted on getting at least one bird with a shot. A heavy toll was also taken of wild-fowl by professional fowlers, who netted them a hundred or more at a time. They paid the sheikhs for the right to use certain ponds where they put down grain. There were many small reserved ponds round Amara alone.

The wild geese used to arrive in the Marshes in October. Greylag and white-front, they came out of the north, returning from their breeding grounds in Siberia, and in their calling was the magic of wild places. Wedge-shaped formations followed each other, strung out across the pale sky, and as I watched I thought of the day when the last wild geese would be gone, and there were no more lions in Africa.

Each morning before starting out we would borrow a kettle, glasses and a dish from our host at Dibin and buy tea, sugar, salt and flour from the merchant. When we felt inclined to stop, we would choose a convenient spot on the edge of a lake, trample down reeds to make a platform to support us on the water, and cook a meal. Hasan roasted on a reed spit whatever birds we had shot, and in the embers Sabaiti baked discs of bread that were soggy and full of ashes. Afterwards we went on brewing tea until the sugar was finished, and I would watch the duck on the lake, or the halcyon kingfishers darting past. Once we noticed two otters playing together a hundred yards away, but Hasan reached for the gun and they saw us. They appeared to stand upright in the water eyeing us for a few seconds, before they dived and disappeared. I was glad they had seen us as otherwise Hasan would certainly have tried to shoot them. Their skins were worth a dinar apiece. His uncle at Bu Mughaifat once shot forty in two months.

Hasan told me that otters were very common round Zikri, where they bred on the floating islands, sometimes as early as January but more often in February or March. Three years later, in 1956, Gavin Maxwell, who wished to write a book about the Marshes, came with me to Iraq, and I took him round in my *tarada* for seven weeks. He had always wanted an otter as a pet, and at last I found him a baby European otter which unfortunately died after a week, towards the end of his visit. He was in Basra preparing to go home when I managed to obtain another, which I sent to him. This, very dark in colour and about six weeks old, proved to be a new species. Gavin took it to England, and the species was named after him.

One afternoon, some days after leaving Dibin, we arrived at a village on the mainland. The sheikh was away looking at his cultivations, but we were shown to his *mudhif* by a boy wearing a head-rope and cloak, with a dagger at his waist. He looked about fifteen and his beautiful face was made even more striking by two long braids of hair on either side. In the past all the Madan wore their hair like that, as the Bedu still did. After the boy had made us coffee and withdrawn, Amara asked, 'Did you realize that was a *mustarjil*?' I had vaguely heard of them, but had not met one before.

'A *mustarjil* is born a woman,' Amara explained. 'She cannot help that; but she has the heart of a man, so she lives like a man.'

'Do men accept her?'

'Certainly. We eat with her and she may sit in the *mudhif*. When she dies, we fire off our rifles to honour her. We never do that for a woman. In Majid's village there is one who fought bravely in the war against Haji Sulaiman.'

'Do they always wear their hair plaited?'

'Usually they cut it short like men.'

'Do *mustarjils* ever marry?'

'No, they sleep with women as we do.'

Once, however, we were in a village for a marriage, when the bride, to everyone's amazement, was in fact a *mustarjil*. In this case she had agreed to wear women's clothes and to sleep with her husband on condition that he never asked her to do women's work. The *mustarjils* were much respected, and their nearest equivalent seemed to be the Amazons of antiquity. I met a number of others during the following years. One man came to me with what I took for his twelve-year-old son, suffering from colic, but when I wanted to examine the child, the father said, 'He is a *mustarjil*.' On another occasion I attended a man with a fractured skull. He had fought with a *mustarjil* whom I knew, and had got the worst of it.

Previously, while staying with Hamud, Majid's brother, I was sitting in the *diwaniya* when a stout middle-aged woman shuffled in, enveloped in the usual black draperies, and asked for treatment. She had a striking, rather masculine face, and lifting her skirt exposed a perfectly normal full-sized male organ. 'Will you cut this off and turn me into a proper woman?' he pleaded. I had to confess that the operation was beyond me. When he had left, Amara asked compassionately, 'Could they not do it for him in Basra? Except for that, he really is a woman, poor thing.' Afterwards I often noticed the same man washing dishes on the river bank with the women. Accepted by them, he seemed quite at home. These people were kinder to him than we would have been in our society. Yet in some ways they were very callous.

Once as we were setting off on one of our daily expeditions, we were asked to look out for the body of a small girl drowned in the river. Coming back in the evening we saw the floating corpse, but when I suggested bringing it on board my companions refused to touch it, or even to have it in the *tarada*, for fear of ritual pollution. 'We should have to wash completely seven times,' Yasin said. 'And anyway it's not our child.' The most they would do was to push the corpse to the river bank and lift it out with their paddles.

In the reedbeds along the Euphrates a new growth was already high among the sapless old, while scented water-crowfoot covered the open water like a fall of snow.

At Azair we left the boat and hired a car to take us to Basra, which I generally visited every two months to collect my mail, have a bath and buy more medicines. A few days in a comfortable house was a pleasant change and my friends at the Consulate were always good to me and my companions. Back once more in our *tarada*, Amara said, 'Now that Falih is dead you must stay with me instead. We have not got much, as you know, but what we have is yours. We will leave Yasin and Hasan with their families and send for them when we are ready to go on again.'

Four days later we entered the canal that led to Rufaiya, Amara's village. The current ran strong. Beyond the banks, men cleared the ground and floated great piles of vegetation farther into the marsh, working knee-deep to waist-deep in water. A tall boy, his shirt round his neck, splashed towards us and called greetings. 'That is Reshiq, my brother,' Amara said. 'Last year he helped others with their rice; this year he has his own land.' The boy washed the mud off his feet and legs, dropped into the *tarada* beside Amara, kissed him and then picked up a pole. Although nice-looking, with a lively rather cheeky expression, he lacked the air of breeding that distinguished his brother. A year younger, and nearly as tall, he appeared gangling but would probably be the more powerful of the two when he filled out. We passed the first houses, and children began to follow us, scampering along the banks till I felt like the Pied Piper. By the time we stopped, a large crowd of them had gathered and were waiting to help us land. 'Hasan, run and tell father that the Sahib comes as our guest,' Amara said to one; and to Reshiq, 'See that the other chicks bring everything to the house, and don't forget the poles.'

Yasin and Hasan had remained for a few days in Bu Mughaifat. Accompanied by Sabaiti, and another lad who had come with us, we walked towards Amara's home on the outskirts of the village. Harvested fields of barley lay beyond, and in the distance a dark clump of palms. Amara's father, Thuqub, was an old man with a weathered face and untroubled eyes. Dressed in a clean white shirt and headcloth, he received us with quiet courtesy. He held himself erect but moved slowly and rather stiffly as he showed us into his house, which was small and low-roofed, each of its five arches only a few reeds thick. A worn carpet was spread on a tattered mat with two cushions. A lively, middle-aged woman with a kindly face greeted me. 'Welcome, Sahib, welcome to your home. Are you not Amara's father? God bless you.' Behind her stood a baby, two small boys and a girl of fifteen who half hid her face.

Amara sent Reshiq off to find a kettle and Sabaiti to his father's shop for sugar and tea. Then, assisted by his small brothers and a crowd of other children, he attempted to capture an old rooster. After escaping from the house and leading them round the village in noisy pursuit, it was finally cornered and slaughtered for lunch. Amara also produced a very stale fish, but in these parts no one minded if a fish smelt. To eat with it, Naga, his mother, baked bread for us in a circular clay oven, slapping the discs of wet dough on the inside wall. On the mainland, one of these ovens was to be seen in front of every house. In the Marshes, the women cooked their bread over a fire on round earthenware platters. Chilaib, another brother, arrived back from the Marshes. A solid silent boy, he was in charge of the buffaloes while Amara was away with me and, although only about twelve, worked from dawn till dusk cutting and fetching *bashish*. Reshiq helped him carry his load to the house from the canoe. In the evening the buffaloes were tethered to pegs before the house. They could not be left loose at night or they would wander into the cultivations. The herd comprised a wild-eyed bull, three cows, a heifer and a calf. Like Chilaib, Amara's heart was with the buffaloes. After milking, he said to me as he fondled a cow, 'Look at this one, she is a real beauty and in calf. I bought her with the money you gave me last year. Soon, God willing, we will have a proper herd.'

The following year Amara consulted me about sending Hasan to school. 'We ought to have someone in the family who can read and write.' I agreed, though rather doubtfully, and next morning we sent him off to a school, which half a dozen boys from the village attended and which was two miles away on the main stream of the Wadiya. There was another school on the Adil below Majid's village, but none inside the Marshes. Hasan was very happy there. He trotted off in the morning with the other children and in the evening showed me his work with pride. When I was next in Basra I bought him a satchel and notebooks, coloured pencils, pens, an inkpot, a ruler and compasses. He was delighted and assured me that none of the others had anything of the kind. Nevertheless, I felt worried about the results. For the next five or six years he would spend the day sitting at a desk inside a house and at midday would be given a special meal as prescribed by UNESCO – an easy existence compared with Chilaib's in the reedbeds or Reshiq's in the rice-fields. But reedbeds and rice-fields would be his lot if he remained on in Rufaiya after leaving school. I only hoped that he would not later drift off to become a corner-boy in one of the towns, the fate of so many of the semi-educated through-out the Middle East today.

Few boys who had been at school were content to remain in their village. For years they had been influenced by teachers who hated the tribal life and encouraged them to think that the only respectable existence was in the towns. 'Take me with you to Basra, Sahib, and find me a good job there,' young men often pleaded. 'I hate it here where we live like animals – it is all right for my parents and brothers but I am educated.' If they stayed at home, such boys soon became bitter and discontented. Their belief that, if only they could escape, their meagre education would give them all they hoped for, was pitiful. They did not realize that there were hundreds of thousands of others in Iraq with the same qualifications. In fact, if they left home, they probably ended by selling newspapers or Coca-Cola in Basra or Baghdad, as well as stealing from cars and pimping for taxi-drivers to keep alive.

Nearly all parents were anxious to send their children to school, but I remember an old man, in a village on the Adil, saying to me, 'My son has a good job with the Government in Basra. We are poor, as you can see. I spent much money keeping him in Amara during the ten years he was at school. Later I thought he would look after us. We were happy with him when he was a child; he is our only son. Now he never comes near us or helps us. This education is a bad thing, Sahib, it steals our children.' An old woman in Qabab, however, whose husband had divorced her and worked in Amara as a nightwatchman, had no such doubts. She was visited by her son who had been to school there. He wore a coat, and trousers with a large hole in the seat, and his hair was smeared with brilliantine and parted European-fashion. When he left, after his two days' visit, his mother went proudly round her neighbours, declaring, 'My son is civilized. He eats with a spoon, and pees standing.' Tribesmen always squat to urinate.

We were out shooting one afternoon when black clouds massed quickly, presaging a tremendous storm. Yasin said anxiously, 'God, I hope there is no hail in that,' and the others echoed his prayer. The storm broke and before we were home we had to bale to keep afloat. My companions were frightened of hail, with good reason. The following year a hailstorm cut a swath right across the northern half of the Marshes, smashing even the largest reeds and killing countless pelicans, geese and other birds. Their corpses were scattered everywhere. It also killed a number of buffalo calves, and battered a man and his son to death on Dima.

'With this high water, we shall kill many pigs this year,' Amara said, and sure enough we did. Before recrossing the Tigris, I had shot two hundred and five. It was always exciting work, and sometimes dangerous, but I did not hunt them solely for sport. They were the Marshman's natural enemy, and I had had to sew up too many men savaged by pigs to feel any compunction killing them. Yet I should have hated to have seen them exterminated here, as the lions had been. Their massive dark shapes, feeding on the edge of the reedbeds at evening, were for me an integral part of the Marsh scene. Without the constant risk of encountering them, life here would have lost much of its excitement.

The pig could be astonishingly bold. Once, in the Amaira country, the villagers assured me that the pig came back to the village with the buffaloes and spent the night in empty houses. I did not believe them until we saw two walking through the shallow water towards the village at sunset. We chased and killed them and, when we got back in the dark, a family who were sitting outside by a fire said quite casually, 'There are some more in there,' pointing to the next-door house a few yards away. I thought they must be joking. However, we landed on the *dibin* and were nearly knocked over by five pig as they charged out and plunged into the water.

Turning north in the *tarada*, Tahir guided us to Auaisij, the long ridge of slightly higher ground that runs parallel with the Tigris. Owing to the unusually high floods, most of it was already awash and great numbers of pig were lying up there by day. My companions were easily able to slide the *tarada* through the sludge in any direction while we were hunting. One afternoon I killed ten that were walking across our front in single file. I was shooting exceptionally well that day and dropped the rearmost each time with a single shot. We found four more. When I killed one, the other three gathered round it as it kicked convulsively on the ground, and for some odd reason remained like that until I had killed them too.

Next day we chased another big boar through water eighteen inches deep. He was only forty yards ahead and we were gaining on him when he whipped round and charged, coming very fast through the water in a smother of spray. I failed to stop him from the still moving *tarada* and he was alongside before I could fire again. Tahir had borrowed a fishing spear that morning and he now drove it straight into the boar's face. From the corner of my eye, I saw him lifted on the end of the shaft, right out of the boat. I fired again and this time the boar collapsed, knocking the *tarada* sideways through the water. Dripping from head to foot with liquid mud, Tahir got up spluttering.

'Why did you jump out of the boat?' Yasin asked him innocently. 'You would have been quite safe in it. Didn't you see the Sahib was getting ready to shoot?' Tahir was not amused.

'Another foot and it would have smashed our *tarada* in half,' Amara remarked. 'Like the boat we saw the other day that a pig had broken up.'

This boar, one of the largest I ever shot, had long matted hair, dark brown in colour. The coats of some were almost black, of others reddish, while a sounder we once saw were all so pale in colour that, for a moment, we wondered if they were sheep. Many, however, had only a few coarse bristles on their bare hides. The piglets, born between March and May and usually five to a litter, had soft striped coats and were attractive little beasts. When shooting pig I found that it was generally useless to stalk them downwind. They had good eyesight, but seemed hard of hearing when they were asleep. Once, hunting them on horseback in tamarisk scrub, some mounted Bani Lam shouted to me to come over to where a large boar was snoring in a bush within a yard or so of a dozen trampling horses. The Madan maintained that pig ate carrion. On Auaisij, I certainly saw the partly devoured bodies of boar I had shot some days before, but they might as easily have been eaten by jackals of which there were many. I was afraid all the jackals would be drowned that year, for there was little ground still uncovered and the floods would continue to rise for at least another two months.

* * *

187

Amara and Sabaiti saw me off from Basra. My plane was due to leave at midnight and we waited at the airport. Eventually the plane landed and a crowd of weary passengers came into the room and settled down to wait while it was refuelled. A waiter handed round Coca-Cola. They had left that morning or the night before from Bangkok or Sydney. Now I should be joining them and after eight hours I should be in London. On the wall opposite an airways poster advised me to see the world from the comfort of an armchair.

The loudspeaker erupted. I could make out odd words, 'Passengers ... BOAC, flight number ... Rome ... London ... passports ... passport control.' There was a general stir. I got up and collected my things. 'I must go now,' I told my companions.

Amara and Sabaiti kissed me farewell and Amara said, 'Come back soon.'

'Next year, if God wills,' I replied, and joined the queue.

Three weeks later I was having tea with friends in Ireland. Someone entered the room. 'Did you hear the four o'clock news? There has been a revolution in Baghdad and the Royal family have been murdered. The mob burnt the British Embassy ...'

I realized that I should never be allowed back, and that another chapter in my life had closed.

from *The Marsh Arabs*

The journey from Loe Pan Ghala, in Chitral, over the Kachi Kuni Pass to Laspur, took more than two days. The first day involved a series of pretty steep climbs, broken by easy going over occasional grassy flats. Near Loe Pan Ghala the hillsides were covered with a small red flower like sorrel. From a distance this gave an effect like heather. Otherwise, flowers were scarce, and then mostly daisies. Further on, the mountainsides were bare rock, with much scree where there had been landslides. The peaks all round us had snow on them and seemed quite close. Here the river was little more than a stream. We rested at midday and cooked a meal over a fire of dry bog myrtle, then carried on over more rocky debris where the going was rough and the cracked, crumbling earth looked as if it would not take much to start another landslide.

By late afternoon we were climbing the mountain itself by a steep scrambling route which, in places, led over small glaciers. Away to our right I saw an ice-fall, at the end of a small glacier, at the head of the valley we had just come up. While it was still light, we pitched the tent on a narrow ledge and cooked our dinner using the solid fuel and water from a stream we found trickling beneath some boulders. The porters made themselves shelters under the rocks.

During the night three or four inches of snow fell and everything was white when I came out of the tent at sunrise. This was very Christmas-like but inopportune. The porters seemed remarkably cheerful despite their night in the open at about 13,000 feet without anything but a blanket apiece. I was afraid they would refuse to go on, but they started without a murmur and without breakfast.

The sky all round looked stormy, the clouds lit red by the rising sun. There were occasional flurries of light snow. We climbed steadily for three hours until we reached the 16,000-foot summit of the Kachi Kuni Pass. For about half the climb we found frozen snow overlaid by last night's fall. I went ahead and cut steps. The rest of the climb was over jumbled boulders also hidden by the fresh snow. I was glad to find that I did not feel the least tired or breathless, except that my arms got tired from step cutting. Several of the porters complained of headaches.

When we got to the top there were fitful glimpses of the sun, but the distant mountains were smothered in cloud. We could see the tarn where we lunched the day before, far below us at the bottom of a black, shadow-filled gorge.

After a brief halt we started off again, over a smooth, snow-covered glacier. One of the porters, who knew the glacier, went ahead with me roped to him. It sloped gradually downhill, but the last hour involved a fairly steep descent to the bottom past an impressive ice-fall on our left.

We continued on following the stream down the valley, which fell quite steeply. We camped eventually under a large, overhanging rock with a few birch trees nearby. Apart from these trees the landscape was very bleak, and the mountainsides to our right and left merely bare rock and earth.

A fine snow-covered mountain dominated the valley behind us. Coming down the glacier we had passed below this mountain, but it had been too close for us to get a proper view.

The following day, after walking for about four hours in bright sunshine down the bare, boulder-strewn valley, we arrived at Laspur, a small village attractively situated beside the stream, bordered here by some very green turf, poplars and fields of wheat. The dak bungalow where we stayed had been used to stable the villagers' animals. Some of the cows I saw had been crossed with yaks.

Several boys carried bows, about two feet long with a double string held apart at one end by a short stick; the strings were joined in the middle by a small leather pouch and the bow was used, like a catapult, to shoot stones. In Chitral, almost all the men and boys carried these bows.

The four porters left to go back to Matiltan and Jahangir Khan and I went on to Mastuj, carrying our kit on two donkeys. I found this a slow and wearisome way of travelling. At one village the women wore skull caps and looked, to me, far more Mongolian in appearance than the men, with their hair in two plaits down each side of their faces. Small herd boys ran about naked in the hot sun.

Mastuj, like all the Chitrali villages, I was told, consisted of a number of scattered farmsteads. The houses were built from stones and mud, each with an orchard inside the stone wall surrounding it. There were poplars, willows, fruit trees and some hemp; and fields of corn, most of which had already been cut. Wild roses grew along the lanes. There was a fine view down the valley of Tirich Mir. This snow-covered mountain with its graceful peak was the highest in the Hindu Kush; its 25,200-foot summit towered over other snowy mountains of 20,000 feet. The mountainsides were very steep, with evidence of many landslides, and the mountain opposite Mastuj had its lower slopes eroded into curious formations.

Swaths of smoky cloud had hidden the mountains from view the previous day and they were still wreathed in cloud when we left early in the morning. As far as I could see the mountains appeared very jagged and steep. There were birch coppices with small streams oozing through them in the valley as far as Dobargar, and quite a lot of juniper, stunted trees between six and eight feet high.

Opposite Nakiadam were some spectacular mountains: snow-covered peaks broken by rocks and precipices and, lower down, long stretches of pale-grey scree only a shade darker than the snow. The mountains here varied in colour from purple-black to red, brick-brown and from almost salmon-pink to ivory. They looked like the sort of mountains where you might expect to find wild sheep, quite different from the precipitous ibex mountains we had seen so far. These mountains were in Yarkhun, the most attractive mountains I had seen so far on this journey.

We passed some cultivated fields and then through woods of poplar, willow and thorn where I noticed the first autumn tints; then out on to a hillside covered with more stunted juniper, a strangely old-looking tree like yew. Coming round the slope of Gharqab we had to unload the horse and donkey and carry the loads along a steep face of scree where there was almost no track. The sun had come out by then but the mountains were still largely hidden in mist and haze.

Generally speaking there were few birds to be seen: an occasional magpie, a few doves, black and white chats and choughs among the cliffs. Where a stream from the west shoulder of Gharqab joined the river, I saw a mallard, two falcons and an eagle with dark plumage and a white-banded tail.

Until the sun was properly up the next day felt bitterly cold. The people themselves, I noticed, wrapped up warmly, but many of the boys and small children went barefoot. A young boy with pronounced Tartar features came with us as far as Wadinkot. Here we found one of the previous night's Afghans and a Kirghiz, very Mongolian in appearance, with a thin straggling beard. I photographed both of them. The villagers gave us some good bread and curds.

I had some magnificent views of the 22,000-foot snow mountains across a glacier further up the valley from Wadinkot. We stopped for the night at a two-roomed house near a bridge, where a munshi with an irregular guard of eight armed men lived for ten months a year. We had passed some stone-built houses inhabited by Wakikh from Warkhand who are now refugees on this side of the border. Some Kazakh also lived in these parts, but mostly Wakikh.

We left at 7 AM accompanied by the munshi Sharwal Jafar Mamad, who rode a horse and carried a Lee-Enfield rifle. We crossed the river by the pole-and-brushwood bridge near the munshi's house and carried on along the bank past small fields of wheat which had just been cut but not gathered, and some stone houses belonging to the Wakikh.

From here we had a fine view of the snowy peaks and also of the Chiantu glacier. The mountains round us were not very high though they had some snow on them; those across the river were higher. We passed no more dwellings until we reached Shuasir. The surrounding country was very bare and here the river divided in small channels, flowing through an expanse of sand and pebbles. The water was a curious chalky colour with sediment in it. We found some yaks at Shuasir, the first I had ever seen; they were mostly black, but one was pure white and several others parti-coloured. At sunset a few men turned up riding on yaks, which they guided by a rope fastened to the yak's nose. A Sarakouli, whom I photographed, wore a curious hat shaped rather like an admiral's.

The next morning, I left the others behind and went on ahead with the Sharwal up the valley to Karumbar; he was riding his horse and I was riding Malung's. It was very cold at first light and there were icicles along the edges of the streams. We arrived at Karumbar at 10, left again at 11, and got back to camp at 3 PM.

The country between Shuasir and Karumbar was most

exhilarating, great tawny mountainsides across which cloud shadows drifted and, higher up, the snows and glaciers very white and clear in the thin, cold mountain air. Here was the space and cleanliness of the desert combined with the great heights and the clear blue sky of Central Asia.

As far as Zhuil we rode along the side of a rather stony mountain, with small hollows below us in which were pools of very blue water and reddish-golden patches of bog laced with a network of little streams. Beyond this was the wide expanse of the river-bed, grey sand and shingle, and behind this the stony, black, snow-sprinkled foothills of the main snow range, whose higher peaks and glaciers stood up against the sky.

The watershed at Karumbar was barely noticeable. The lake, about three miles long, with its deep blue waters, lay on the far side of it. The map gave the lake's altitude at 14,250 feet. The mountains immediately above the lake on its south side were thickly covered with snow and a few patches lay near the lake.

At its west end, by a small stone shelter built under a rock with a cairn on top of it, we found a man with very Mongolian features, well dressed in a mulberry-coloured surcoat, high boots and a fur-lined cap with ear-flaps. With him was a bearded Afghan mullah, and their young servant, a boy in Chitrali clothes. They had two horses with them, one of which had a good Kazakh saddle decorated with silver. They were eating dried bread and drinking a weak, straw-coloured, sugar-less tea when we arrived. I said in English, 'Good morning, gentlemen.' It seemed silly to say *Salaam alaikum*, and not to be able to follow it up in Persian, Turki or whatever language they spoke. The Mongol, who later told me he was called Ahmed, smiled and asked us in English to come and join them.

While I was drinking tea from one of their small, handleless cups, he asked me if I spoke German. I said, 'Only French and Arabic, I am afraid,' and he replied, 'My friend the mullah speaks Arabic.' Shades of *Kim* and the 'Great Game', I thought. I gathered that they were on their way to Kashgar, where Shipton had been Consul after the Second World War. I would have given much to have travelled with them, but times had changed and the boundaries of our world had closed in. At first Ahmed refused to be photographed but then suddenly agreed.

We left them and rode back to Shuasir. I had bought a sheep that morning for fifteen rupees and had told Jahangir Khan to keep it tied up. But after I left for Karumbar he loosed it and sent it off with the rest of the flock. The result was that we could not get hold of it again until nearly sunset, and Jahangir Khan produced a filthy dinner in the dark, which made me angry.

Sharwal Jafar Mamad and I left at 7 AM the next morning for the Boroghil Pass, both of us riding his horse. There was a strong, very cold wind blowing and I soon found it too cold to ride. We went up over a broken, rocky hillside, past a small, crystal clear lake in a damp hollow, to the pass. From the top of the pass, gazing out over the mountains of Wakhan, I could see in the far distance the glinting waters of the Oxus, which the Sharwal called Ab-i-Panja, flowing through a broad shingle bed at the foot of some dark mountains. We then descended past several small lakes, very clear and in certain lights looking almost indigo-coloured. They were edged with golden-coloured bog and some had reeds growing round their sides.

The views of the snow range south of Boroghil were magnificent. Its higher peaks towered into a cloudless and very blue sky. On the way back we stopped at a house for some dried bread and tea which the locals drank with milk and flavoured with salt. We rested in the hot mid-morning sun, watching some yaks and cows grazing, while the occupants of the house drove their sheep and goats out to pasture. When we got back to the munshi's house in the valley by the bridge, we saw men and women in the fields, trying to keep the pigeons and ubiquitous choughs off their harvest of cut and standing corn.

Early the following morning, we set off from the munshi's house and after two hours arrived back at Wadinkot, where we had stayed the previous week. For the first time I saw a man smoking opium. He heated a small quantity of powdered opium over a flame and then put it into a pipe, using a needle. Further on, at Khankhon, where we stopped for the night at a Sayid's house, a field nearby was full of poppies and hemp. Many houses in this area grew a patch of poppies for opium. The Sayid had dysentery and his brother had died of it ten days before, so I gave him some Chloromycetin.

At Yoshkish, high up on the mountainside near Nakiadam, I had a fine view of the snow-white mountains above Khankhon, and a really magnificent prospect of other snow peaks down the valley. Yoshkish occupied an attractive position at the head of some terraced fields. Poplars and willows, all turning to gold, grew round the scattered houses; as elsewhere, the corn had been cut but still not gathered in. All we got to eat here were some unripe apples. Coming from Lasht to Yoshkish we passed a succession of farmsteads and fields, with the Yarkhun mountains always above us. Twice on the way, at the far end of the gorge, I glimpsed the 22,500-foot summit of the range.

We were told that the path over the Shah jin Ali Pass was bad, so the local Hakim came with us, and six men to carry the loads and save our animals.

We left early, climbing steadily and steeply by a fair track, with only one pitch of 300 yards that was really severe along the edge of the stream. I saw a number of petroglyphs, crude rock carvings featuring representations of ibex with large horns; these showed no sign of weathering and stood out very white on the grey rock. We left the main stream and followed a smaller one, veering to the right, after about three miles. Steep cliffs rose up on both sides of the gorge where we came across some juniper and birch.

Behind the pastel-coloured granite peaks to the north-west lay a great, rounded black mass of mountains with two great snow-caps on their summit. Down the valley of the Rich Gul, the graceful peak of Tirich Mir seemed to tower over everything in its vicinity, even mountains of 24,000 feet. Nearby, another range of jagged peaks sprinkled with snow shut out the view to the south. Undulating grassland stretched away to the east, while to the south-west I could see golden-brown patches of bog and the glitter of water. It was probably the finest view I had ever seen in my life.

We descended to the valley of Rich Gul down the stony, grass-covered mountainside, patched with golden bog-myrtle and other shrubs turned to a flaming red. The stones in the beds of streams we passed had been laid flat by glaciers which had long since dispersed. Continuing down the Rich Gul, we passed small stands of birch wherever streams flowed down the hillside and in one of these coppices we camped for the night.

At dawn the next day we were making our way in the cold shadows along the grassy hillside through more clusters of birch. Light and graceful trees, their leaves by now had turned to pure gold. Streams of foaming water, the icy melt from the snow peaks high above, rushed past us; numbingly cold like the Rich Gul which we later had to ford thigh-deep.

We then came to a most spectacular gorge framing a snow range 20,000 feet high. Here we had to carry the loads down as the path was very steep. Jahangir Khan annoyed me by taking only a 10-pound bag of flour. The rest of us were each carrying some 60 pounds. On a mountain, Jahangir was like a sick old woman allowed out for the first time.

We recrossed the river by a bridge and then stopped for lunch at 11, where the valley began to open out. Here, glacier-fed streams mingled with the river; high granite precipices rose very sheer above us; and, opposite, across the Rich Gul, were the towering snow peaks.

Further down the wide, boulder-strewn valley we crossed the river again by a bridge. Soon after this, we saw some cultivation and a few houses on the south bank, and then some more on our side. Recrossing the river by another bridge, we passed through a number of farms until we reached the Hakim's house an hour before nightfall.

The Black Kafirs, who called themselves Kalash Gum, lived in the three valleys of Brumboret, Rambor and Barir. People there still worshipped the old gods, grew grapes for wine, and set up carved wooden figures where they buried their dead. Their kinsmen across the border had been forcibly converted to Islam by Abd er Rahman, Amir of Afghanistan, at the end of the last century, and their land, once known as Kafiristan, was now called Nuristan, 'Land of Light'. Many of the Muslims living in Chitral were descendants of Red Kafir refugees who had fled from Kafiristan in 1897. Some years later I was to travel through Nuristan, but I am glad that I saw the people here as they once had been throughout Kafiristan.

After a few days' rest, I visited the Kafirs, accompanied by the political agent, Mir Ajam, who took me by jeep to Aijun, a Red Kafir village, which he assured me was the largest village in Chitral. From Aijun I continued on foot up a narrow valley where a stream of clear water flowed down from the north-west. The steep, rocky hillsides on both sides were covered with trees, among them a species of scrub oak with leaves like holly but recognizable as oak from its acorns. We crossed and recrossed the stream by bridges, each made of a single plank. After about an hour and a half, we turned up the valley of the Brumboret, the southernmost of two tributaries. The other tributary, above the Brumboret, was called Rambor.

We met many parties of men and boys bringing sacks of walnuts down to Aijun. They carried long poles for knocking down the walnuts, which they shelled on the spot.

Further up, in Brumboret, we came to a succession of farms and terraced fields of rice and Indian corn, both of which were being cut. I saw a great many walnut trees, besides other fruit trees and some very big mulberry trees.

The valley here was rather wider and more level, the hillsides steep and rocky with scrub oak and, above this, forests of pine and fir. The villages in Brumboret were inhabited by both Muslims and Black Kafirs. We stopped at Batrik where there were about a dozen well-built Black Kafir houses in a side valley. The men dressed like Muslims, but the Kafir women and small girls wore a distinctive head-dress ornamented with tiny shells. All the women and girls wore a dark-brown, loose garment girdled in round the waist.

I took a number of photographs of Kafir men, women and children and two carved wooden statues, about six feet high, where they had placed dead bodies. Corpses were laid out in wooden coffins and then taken to a corner of a field and left there to disintegrate above ground. The statues were apparently commemorative, but the people had no objection to moving them into a better light to be photographed, indeed they rather chucked them about. The façades of the Kafir houses were also decorated with some simple carving.

From Brumboret, the way to the valley of Barir led uphill by a very steep track through scrub oaks, then extensive forests of pine and deodar. I saw few birds here; some fresh droppings I noticed on the track were probably those of markhor. The descent to Barir was much steeper and in places the track was barely discernible.

At the foot of a narrow, rocky gorge we found some Kafir houses surrounded by fields of rice and millet, fruit trees and large vines. We rested here for about half an hour and devoured quantities of small, sweet-tasting, purple grapes picked from a vine which must have been thirty feet high. We then continued on down the valley to Gurru, where the houses appeared to hang from a steep hillside above the stream.

I found the Barir valley more attractive than Brumboret. The first group of houses we encountered had been occupied by Muslims as well as Kafirs, although I gathered that Kafirs predominated here. As usual, the recently converted Muslims were very regular with their calls to prayer. In and around Gurru, all the houses were owned by Kafirs. I noticed certain dissimilarities between these people and the Chitralis. For instance, unlike the Chitrali men and boys, none of the Kafirs or Muslims carried catapult bows and, instead of a funnel above the hearth, the smoke from their fires had no outlet but the door. The Kafir villages were, besides, rather dirty and at Gurru I counted about sixty bed-bugs in my sleeping-bag.

*　　*　　*

We were off again at sunrise, marching along under over-hanging mountains whose barren, rocky slopes, apart from scattered conifers and juniper, were almost devoid of vegetation. I now had my first glimpses of Rakaposhi, the brilliant white snow mantling its shoulders contrasting with a cloudless, deep blue sky.

Another three hours' walking brought us to Chalt, an attractive village set among poplars, fruit trees and terraced fields of rice at the end of a bare stretch of the valley. We bought some excellent grapes here from a donkey-caravan loaded with panniers from Hunza, and spent the night in the rest-house at the far end of the village.

Leaving Chalt at first light, we had to make a detour to get to the bridge over a wide stream flowing down from a large valley on our left. From here Rakaposhi, 25,550 feet high, dominated everything. It was a magnificent mountain, a great white pyramid of ice, towering over its surroundings. We had an unbroken view of the whole side of the mountain which was now right over our heads.

For the next three days we could see this incredible mountain rising abruptly from the far side of the great valley up which we travelled. I remembered Shipton describing Rakaposhi in the Travellers' Club, and how this had fired me with desire to see it. Now I had done so: whatever lay ahead, the journey had been worthwhile.

We passed through a succession of orchards and farmsteads clinging on to the lower slopes of the mountains above cliffs that fell sheer to the river. Rivulets of cold, dirty-grey glacier water, with snow-crystals swirling in it, irrigated the fields. Everyone we met saluted us and seemed very friendly. Some lads carrying panniers of fruit to Gilgit gave us excellent peaches, and in one place the villagers brought us delicious grapes which we stopped to eat at leisure. At Maiyun, ten miles beyond Chalt, we rested for a couple of hours. Rakaposhi loomed directly above us, but was rather foreshortened from this angle so that one of its lower peaks looked higher than the actual summit.

I stayed on at Hindi until the sun was on Rakaposhi, so that I could photograph it. From here, the track to Aliabad and Baltit led through fields and orchards. Rakaposhi was in sight for most of the time, and I had a good view of the high snow peaks, from Aliabad, up the Hunza river valley beyond the Hispar glacier. We reached Karimabad, the Mir's residence just below his old residence at Baltit, soon after midday. The scenery here was superb: Rakaposhi, the snow peaks of Hispar and the snow-covered, bare, sheer-sided mountain rising straight up behind the village. The slopes above the Hunza river were covered with terraced fields, farms and orchards. There were no markhor, I was told, this side of Chalt, and no black bear, but numbers of ibex, urial, brown bear and snow leopard. *Ovis poli*, a variety of wild sheep named after Marco Polo, were found near the Mantaka Pass, at the Sinkiang border on the road to Kashgar.

Here among the mountains I found that I slept very little. Most of the night I would doze on an imperceptible line between sleep and waking, yet in the morning I would feel quite rested. This night at the foot of the pass had been no exception. I rose and made tea at 4 AM, but could not get the porters under way until after five.

Despite a cloudy start to the day, the weather looked promising. We brought the yaks as far as the shoulder of the mountain, but we had to abandon them where a rocky defile proved too narrow for them to pass, even without their loads. In this arctic landscape there seemed nothing for them to eat, but the porters assured me that the yaks would scratch about and find enough beneath the snow, and be all right until they came back for them. The porters now carried loads of about 60 pounds apiece, together with their own rations.

Beyond this point the going was reasonably easy, much of it up a glacier. Ploughing upwards, knee-deep, through the snow, I was worried about crevasses but the porters appeared unconcerned; they trudged steadily ahead and rested often. We reached the top of the pass at one o'clock and rested there a while, gazing over range upon range of mountains, some in heavy shadow, all of which Tilman, who had crossed the Chilinji Pass some years before, had described as looking 'eminently unclimbable'.

But we had to get down into the valley before night fell. Immediately beneath us was a very steep slope of snow-covered scree. At first glance it looked impassable, but luckily the snow was soft and we slipped and slithered down for 2,000 feet, falling frequently. Had the snow been frozen I do not think we should ever have got down.

The porters were exhausted by the time we reached the bottom and Faiz was in equally poor shape. However, I felt hardly tired and took a load and went on with Mirza Khan, the strongest of my party, as we had to get to the 'jungle' in the valley below for firewood. After the very steep 2,000-foot slope the going was easy until we came to the last 1,000 feet which were steep and rocky.

By the late afternoon Mirza and I arrived in the 'jungle', the upper fringes of a belt of willow extending down into the valley; here there was abundant firewood. The others eventually struggled in and hot tea and a meal soon had everybody happy. We made a huge fire and slept round it on rather rocky ground under the stars.

The next day, I delayed setting off until the porters had mended the soles of their soft leather boots which were much the worse for wear after the previous day's scramble. The day was cold and cheerless with flurries of snow at intervals.

On the cliffs around us we heard ibex (which the porters called markhor) whistling continually, a bird-like note rather like a curlew. Also a lot of chikhor were calling on the mountain tops.

We saw tracks of ibex everywhere on our way down the valley. We followed a stream whose banks were clothed with thickets of golden birch and willow. The mountains around us were shrouded in mist; when we camped at midday, we chose a place where a jutting rock would give us shelter if it snowed. I decided to go to Ishkoman from here, and then to Darkot, instead of Boroghil, where if the weather broke we could not hope to get across the Darkot Pass. In any case, I had already seen the country beyond Karumbar the previous year.

It snowed throughout the night and for the whole of the next day. About three feet of snow had fallen by the time we started and visibility was down to fifty yards. We struggled through the deep snow down the valley for a mile and a half to an over-hanging rock with a low cave under it. The cave was nowhere more than three feet high and in consequence the smoke was troublesome when we lit a fire. We stayed there for the rest of the day; I slept in my tent away from the smoke.

The following morning we started early and struggled down to the main valley again through deep snow which made it difficult to pick a way through large boulders. The weather, however, was now clear and bright. The juniper and birch were laden with snow. For a mile or two we followed the tracks of a snow leopard which had chosen the easiest route. Then we crossed the stream and halted in a forest of large, blasted juniper on a terrace above the river below some high, precipitous cliffs. Here an Uzbek had built two or three rough log cabins round the juniper trees. He had large flocks of sheep and goats, a few small black cows and a couple of large, well-kept, friendly dogs. He was out hunting when we arrived but turned up later and seemed very hospitable. He gave us excellent curds, butter with bread and a meat stew for lunch. The Uzbek was a refugee from Russia who had been living in India for the past twenty years. He had bought this patch of forest three years ago. His family included two or three small boys and some women whom we did not see.

We spent an extremely pleasant day with the Uzbek; the sun was hot but all the time it was freezing hard in the shade. Beyond his encampment was a thick wood of golden birch and a fine view of the Chilinji Pass and the high peaks above it, and on the other side of the valley.

A Kirghiz arrived on a horse very heavily laden with sacks of flour. He was on his way back to the Pamirs but, because of the weather, would probably have to remain here for another week or two. In the evening two Wakhis, servants of our Uzbek host, turned up with a small flock of goats. They had just returned from the Pamirs and told us that the snow there was waist-deep.

That night we had an enormous fire of juniper branches. I bought a sheep for twelve rupees, and after dinner the men danced round the fire to tunes which one of our porters played skilfully on a pipe. Despite a very hard frost I slept snugly in my two flea-bags on the snow at some distance from the fire to avoid the sparks, which are bad with juniper wood.

I rose to the sound of ibex whistling on the cliffs above our camp; we were to see many of them further on. We crossed the river again and followed it downstream through thickets of juniper, willow, wild rose and birch, under sheer cliffs of bare rock which disappeared into the clouds thousands of feet above us. Occasionally stones came rattling down as the mountainside warmed in the sun. After we had forded the river a second time, we had some difficulty crossing another fast-flowing torrent, over frozen rocks. Faiz waded the torrent in his boots which made me angry; I told him this was just the way to do his feet in properly.

We halted briefly at Buk, near some hovels; then we crossed the main river again and carried on over the jumbled moraine of a glacier, along a wide, gloomy, boulder-strewn valley to Matramza.

We had to pick our way over the debris of two smaller glaciers before we reached Baihan near Bad Swat, a large terraced settlement further up the valley. By mid-afternoon low cloud had blotted out the view up the main glacier, and a storm of wind and rain broke soon after we arrived at the village. I found the inhabitants of Bad Swat welcoming and hospitable. The Wazir's son, a boy of about seventeen, turned up at sunset by which time the storm had abated.

Next morning we continued on to Imit, quite a small village attractively positioned in the Ishkoman valley. Except for some houses and cultivated fields, Ishkoman itself was in ruins; the Mir, Sultan Ghazi, now lived permanently at Imit where there was a small mosque and a guest-house. On the way along the valley I had seen a peregrine falcon and here, for the first time, I saw many smaller birds, mostly warblers. The Mir kept a sparrow-hawk which he used for hunting partridges; he was very friendly and provided us with fruit and other food.

The Ishkoman Pass was only 14,000 feet high, but the Mir warned me that after the recent snow we might find it impassable, so I decided to engage four extra porters to help us carry our loads over the pass. I planned to spend the following night on the near side of the pass and arrive at Darkot the day after that.

The Mir and some of his retainers accompanied us for about two miles, as far as the river which we crossed with the help of their ponies. We went up a side valley to a small village, beyond the ruins of Ishkoman, where we exchanged the pony we had brought from Matramza for four porters.

Higher up the valley, we came to a forest of juniper, where many large branches had been broken by the weight of snow. In several villages, I saw houses built like wigwams, of tree trunks and large branches, some of them with a rough stone wall round the bottom. After seven hours' march, we eventually arrived at a deserted village on the snow-line. This village was only occupied during the summer, so there were four or five empty houses now, in one of which we slept.

We kept a fire burning all night but even so, by morning, some water which had been left in a cup within two feet of the fire was frozen over.

Starting at sunrise we went up the south side of the valley where the snow lay about a foot deep. The porters went slowly with constant halts. After about three hours we reached the last of the trees. The porters wanted to camp here and cross the pass the next day, saying it was a very long way to the top.

I refused and insisted on going on as I was afraid the weather might break; true, it showed no signs of doing so, being a perfect, cloudless day, but from experience I knew that it could cloud over without warning. Besides, everyone we asked had assured us that we could get to Darkot that same day. From where we were to the top of the pass looked close and easy; I expected to reach the summit by noon.

We now got on to a flat, snow-covered plain about three miles across. This proved heavy going, the snow being about eighteen inches deep, and it took us two hours to cross it. Beyond this came a succession of ascents and depressions, none of them very steep, but heavy going through two or three feet of snow.

The top of the pass remained elusive. We climbed up to what I had taken to be the top, only to have to work all the way back to our right, towards what looked like yet another summit, and then back again behind a rocky ridge to our left. The last stage consisted of a series of steep ascents and descents into small, snow-covered basins. In places the snow lay waist-deep.

Mirza and I went on ahead to break a trail while the porters lagged behind leaving us uncertain of the road, and Faiz Muhammad, who was nearly in tears, set the porters a rotten example by sitting down after every few steps.

The sun had disappeared over the ridge and by now it was getting very cold. We finally struggled to the last crest at 5.15 PM, about half an hour before sunset. On the snow near the summit I noticed a single comatose fly.

On the far side was a steep, snow-covered descent. The porters warned us to keep well to our right, off the glacier and clear of any crevasses. Again Mirza and I led the way. Faiz, now in tears and almost hysterical, begged me to stop and sleep

208

where we were but I told him and the porters that we must get down to the 'jungle'.

At the top of the pass I noticed some large tracks but had been too preoccupied to pay them any attention. When I asked Mirza what they were he said they were the fresh tracks of a very large brown bear. The sight of them had a considerable effect in getting the porters down the hill.

The going was difficult; in some places I broke through more than waist-deep. Mirza and I went on ahead with Latif as a connecting link with the porters. At about 7.30 PM we stopped, having lost touch with Latif. Mirza was all for pushing on down to the 'jungle', but this I refused to do until I had established contact with the others, angry that even if we went on we stupidly had no matches with us to light a fire. Mirza finally disappeared and I was left by myself on the frozen mountainside, half expecting to have to sleep on the snow without any covering. I called and called and after about an hour heard an answering shout, so started back uphill. Suddenly the four porters loomed out of the night. They said Faiz had bedded down under a rock and that Latif was with him. Since there were two of them and Faiz had ample bedding with him and Latif an overcoat and a cloak I was not worried. I therefore went on slowly downhill with the four porters, trying to pick the best way by starlight. Owing to the snow there was quite a lot of light.

We came to one frighteningly steep face which never seemed to end, but the snow was crisp and frozen and held well, and eventually we got down to the bottom. I then found that one of the porters had stayed at the top behind a rock. I knew I could never get back up to fetch him, so went on down to the stream with the other three. After going some way along the stream we came to a little scattered shrub and some rough sheepfolds. It was after midnight by the time the porters lit a fire and I crawled into my sleeping bags. Lying awake, I knew that I had made a mess of things by ignoring local advice.

During the night the snow melted through my sleeping bags. I had taken off my trousers and socks which were lumps of ice and my feet remained very cold. I stayed where I was till the sun reached me, then I gave the three porters a tin of bully beef and tea (Mirza had the sugar with him) and I made myself some Bovril. We stayed where we were, drying our things and getting warm, until 10 AM. The missing porter meanwhile turned up at 8.30 AM. I then took the porters down the valley for about three miles to an empty village, within sight of Darkot, where we found Mirza. His feet were slightly frostbitten. He would have done better to have stayed with me. We had a cup of tea and then, taking my pack with my sleeping bags, groundsheet and some tinned food, I started back up the hill to look for Faiz and Latif. I was nearly back at our last night's stopping place when I found them. Latif was all right, but Faiz's feet were a little frostbitten.

As we approached the village where I had spent the night we met three locals who had heard we were missing and were coming to our assistance. We had some more tea and then went down to their village about two miles away. The headman was most hospitable and insisted on slaughtering a sheep for us, despite our protests.

It was pleasant to be all collected together again; the night before I had felt like one of a scattered covey of partridges.

The Hazaras of the Koli Barit valley, in Surkh-o-Parsa, camped in their fields in black tents or, in some cases, circular dwellings like *yurts* made of a framework of willow saplings covered with mats and branches. One Hazara told me that they moved out of their houses to escape from the bugs, but others said they did this every autumn to allow their livestock to manure the harvested fields when they were brought inside the tents at night and kept tied up until morning. By constantly moving the site of their tents, they were able to manure the greater part of their fields: all the fields were small, the valleys on the northern slopes of the Paghman range being steep and narrow.

Travelling in the Hazarajat, Afghanistan, in 1954, at the junction of the Koli Barit and Colom Bela valleys, we stopped at some Hazara tents. From there we marched up the valley of Colom Bela, then up a side-valley, where we camped on the hillside near a solitary house. Coming up the Colom Bela, I noticed a tall, solid stone building like a monastery, evidently divided into separate dwellings whose windows looked out from the high wall. Further along I saw another curious sight, a sort of natural rock gateway where the Colom Bela stream had cut through granite cliffs, producing some oddly shaped pinnacles.

That evening Jan Baz and I decided to climb up and see the sacred Hauz-i-Khas pools, a place of pilgrimage near the 15,600-foot summit of Takht-i-Turkoman; meanwhile, the Sayid would take our pony from Colom Bela, directly over the pass, to Paghman. We would have to come down by way of Shakar Dara, as we had been told that, owing to sheer cliffs, there was no way of getting round the pools to the Paghman Pass.

It was bitterly cold when Jan Baz and I started off at daybreak up the valley. The Hazaras in Colom Bela had asked too high a price to show us the way to the pools, but an Ibrahim Khel from a Kuchi encampment higher up came with us. At this altitude the mountain streams were frozen over.

211

After a long, steep scramble, which, though tiring, had not been very difficult, we arrived at the pools, a thousand feet or so below the summit of Takht-i-Turkoman. Two of them were the size of small ponds; the third, and largest, which had some mallard swimming about on it, was about 120 yards across. The pools had been formed by melted snow; in consequence their dimensions varied considerably according to the season. The pools were ringed round, except on the north-east, by granite cliffs and scree streaked with snow, and lay among a tumbled mass of granite boulders and slabs covered with a very dark, almost black patina, which from a distance looked volcanic. Nearby were several small springs, and patches of fresh green grass dotted with flowers including a sort of Canterbury bell.

Every year Hindus from Kabul made a pilgrimage to Hauz-i-Khas. Ten days before we arrived more than a hundred of them, and for the first time some Sikhs, had undertaken this pilgrimage. They had spent two nights beside the pools, 14,000 feet above sea-level; getting there must have been a stiff climb for a Hindu shopkeeper.

Jan Baz and I climbed with some effort up a rough, boulderstrewn face to the summit of Takht-i-Turkoman. Despite the hazy atmosphere, which diminished a magnificent view, I could still discern the outline of the distant Nuristan mountains.

from *Among the Mountains*

I first visited Persia in 1949 on my way back to England from Oman, and I did not return until June 1964, when I stayed for six months. I made three long journeys on foot. First I travelled some four hundred and fifty miles through the Elburz mountains from Bujnurd to Alamut. Then, in September, I joined the Bakhtiari tribe on their autumn migration from the Zagros mountains down to the coastal plains. Finally I crossed the Dasht-i-Lut desert from Tabas to Yazd, a distance of over two hundred miles. I was greatly helped by Lew Tamp, a Russian émigré who lived in Tehran and knew Persia intimately. He gave me invaluable advice and took me to the starting point of each journey.

Before my first journey I visited with him the Turkoman in their *yurts*, or felt tents, on the Gorgan steppes; I saw the ancient brick-built tower of Gunbad-i-Qabus, which Robert Byron in *The Road to Oxiana* asserted to be finer than the Taj Mahal; and I looked across the Russian frontier at the wire fences and watch-towers, a chilling experience. Then we went to Bujnurd, where I bought two pack mules.

On this journey I was accompanied by a muleteer, and a Kurdish school-teacher who acted as my interpreter. On our first day's march the school-teacher, in poor condition, lagged further and further behind. Eventually I waited for him to catch up. When he did he gasped, 'I am very hot, very thirsty and very tired!' Exasperated, I said, 'I told you it was a long way. We still have more than four hundred miles to go. What is the furthest you have ever walked?' 'From my bedroom to the bathroom, I suppose.' His feet soon blistered so we mounted him on one of the mules which was already heavily laden. But as soon as his blisters were healed he insisted on walking. I found him a good companion, humorous and informative.

Week after week we walked over a bare, tawny land; we crossed wide plains covered with stones, and climbed high windswept passes. We sometimes passed the ruins of a castle on a hill-top, or the black tents of shepherd tribes, their sheep standing each with its head in the shade of another sheep's body. Wherever a stream issued from a hillside was a village, with cultivated fields, fruit trees, poplars, walnuts and magnificent *chenar*, the Persian plane trees. But such villages appeared as isolated dots or ribbons of green, in the immense desert setting.

Usually the shepherds were welcoming, but the villagers were almost always churlish and inhospitable. We carried some food with us and paid for anything else. Time and again we hung about on the outskirts of a village, the loads still on our tired mules, while Taj Ali the muleteer tried to find someone who would allow us to sleep on the roof of his house. It annoyed me when the owner invariably turned up to share our meal and eat the chicken for which he had overcharged us, especially as I knew he would demand yet more money for letting us sleep on his roof, or for the oil in the lamp we used. Taj Ali had a heated argument with a man demanding money for the grass the mules had eaten on a hillside near his village. I did not like these people, and this reduced my pleasure in the journey. To me it is always the people rather than the places that matter.

We reached the Lar valley, and spent a few restful days in the Embassy camp, where Sir Denis Wright made us very welcome. There were trout in the river and a view of Demavend, eighteen thousand feet high, framed by the sides of the valley. Then we went on again through bare country even bigger than that through which we had come. We climbed six or seven high passes, coming at last to the final one above Alamut, the Valley of the Assassins. Men were gathering mule-loads of thistles and fennel, all that grew among the rusty red rocks. Around us, and far into the distance, rose great ranges of mountains. In the morning we went down into the valley, through a bank of cloud that emphasized the savage desolation of the scene, to a village perched on a shelf beyond the gorge. Above the village

The Yemen, 1966: a young man, smoking a water-pipe, wears the conical, plaited cap peculiar to the region.

The Chamar Pass above Nuristan, 1965. 'Higher up on the northern face, the snow had been eroded into frozen pinnacles, two feet high and a foot or so apart, the formation known to mountaineers as *névés pénitents*, laborious to cross.' These formations of porous ice are so named because of their resemblance to cowled monks.

Thesiger's Tajik porters on the Nuristan side of the Chamar Pass.

Badakhshan, northeast Afghanistan, August 1965. Kandari nomads winding down towards the plains from their summer camp near Lake Shiva, above the Oxus valley.

'One of my favourite compositions': Thesiger photographed this group of boys at Qalat Razih, Yemen, soon after its recapture by Royalist forces, during the Civil War.

Left Thesiger's Samburu adoptive son, Lawi Leboyare, after Lawi's circumcision, in 1976. Lawi has a black ostrich-feather fastened on either side of his head; he wears the initiate's goatskin cape made of three skins dyed black with charcoal mixed with animal fat. *Right* A Samburu *moran*, or warrior, being decorated by another.

Mount Kenya from the Teleki Valley, with giant groundsel in the foreground. In February 1971, Thesiger made a circuit of the mountain in a single day. The twin peaks, Nelion (17, 022 ft) and Batian (17, 058 ft), were climbed by Eric Shipton in 1929, thirty years after Sir Halford Mackinder's pioneering ascent. Teleki Valley is named after Count Samuel Teleki who, with Lt Ludwig von Höhnel, discovered Lake Rudolf (now Lake Turkana) and Lake Stefanie, in 1888.

Nerags, near the Zanskar river, photographed during Thesiger's journey in Ladakh, with Sir Robert ffolkes, in September-October 1983.

the scant ruins of a castle sat on a fang of rock, accessible only by a precarious path above a two-hundred-foot drop. From this seemingly impregnable stronghold Hassan-i-Sabbah, the 'Old Man of the Mountains', had ruled his Ismaili sect and despatched his Assassins on their missions of death; there he and his successors had sat like spiders at the centre of their web, for one hundred and seventy years until Hulagu and his Mongols stormed over the pass.

Next day we followed the track down the valley, fording the river six times in one mile, and two days later, 2 September, we arrived at the Qazvin road. We had been travelling for forty-six days.

I was in Tehran for a fortnight before I was given permission to accompany the Bakhtiari on their migration. Both the Bakhtiari and the Qashgai tribes migrate each spring from the low country along the Persian Gulf to the Zagros mountains, where they remain till the autumn before returning to the plains for the winter. They are perhaps the last two tribes who regularly over great distances migrate in a manner unchanged through the centuries. The Bakhtiari nomads numbered about fifty thousand. Both tribes had been virtually independent until Reza Shah ruthlessly curtailed their power in the twenties. Even after that they gave periodic trouble to the Government: consequently it was not easy to get permission to visit them.

I hired two mules at a village called Shashmeh to the west of Isfahan, and on 22 September left there with a muleteer, also a policeman who had been sent with me from Tehran. The main body of the migration was ahead and we hurried to catch up with them, passing many smaller groups. Some of them pitched small black tents when they halted; others were content with shelters of branches. The men wore round black felt caps, sleeveless white coats to their knees with a dark pattern down

215

the back, dark long-sleeved shirts, and very wide trousers. The women wore long, loose dresses, often of red, blue or green velvet, with a kerchief attached to a small cap, hanging down behind almost to the ground. The various families we stopped with were hospitable and friendly. The route they were following was hard indeed, often a twisting track through and over piles of rock fallen from the precipice above, or along a narrow shelf across a wide limestone face with a sheer drop hundreds of feet below. Sometimes the track crossed and recrossed a river, or climbed through dense oak woods, then went steeply up a bare mountainside to some high pass, where the limestone, polished over the centuries, was slippery as glass. From the passes we looked across successive ranges of the Zagros mountains, their summits high in cloudless skies where ravens tumbled.

After five days we came up with the main body and moved with them, usually camping with a different family each night, having been separated from the previous one during the march. I remember one day that typified the whole migration. Many families had camped the night before near a wood on the lower slopes of a very steep ridge which we had to cross. All around us were the watch-fires. Water was scarce and the flocks and herds were restless. Dogs barked; men shouted at intervals; there was uproar when a wolf attacked a sheep and mauled it. All night I heard the music of the bells, some deep-toned, others of higher pitch, that hung round the necks of sheep and goats; and at intervals the sound of pipes played by shepherd boys. We moved off at half past three, soon after the moon had risen; others had already left. I climbed above the wood and sat beside the track, to watch the migration pass. Below me were the lights of many fires, and from the darkness of the waking valley I heard a rising, falling roar, a flowing river of sound, as the migration moved forward. Flocks of sheep pushed past, their fleeces luminous in the near dark; and separate flocks of black goats, a moving darkness, darker than the hillside. Men and boys passed, pale figures in white coats; and dark, barely discernible women interspersed with scrambling, straining mules and cattle. The light grew stronger. I could distinguish tents and bedding, pots and pans, sacks of grain loaded on mules and cattle, a puppy on a cow's back, babies in cradles or bundles, carried by the women. Then the birds began to sing in the wood, and the sun came over the mountains. I climbed to the pass; ahead, the track was solid for miles with a thread of slowly moving men and animals.

A few days later we came to the ancient shrine at Shahabad, under its curious white cone. Next day we reached the Karun river, and there I left the Bakhtiari.

I was anxious to cross the Dasht-i-Lut, or Desert of Lot, before I returned to England. The very name was intriguing. Lew Tamp took me in his Land Rover at the end of October to Tabas, where I hired two camels and a man to look after them. The captain of the gendarmes insisted on sending three of his men with me. When given the order they protested volubly. 'What crime have we committed that you send us into the Dasht-i-Lut?' This was actually much ado about nothing. It took us ten days to reach Yazd and on seven of those days we found water, though sometimes brackish. My own camel was a large baggage camel with a wrenching stride which I soon realized would incapacitate me: I had slipped a disc in my back some years before and was still liable to trouble. I therefore walked upwards of two hundred miles to Yazd. The weather, cool by day, was bitterly cold at night; several times the water-skins froze solid.

We crossed gravel plains and low, bare hills, sometimes

gashed by deep watercourses. In places there were drifts of sand, and small salt flats; there was little vegetation except occasional tamarisk bushes. Here we saw four onager or wild ass. They were quite close and although donkeys are unlawful food for Muslims the gendarmes wanted to shoot them for meat. I deliberately raised my voice in protest; the onager galloped off and the gendarmes sulked. We also saw occasional gazelle and found the skull of a moufflon. Then, after skirting some jagged black mountains we came to the small village of Zaraigan, where there were fruit trees and a little cultivation; and the next day to Shah Kevir, another village of half a dozen houses with a few palms. Beyond this village we marched for ten miles or more across a plain, the surface consisting of salt encrusted with dry mud. Finally we reached an extensive gravel plain with mountains on either side, and arrived at Yazd.

This journey had been a slog through dull country. It lacked the sense of comradeship, of hardship or of danger which would have made it rewarding. Nonetheless I had reached my goal.

from *Desert, Marsh and Mountain*

At Puchal we put up the tent beneath some mulberry trees. Unlike my previous visits, this time everyone in the village including the mullahs – even the mullah who had cursed me – was welcoming and friendly.

Throughout this journey I remained on good terms with the Nuristanis. Unlike Robertson, I never had anything stolen by them, nor did I find them avaricious. They would drive a hard bargain, but many of them, especially in villages unused to Europeans, were exceedingly hospitable.

* * *

We left the main village an hour after sunrise, heading for Kulam. A little further downstream, we stopped at the smaller group of a dozen dwellings forming lower Puchal, where I had stayed in 1956. We then crossed the river by the bridge and climbed for two hours up the mountainside. Higher up the mountain, there was no sign of water until we reached an ailoq surrounded by drifts of snow.

That evening two Tajiks turned up, and they and the porters bought a goat from the owner of the ailoq. They ate it all, after giving Baz Muhammad and me as much meat as we wanted. After dinner, two Nuristani herd-boys sang and so did one of the Tajiks.

At dawn a thick blanket of low cloud hid the mountains. We set off just as it was getting light, and climbed to the top of the Purdam Pass. The way up involved a steady slog for three hours over hard snow, scree and boulders, and the descent from the pass was very steep, but we found hardly any snow lying on the Kulam side except in the gullies. Further down, we came to an ailoq built of tree-trunks. Thick forests covered the lower slopes, with water everywhere and green grass strewn with pink asphodels and other flowers beneath the trees which included some magnificent large junipers and pines.

We halted at a village on a spur above the confluence of two rivers, the Goulata, also known as the Purdam, and the Bedetsau. The villager who put us up for the night had recently killed his wife and her lover, a man from across the valley. The ensuing blood-feud between our host's family and the family of the dead man had already resulted in some shooting the day before, and reinforcements turned up soon after we got here.

I found these people very hospitable. They gave us lunch as soon as we arrived, then dinner; and the following morning they gave us a very good breakfast. As we were leaving, the villagers became very excited, having spotted our host's enemies on the mountainside opposite.

The local chief, Habib Allah Khan, who stood six foot four, invited us to stay at his house further down the river. From midday, when we arrived there, until the late evening he left us with nothing to eat; in consequence everyone felt browned off. Instead, the wretched man spent his time trying to make me give him my wrist-watch.

Next morning we set off at daybreak and marched downstream for three hours to the junction with Derai Shuk, a big river-valley with a pass at the head of it which led into Kantiwar. We crossed the river and went on east up the Shuk valley as far as Taurich, a small village high up on the mountainside. Here occurred the only real disagreement I ever had with the Nuristanis. The people gave us food on our arrival; we gorged on mulberries with bread and curds. Unwilling to impose eight of us on them again in the evening, I bought with difficulty a chicken which we cooked and ate with some boiled rice for dinner. This gave great offence: although we had camped on a roof instead of sleeping in someone's house, the furious villagers maintained we were their guests and said we had scorned their hospitality.

The villagers refused to see us off the following morning. We left Taurich at 6 AM and marched up the valley for two hours until we reached Shuk, an attractive village clinging to the mountainside, where we rested under some trees by the mosque. All the villagers, including the mullah, were very friendly. In the afternoon we moved the loads to a nearby roof and set up the tent beside them. The views from here up and down the valley were magnificent, among the finest I have ever seen. Nuristan was a land of great contrasts, reminding me sometimes of Kurdistan but on a vaster scale. Across the river, forests of holly-oak covered the steep mountainsides; pine trees grew higher up on the ridges, and all round us the mountain peaks glistened white with snow.

Some bundles of wheat cut by the women had been spread on another roof, and children romped in the wheat to thresh it. In Nuristan, only men and boys went up to the ailoqs and only the women and girls worked in the fields.

After a steady, but relatively easy climb over hard snow, we reached the top of the pass overlooking Kantiwar. On the far side of the mountain, we descended from the pass through deep, soft snow until we came to an empty ailoq on a patch of turf scattered with flowers. We rested here, and rested again at another empty ailoq lower down, where we made tea over a fire of dry dung.

The way from here, down the face of the mountain to the valley floor, was steep and difficult. The scenery was magnificent: snow-covered mountains; a deep gorge with a racing river, and high up in the valley, flocks of sheep and goats tended by Gujurs.

Massive drifts of snow lay in the valley bottom. We crossed the icy torrent on a snow bridge and camped in the shelter of some rocks; the bushes nearby provided us with firewood. Huddled round the fire under a full moon, the porters worried that we might have been followed by Gujur bandits.

The following morning we marched down the valley through a wood of large birch trees and willows, then across open grassy meadows intersected by streams. After about an hour, we stopped beside a Nuristani ailoq. The shepherds in the ailoq welcomed us; one of them said that they had been asked not to kill strangers.

We pitched the tent close to the river which was wider here, slow-flowing and very clear. Known as Chaman, this was a delectable place where the untroubled water idled past, dragging at the overhanging willow in the current; where black cattle, watched by boys with flutes, grazed on rich pasture among banks of lilac primulas, wild roses, purple orchids, asphodel and grass of Parnassus.

At sunrise, we rode high up into the rolling sweep of bare mountains above the plain. I had hoped to find the Kandaris at their massed encampments beyond the pass above the Oxus valley, near Lake Shiva, but we were too late. These nomads arrived at Shiva at the end of May; now, at the beginning of August, they had already left the lake where, it was said, two hundred thousand of them congregated with their flocks. Down slopes that were almost colourless in the hazy light, but for the vagrant shadows of scattered clouds, there came winding towards us a continuous thread of men and camels. They followed no apparent course, turning, twisting, disappearing into hollows and reappearing. The weather was still broken after heavy rain the previous day which had brought the mountain streams crashing down in spate.

We dismounted and stood aside to let them pass: camels tied head to tail, laden with tents, poles and the scanty furnishings and possessions of a nomad people; each camel decorated with tufted woollen head-stalls and wide tasselled neckbands; many with bells fastened above their knees; laden donkeys and horses; small children and a woman or two perched on the loads; women in voluminous clothes with black draperies over their heads, leading strings of camels; bearded men and smooth-faced youths striding past, in turbans, patterned waist-coats and long cloaks; and guard dogs padding by, formidable brutes that could kill a wolf. I had seen the great tribes of northern Arabia – the Bakhtiari of Persia, the Herki of Kurdistan, and the Powindah coming down to Pakistan – yet for some reason, perhaps the landscape, my memory of these Kandaris remains the most vivid of them all.

On my journeys among the mountains of Kurdistan, Pakistan and Afghanistan, I had passed through some of the most spectacular country in the world and I had encountered people of many different races and origins, from Mongols to Nuristanis and Pathans. They varied greatly in their customs, the clothes they wore and in the lives they led; but all were Muslims, and this gave me a basic understanding of their behaviour. Though I had managed, in Peshawar and Kabul, to find someone who spoke English and was willing to accompany me, my inability to speak any of their languages kept me apart from my porters on these journeys and deprived me of the sense of comradeship I had known in Arabia and among the Madan in Iraq.

I went to India in 1983 and spent two months in Ladakh. For me this was a totally new experience, for here I was among Buddhists and with a people akin to the Tibetans.

Sir Robert ffolkes had been in Ladakh for the past five years, in charge of the Save the Children organization and he had invited me to join him there. He had advised me not to come before the beginning of September as the tourists would have left by then.

He met me in Srinagar on 4 September and a few days later he motored me by way of the Zoji-la Pass and Kargil, to Leh.

We set off from Leh on 17 September and for the next six weeks we travelled with ponies or yaks from one village to another. We crossed many passes, among them the Sisir-la, Kupa-la, and the 17,000-foot-high Sengyyi-la where a little snow still lingered. After descending from them in the bitter cold we sometimes arrived in a village after dark. Only in the

Tibesti mountains in the Sahara had I seen a landscape as barren. We travelled incessantly over rocks and stones where the only vegetation was an occasional artemisia plant. Sometimes we crossed two passes a day, or skirted tremendous gorges. At last we would reach a small village with some cultivation along a stream, perhaps bordered by tamarisk and willow. Many of the villages had such strange, yet evocative names: Photoksar, Yulchung, Linkshet, Hanupata. Everywhere we were welcomed, for Robert ffolkes had done much to help these people. We would stay in a village for a day or two, and each night sit round a hearth in the increasing cold and drink their buttered tea. Some of these people, especially the old women, had striking faces. I was happy to be accepted by them, able to take what photographs I wanted with no feeling of restraint.

We returned briefly to Leh and visited the great monastery of Hemis; then we travelled through more of Ladakh's spectacular mountain valleys until in the last week of October we ended our journey back again once more near Leh, at the impressive Spituk monastery.

From Ladakh I went on to Jaipur, Pushkar and Jaisalmer in Rajasthan, Bandhavgarh in Bhopal, and Hyderabad; before returning to England from India the following year I spent a month in Nepal. I deliberately went to Nepal in March and April, being anxious to see the rhododendrons, but for some reason they were not in flower that year. I was aware that this was not a suitable time to see the Himalayas, which were then usually obscured by haze. I once caught a glimpse of the Annapurna range, clearcut and beautiful after a fall of rain. This was the vision I took away with me from the Himalayas, more than thirty years after I first travelled among the mountains.

from *Among the Mountains*

PART THREE
1960–94

For two months in 1959 I had been travelling with mule transport from Addis Ababa to the Kenya frontier. I was disappointed by the lack of game animals seen on the way to Mega, a small township some forty miles from the Kenya frontier, since wild animals had been abundant there in the accounts which I had read about this country as a boy. By now they had been virtually exterminated. I travelled through country conquered by Menelik at the end of the nineteenth century and added to the Ethiopian empire. It bore no resemblance to the five historic provinces of the north – Tigre, Begemger, Gojjam, Wollo, Amhara – with which I was familiar.

By the time I reached Mega, a journey of some four hundred miles, my shoes were worn out but the Vice-Consul in Mega, Ian Reeman, advised me to go to Moyale where he thought I would be able to get others. I did not have a permit to cross the frontier from Ethiopia into Kenya, but at Moyale the DC, George Webb, made me welcome. I told him that I must get another pair of shoes, and that evening George Webb sent for a cobbler, told him to measure my feet and to have a pair of strong *chapli* sandals ready by breakfast time. I found George Webb a quite exceptionally able linguist, a man dedicated to the work he was doing and fascinating to talk to. Ever since I was a boy I had been interested in the Northern Frontier District of Kenya (the NFD as it was more generally known). While I was a child in Addis Ababa British officials serving on the frontiers of the Sudan, Kenya and British Somaliland came up on various occasions to see my father to discuss tribal raids and other problems they were having with the Ethiopians. While staying with us, such men as Arnold Hodson, Consul in southern Ethiopia, had told me stories of tribal raids and lion hunts and I had felt that this would be the life for me. As a boy in Ethiopia and later at school I had dreamt of exploration and of hunting big game. In the Sudan, five years before the Second World War, I took every opportunity to hunt and I shot elephant, buffalo and many lion. Now, however, I only wished to shoot an occasional animal for food. Over the years I had read a number of books about the NFD and the tribes that lived there – for instance, *The Ivory Raiders* by Major H. Rayne which my mother had given me for my fourteenth birthday. Now talking to George Webb in the evenings I heard a lot at first hand about tribes such as the Boran, Turkana and Rendille who lived there. He told me that a special permit was needed before anyone who was not a government official was allowed into that area, and this of course added to my determination to go there.

From Moyale I trekked back to Addis Ababa along the east side of the Rift Valley and its lakes. The next year, 1960, I made an arduous journey lasting several months from Addis Ababa, following the east side of the Blue Nile to Lake Tana; from there, I travelled through the Simien Mountains and then back to Addis Ababa by way of Lalibela and Magdala. Later the same year Frank Steele and I planned to travel to Lake Rudolf in the NFD.

I had met Frank Steele in 1951 in Iraq where he was the Vice-Consul in Basra, while I was living in the Marshes. I went into Basra occasionally to stay with him and his wife Angela to get a hot bath and a civilized meal in their house. Frank visited me in the Marshes and spent several days with me travelling about in my canoe. After the War, he had served for two years in northern Uganda where he had hunted, particularly elephant, and done some game control and conservation work. Like me, Frank enjoyed travelling simply in remote places. I had always preferred to travel on my own, but I felt that here was somebody I could happily travel with. We soon became close friends.

We started our journey from Kula Mawe, east of Isiolo, where we hired six camels and five men, two of whom were Somali camelmen. Kula Mawe acquired its strange name ('eat a stone') when some years previously a policeman and his young son were travelling to Garba Tula. Too late to get there that day, the policeman decided they should spend the night under a tree. They had no food with them and his son asked him what they were going to eat. The impatient father turned on him and said 'Kula mawe!' ('Eat a stone!'), a name remembered when, soon afterwards, a village was built there.

From Kula Mawe we took four days to reach Archer's Post, where a bridge crosses the Uaso Nyiro River, travelling through rolling country sometimes covered with scrub and sometimes open and grassy. We saw a lot of game: a cheetah and many oryx, eland, Grant's gazelle, impala and zebra. The zebra were very tame. Archer's Post had been established by Geoffrey Archer in 1909 as a forward post for the administration. Now it was a small village. As a boy, I had known Sir Geoffrey Archer when he was the Commissioner in British Somaliland and he had come to Addis Ababa for Zauditu's coronation as Empress in 1917. Later we had stayed with him in Berbera on our way to India, the first British children ever to have been in British Somaliland. A great giant of a man, he had been especially kind to my brother Brian and me, taking us on expeditions along the coast where we shot birds with the .410 which he lent us.

I left Frank at Archer's Post to get the camels injected against tsetse fly while I went on ahead by lorry to Wamba. At Wamba, a pleasing cluster of houses at the southern end of the Mathews

Range, I stayed with the District Officer, David Bennett, who had been an instructor in an Outward Bound school in Cumberland. Together we climbed through thick forest to the top of Warges, the 9000-foot mountain immediately behind Wamba which dominated the town, and from there we had a magnificent view. In the forest were some enormous podocarpus, a tree I remembered from Ethiopia, large juniper trees, crotons, wild olives and others which I did not recognize. The podocarpus trees were covered with lichen and we saw a lot of colobus monkeys and the tracks and droppings of what we thought was a giant forest hog. We also found tracks of several herds of buffalo and masses of elephant droppings, but these were two or three days old. Next day we climbed another, rather difficult peak, and then did a twenty-mile walk northwards through the forest. There were elephant all round us in the forest and the guides saw two. We also heard a rhino. Eventually, we were picked up at the end of the forest in Bennett's Land Rover. We had to search for the Land Rover for some time before we found it and were half-expecting to have to walk all the way back to Wamba. I was glad to have seen this forest for I had not seen its like before. Frank arrived the following day from Archer's Post and the next day we set off on foot with our camels.

As on all my journeys travelling on foot with animals in Kenya, we lived simply. We had no tables, chairs or lamps; we had a tent but seldom used it. We slept in the open in a group with our men and the camels. On one occasion, when it rained heavily, we covered our food, kit and ourselves with the cow hides from the camel harnesses. We carried water between water holes which were never more than four days from one to the next, unlike in Arabia where wells could be as much as fourteen days apart. Sometimes we drank from running streams

230

but at other times water that was so polluted and foul as to be barely drinkable.

As our men loaded the camels at dawn we drank some coffee but ate nothing, and then moved off. At the midday halt, we drank a lot of tea but generally our only meal was in the evening and consisted of rice and stew. On one occasion when I had cooked sandgrouse, Frank maintained it was the best meal he had ever eaten; he remembers the meal to this day.

Most of the time we were in no particular hurry; and seldom did more than about seven hours a day, with a midday halt, but sometimes we kept going without a break, and occasionally we travelled at night to avoid the heat. We camped on water whenever possible; if we stopped at midday, we chose a spot where there was shade, and grazing for the camels. When we had camped, Frank and I might wander up a nearby hill for the view or go to look for elephant or try and shoot something for the pot.

All the tribes in northern Kenya, other than the cattle-owning Samburu living in the Highlands, owned large herds of camels. None of these tribes ever rode on camels; they used some of them for carrying their possessions, and sometimes women and children while they were on the move. The exception to this were the Turkana who never loaded their camels, even to fetch water. It has always seemed strange to me that the Somalis have never ridden camels, in view of their association with the Arabs in southern Arabia. We walked beside our loaded camels. Nowadays tourists visiting this area can ride camels on specially organized camel safaris.

On our way to the Mathews Range, we went through hilly, stony country, some of it thickly covered with bush, and then continued northwards with the Range on our right, the mountains sometimes appearing high above us. Rather unexpectedly, we passed a big bull elephant, the first I had seen in Kenya, only fifty yards off the path. We camped for Christmas in a picturesque valley called the Ngaro Narok where there were big trees, acacias and tamarinds, and green, grassy glades, and here I saw two more elephant. That night, we heard elephant and rhino and, of course, hyenas. One rhino coming down to water almost walked into our camp in the dark and made off with a loud snort. Looking for elephant the next morning, I got within thirty yards of a black rhinoceros, the first I had ever seen, although I had previously seen a white rhino in the southern Sudan. He looked formidable as he went past, peering suspiciously in every direction.

At one camp near a luggah, some wild dogs ran along the other side and, after watching us and our camels for a while, trotted on quietly. The country appeared to be stiff with rhino. Either Frank or I went ahead to prevent our camels, tied head to tail, blundering into one of them.

We went on until we came to the Milgis, a very wide, dry watercourse which separates the Mathews Range from the Ndoto Mountains. We then made our way up a track which took us along the top of the Ndotos. After working our way along the mountain for three days we descended by Ndigiri Alauri, the 'Pass of the Camels' to the hot, scrub-covered country below.

Looking northwards from the pass, I had realized that there was nothing ahead of us but desert country to the Ethiopian frontier and far beyond. This gave me the satisfaction of knowing that all the farms, ranches and towns were far behind and that ahead of us were only scattered wells, the encampments of nomads, and wild animals. Above all, it was the wild animals which made travelling in this country so much more interesting than in southern Ethiopia, which it otherwise resembled. Here, at any time, you half-expected to walk into an elephant or a rhino. At the foot of the pass, within a yard of where I slept, there had been a great pile of elephant droppings. The mountains covered with forest and giant euphorbia gave a background to the scene, but I craved to get back to this desert country. I could picture it to the north with its space, solitude and silence.

We seemed to have collected a good lot of men, the two Somali camelmen, an elderly Galla from the Boran tribe and two Turkana boys, one of whom, a powerfully-built lad called Ekwar, did the cooking. He remained with me for several years. We had been feeding well, with one good meal a day, and when we were near their encampments the Samburu usually gave us a goat.

I had been trying to learn Swahili so that I could manage when Frank had to leave me at Marsabit. I am not a natural linguist, although after eleven years living on my own with Arabs in southern Arabia and the Marshes of Iraq I had become fluent in that language. Struggling to learn Latin at Eton destroyed for ever any enthusiasm I might have had for conscientiously learning languages.

In the far distance to the west were the mountains on either side of South Horr for which we were heading. When we got there, South Horr was particularly attractive. It lay in the valley between Nyiru, nearly 10,000 foot high, to the west and the jagged peaks of Ol Doinyo Mara, 7000 foot high, to the east. We camped in a beautiful grove of tall, slender acacias with a clear stream of running water nearby. Today there is a large village there with some shops and cultivation; then there was nothing other than a small Somali *duka* tucked away; there we replenished our *posho* and sugar. Frank climbed Ol Doinyo Mara, but I did not accompany him because I had strained an

233

Achilles tendon. He came back tired and thirsty, saying that the mountain seemed to consist entirely of rocks and thorn bushes and that the going had been hard and hot. But from the top, he had had a magnificent view of the desert country to the north and north-east, shimmering in the heat, and his description of this whetted my appetite for the days to come.

While Frank had been away, in the nearby forest two hundred yards from our camp, I came across a bull elephant with tusks which must have weighed 100 lb each. I got up to within twenty yards of him while he was dozing and had a good look at him, then withdrew.

After South Horr, we travelled for three hours up the valley until we came to Kurungu, a dry watercourse with a pool of water. Here we encountered four young Turkana who came into our camp, and I was surprised to see how graceful and handsome these young men were. I had not expected to find such classical features among the Turkana and, indeed, I learned later that few Turkana were as good-looking. I looked forward to seeing more of the Turkana on my return journey from Marsabit. We had been travelling through Samburu country so far; the Samburu were a tall, strikingly handsome people, I hoped that I had got some good photographs of them.

Beyond South Horr, we had a long, tiring trek. Luckily, my foot stood up well to this. Frank had made enquiries about tracks and distances to the lake and had got a frustrating variety of answers. In fact, it took us three more days. On the last two, it was hard-going, for the surrounding country was one vast lava field of boulders, red or black in colour, and we had to push on for there was no water anywhere except for what we carried. Conscious that we were approaching the lake, we expected to see it as we topped each new rise, but never seemed to do so.

Suddenly, it was there below us. Few other sights have made a greater impact on me. I saw the lake spread out beneath me, stretching towards the Ethiopian frontier where it ended 150 miles away. We had come a long way from Kula Mawe on foot and now felt a sense of achievement. I found it easy to imagine what this sight must have meant to Teleki and Von Höhnel in 1888, as they stood, surrounded by their valiant but exhausted porters, having at last reached this hitherto unknown lake after their long and perilous journey from the coast.

From [Marsabit] I sent back my Boran camels to Kula Mawe with the Boran, a delightful old man whom I was sorry to lose. We had been lucky with our men, especially Ekwar, the Turkana cook-boy, and the two Somalis. From Marsabit, I kept the two Somali camelmen, Ekwar, whom I liked, and Soiyah, a well-meaning Turkana who had occasionally infuriated Frank and me by his oafishness. I took on Rendille camels and two Rendille camelmen for the rest of my journey to Lodwar, Lake Baringo and Maralal.

We made our way down from the cool, beautifully wooded mountain back to the desert. We crossed from there to Ilaut. The wells at Ilaut are deep and, I believe, never go dry: for this reason, they are of great importance, particularly to the Rendille, in times of drought.

At Ilaut we found a small shop kept by a friendly young Somali whose father had recently been killed. He was very hospitable and fed me on good food during the two days I spent there to rest the camels and myself. The wells here were close to a tree under which we camped and at night elephant came down to them to drink. Three passed within thirty yards of our camp; noiseless grey shapes in the moonlight. Zebra, too, went past, their hooves noisy on the rocks. High above our camp were the spectacular sheer-sided peaks of the Ndotos. From Ilaut, I travelled round the northern end of the Ndotos towards Baringo, through bush country which was full of rhino tracks, but we saw none. We travelled slowly, for now at last there had been rain and pools of water lay around, more than welcome after years of drought. We encountered more of the Rendille, a tribe I had immediately liked and assumed to be akin to the Somali, but who dressed like the Samburu. They were gathered here in large numbers with their camels and goats. Unlike the Samburu who own large herds of cattle, the Rendille are a camel-owning people and I enjoyed once more seeing herds of camels which for years have been my favourite animal. On more than one occasion when I was travelling in the Empty Quarter of Arabia our lives had depended on our camels' endurance. Had they collapsed we should have died. The Rashid speak of them as *ata Allah* (God's gift). My companions had an intense affection for their camels and would always undergo hardship themselves to spare them if possible. Living with the Rashid as one of them, I had learned to some extent to share their feelings.

The Rendille lived in easily moved mat shelters, similar to those I had seen when travelling in 1933–34 among the Danakil. I found the Rendille friendly and welcoming. At each encampment they gave me a sheep or a goat.

The moon was full and at one of these Rendille encampments they had a dance which started near midnight. It was spectacularly effective, with camels couched all round and the dancers' spears stuck upright in the ground. The songs were rousing and the dancing very energetic in short bursts, men and women together.

We were now on the edge of the Turkana country. At Baragoi, it had rained recently and the country was very green, as it had been all the way across from Marsabit. From here I planned to cross the Suguta valley and go to Kangetet, then down the Kerio river to Rudolf, and from there to follow the Turkwel river from its mouth to Lodwar. The 1960 drought had been especially severe among the Turkana, but by going this way we should not be short of water. By now I was talking some Swahili, what is known as 'up-country Swahili', an easily learned variant of the language. The men I had with me were excellent, cooperative and friendly among themselves; and I had already got rid of the only one I had disliked.

I was fascinated to see the Turkana, a numerous, virile tribe with a warlike reputation. Many of the men and boys were naked. When I reached the Kerio, I woke up one morning to find six elders waiting under a nearby tree. They were sitting on their wooden headstools which they use as pillows when they sleep. The only clothing they had between them were two European felt hats. As a result of the drought many of the Turkana were nearly starving but, moving about in small family groups, they kept their goats alive by cutting off branches from trees. They themselves survived largely by eating the husks of doum nuts, berries and other wild fruits, and by trapping and killing wild animals.

The drought had not, however, affected my journey, and would not, for I was following the big river beds where there was water in wells every few miles and we were carrying food for ourselves. From Baragoi to Lodwar we only once had to carry water for the night. Beyond Baragoi I travelled west to Kangetet across the Suguta, where brackish water was flowing two feet deep and fifty yards across; and then I went down the Kerio to within a few miles of Lake Rudolf, and from there across to the nearby mouth of the Turkwel and followed it up to Lodwar. The Kerio was a big riverbed fringed with bush, large acacias and doum palms on both banks. Near Kangetet, there was a strange and extensive forest of dead trees, many of them large, and I was surprised to find here the fresh tracks of elephant, one of them with a small calf, and several single ones. Otherwise I had seen almost nothing in the way of wildlife, a few Grant's gazelle and that was all. By contrast, on my journey to Marsabit with Frank Steele, we had encountered elephant, rhino, lion and hyenas, many small herds of Grant's gazelle and some oryx. The Turkana kill wild animals for food, whereas the Samburu do not and unlike the other tribes in the NFD the Turkana will eat donkeys and drink their milk. However, I was told there were elephant and buffalo along the Turkwel above Lodwar.

At Lodwar, I spent an enjoyable few days with the DC, Geoffrey Hill. In this vast arid region, Lodwar had been an important administrative centre ever since the Turkana had been taken over and administered by the British. From 1906 onwards Lodwar had been the base from which frequent Ethiopian raids had been countered by Major Rayne and others. I was familiar with this area from Rayne's book, *The Ivory Raiders*, published in 1923. Lodwar was a surprisingly small town; a few European-style houses on a small hill overlooked the dry bed of the Turkwel. Behind them was a Turkana village. In those days the forest bordering the Turkwel upstream of Lodwar reached almost to the town. Jomo Kenyatta, who after independence was to become the first president of Kenya, was in detention at Lodwar when I arrived there, but he was to be moved later to Maralal. An impressive-looking man, I saw him on a number of occasions when he reported each morning to the DC's office. I stayed on at Lodwar for two more days to get my camels injected against fly and give them time to get over the inoculation.

The last part of my trip was particularly interesting. From Lodwar, as far south as Kaputir, we travelled up the Turkwel, a large riverbed, dry at this time of year and with dense forests along both banks. One day we were marching up the riverbed when we encountered a large bull elephant and two smaller ones. They looked threatening, so we turned back, and we had to go some distance before we found a way through the forest to get round them. As there were plenty of wells in the Turkwel we were never short of water. Many naked, wild-looking Turkana were on these wells. There were evidently many buffalo in the forests along the river banks, some of which the Turkana caught with snares and drag-logs. One morning, I and a party of a dozen Turkana followed the tracks of a buffalo, with a log caught on one of its feet, through really horrid, thick bush. I was amazed that the buffalo was strong enough to prevent the log from getting entangled and bringing it to a halt. Eventually the log came loose and, as a result, we did not catch up with the buffalo.

We usually started off each morning by moonlight, an hour or so before dawn. I now went on ahead of the camels to make sure they did not walk into buffalo or elephant. One morning, we found six buffalo in the middle of the riverbed and had to shout at them to get them to move. From Kaputir, I crossed the intervening country to the Kerio at Kalosia and went up the Kerio to the foot of the Cherangani Hills, an 11,000-foot range, and then followed the edge of the escarpment southwards. This was the country of the Pokot, or the Suk as they were then called. To me they resembled the Turkana in appearance except that they were circumcised whereas the Turkana were not. It is curious how often tribes have been known for years by the wrong name. For instance, it is only recently that the Suk have been accorded their proper name, the Pokot, by

Europeans. The Danakil, as they were previously called, are now correctly called the Afar; and the Toubou of Tibesti are now known as the Tedda.

Eventually I reached the north end of Lake Baringo. We had a long and rather tiring march to the lake across a dry, dusty expanse of wait-a-bit thorn scrub through which we had, occasionally, to cut our way, but it was well worth it when we got there. Ahead of us were large, green trees and beyond them a white beach of pebbles and a very blue lake. We could see small, wooded islands and creeks, and in the distance high mountains on the eastern and western sides of the lake. There were some hippo in the lake near our camp and I enjoyed watching them and hearing them grunt. I also saw occasional crocodiles, and a pair of fish eagles that screamed as they sat in the trees. The colours of the lake kept changing every minute for there was a lot of cloud about. Some men and boys belonging to the Tugen tribe brought us in plenty of fish called tilapia, resembling perch and weighing about a pound, which were excellent eating. They fished for them in small *ambach* canoes made like the *tankwa* on Lake Tana. Some carried bows with poisoned arrows. We stayed at Baringo for two days. We were still among the Pokot until we reached the edge of the escarpment on which Maralal lies. We had seen zebra and impala on our way.

Maralal was an attractive station, the headquarters of the Samburu district, situated on the plateau at about 7000 feet. The hills going up behind the station and elsewhere were partly covered with forests of wild olives and juniper, while acacia woodlands covered much of the lower ground. Maralal is only eighty miles north of the Equator and consequently it has no summer and winter. Instead, the long rains lasting from March into June and the short rains falling in October and November are separated by the dry seasons. Being virtually on the Equator, the temperature in the NFD is governed by the altitude and varies little throughout the year. I arrived in Maralal for Easter.

Three days after my arrival in Nairobi from Maralal, I went to stay with John Newbould who was working as a Pasture Research Officer at Ngorongoro, a reserve adjoining the Serengeti National Park. Five years earlier, when he was on an Oxford University expedition in Morocco, we had travelled together on foot in the High Atlas and climbed to the summit of the Toubkal massif. Since then he had suggested that when I went back to Kenya I should come and stay with him at Ngorongoro, which I now proceeded to do. It was now the middle of April. John was living in a three-roomed shack on the very edge of the Ngorongoro crater. This enormous crater was 2000 feet deep and almost ten miles across. Further along the crater rim the only road led down to the floor of the crater. At that time few people visited Ngorongoro and, looking down into it from John's house, if we saw a car we could be almost certain that it belonged to the Warden. Sometimes John motored me down there, at other times we went down on foot and wandered about among the animals which we enjoyed far more than being in a car. But there is no denying that in a car one can get infinitely closer to lion, for instance, which will continue to lie undisturbed within a few feet of the vehicle itself. But I have always felt this to be unnatural.

On the green, grassy floor of the crater there was a salt lake, numerous pans of fresh water, a stream fringed with reed beds and a patch of forest, the whole scene rimmed by the steep walls of the crater. This restricted area was covered with animals: herds of wildebeest, heraldic-looking creatures that grunted and frisked about, mixed with zebra and gazelle; and frequently we saw buffalo, rhino and, above all, lion, including the first black-maned lion I had ever seen. Maasai still lived here with their cattle, and I felt that they belonged here and were a traditional part of the scene, which would be diminished if they were turned out. The Maasai do not hunt and kill animals for food, though spearing lion is a challenge and is accepted as a test of courage. John and I visited one of their *manyattas* to hire donkeys for a journey in the neighbourhood. There were many *moran* here who were on good terms with John and consequently friendly.

I had often heard that the Maasai were remarkably beautiful and many of them certainly were. The warriors wore a single piece of cloth, dyed a soft, reddish brown, which fell from one shoulder over their graceful, naked bodies. All of them carried heavy, long-bladed spears and some had buffalo-hide shields decorated with coloured heraldic designs. At dawn the following day, we watched two boys being circumcised, just outside the huts in which they lived. The initiation ceremonies among the Maasai and the Samburu are similar except that the Maasai circumcise boys individually in the encampment where they live, whereas among the Samburu each clan assembles the initiates and their families in specially-built circumcision camps known as *lororas*, where they live throughout the ceremonies involved and which are burnt when they are over. Not a muscle twitched on either of the boys' faces during the long and painful operation, which is performed in a curious, complicated manner by both the Maasai and the Samburu.

During the time I was at Ngorongoro, I spent two interesting days camped in the crater with the Game Warden. As he walked back the last evening by the way we had come, he saw a black leopard. I would have given much to have seen it myself, for I have never seen one. Before I left, John and I travelled for a month with donkeys in the country surrounding the crater. Both the long and short rains had failed and the country was now drought-stricken; in consequence, we did not see as many animals as I had hoped. This year it seemed inevitable that the Maasai would lose most of their cattle.

I returned to Kenya in February 1962. George Webb and I had already planned to climb Kilimanjaro and we set off two days after my arrival, motoring to Moshi in Tanganyika. We spent the first night in the Kibo Hotel at the foot of the mountain, on the south side, about twenty miles from the lowest hut which was just a bare shed with bunks. We had six porters with us and a guide from the Chagga tribe, a Bantu people who live on the southern slopes of the mountain. I liked them – a cheerful people, very eager to help. We went slowly to begin with, to get ourselves acclimatized. When we got to the next hut, we met an RAF mountain-rescue expedition from Cyprus that had got into trouble. They had climbed the mountain too fast and camped in the crater at 18,500 feet. Two of them (there were eight in all) had collapsed during the night and become unconscious. The others, with their Chagga porters, had difficulty in getting them down from the crater. The two sick men were paralysed from the waist down and it looked to me as if one of them had pneumonia. It was rather a daunting start for us to meet these experts driven down off the mountain like this.

Kilimanjaro has two peaks: Kibo, a huge crater, a great dome of ice and snow 19,340 foot high; and Mawenzi, a deeply eroded, steep, jagged mountain 16,900 foot high. At 15,000 feet, they are separated by a bare stony plain, the saddle of Kilimanjaro. Here, we spent the last night in the hut at the foot of Kibo. It was bitterly cold, with snow lying about in patches on the mountainside. There had been more snow on the mountain this year than for years. The hut was cold and draughty. We spent a wretched night there and neither of us slept a wink owing to the altitude. The guide called us at 1 a.m. We had some tea and biscuits and then started off up the mountain in the dark, following his hurricane lamp. There was ashy scree at first, and then, after about 3000 feet, the slope became very steep and covered with frozen snow into which we kicked steps. This was better than it might have been, for without snow it would have been loose scree which slips back as you climb it. We toiled up this for four hours, going slowly to save ourselves and stopping every now and then for a rest, but it was too cold to stop long.

We reached the crater rim at Gilman's Point, 19,000 foot high, just as the sun rose, an orange ball seen through the blanket of cloud on the horizon, above which towered the black, jagged outline of Mawenzi. A minute or two later and the sun was clear of the cloud and flooding the slope on which we sat. Behind us was a great wall of green ice. Both of us were feeling perfectly all right, no headaches or sickness. Round the rim of the crater, the summit looked only twenty minutes away. In fact it took us two very hard hours to get there through soft snow. The last 500 feet were a desperate effort. We would go a few yards and sink down again to rest. Here we saw five wild dogs. They followed us about a hundred yards away, keeping parallel with us along the glacier on our left. It was an amazing thing to have found wild dogs at 19,000 feet, about 10,000 feet higher than they normally ever go. They looked like wolves in the snow as they followed us, or sat and watched us. I have often wondered if there is any record of mammals having been found at a higher altitude.

From the summit we had a wonderful view down into the crater: black rock, great walls of green ice and white snow. The country below us was hidden in mist and cloud so that we were above it in a world of our own. Nearby, Mawenzi rose up out of the cloud. We had a sense of achievement when we reached the summit cairn marking Kaiser Wilhelm Spitz. The wild dogs were still watching us and their tracks were then quite close to the cairn. I wondered whether they had come up in the dark or spent the night on the summit. Going down, the snow had softened in the sun so that we could descend fast, but even so it was hard work. I was glad we had come up in the dark. It would have been daunting if we could have seen the interminable slope above us. In 1953 I travelled in Hunza where I had probably been as high as the summit of Kilimanjaro when I reached the Babaghundi Pass. We were back in the hut nine hours after leaving it. Here we rested for a bit and I noticed a lammergeyer circling above us. Whereas lammergeyers are frequently seen in Ethiopia, where I once saw six, circling together over a rubbish tip in Dessie, they are rare in Kenya and Tanzania. I have only seen them there three times – once on this occasion, another time on Mount Kenya and again at Hell's Gate near Naivasha where a pair nested in the cliffs until someone took their eggs. In the Samburu district, vultures and kites are equally uncommon and in all the years I have been there I have hardly ever seen one. In 1976, when perhaps two hundred cattle were slaughtered on a hillside during a Samburu initiation ceremony, only two vultures turned up and sat in one of the trees. Elsewhere, for instance, in the Maasai Mara, scores of vultures will cluster on any dead animal.

We then went down ten miles to the next hut, where we were back in the giant heath and giant groundsel country. The giant groundsel is an extraordinary plant with leaves like a cabbage on the top of a thick bare stem eight feet high made of old dead leaves. The following day we walked the twenty miles down through the forest to the hotel and from there we motored back to Nairobi.

In May the following year, John Newbould met me in Nairobi and took me back to Ngorongoro. Before starting on our journey south across Maasailand, we went by car into the Serengeti hoping to see the start of the wildebeest migration. Two million or more wildebeest were reliably estimated to take part in this annual migration which goes as far north as the Maasai Mara in Kenya before turning back. When we caught up with the beginning of this migration, they were still in huge scattered herds all moving in the same direction. Though the wildebeest were moving through bush country I got some impression of the vast numbers of animals involved, which included zebra and gazelle. On our way back to Ngorongoro, we encountered another vast collection of wildebeest in more open country, all drifting northwards, and the same day counted nineteen lion which were following them. The weather had been unsettled and back at Ngorongoro there was a tremendous storm of rain with thunder and lightning.

We started off on 21 June 1963 with fifteen donkeys. With us we had Ibach and five other men, one of them a Maasai, with all of whom John was well acquainted. At first we travelled for a week across grassy uplands towards the Embagai crater. We camped on the crater's edge by a pool in a forest of hagenia and juniper trees that covered the slopes of the crater. Two Maasai turned up in our camp with a small black-and-white dog resembling a terrier. It immediately came over and joined us and refused to go back to them. They said we could keep it if we gave them a shilling; our men immediately christened it 'Shillingi'. From now on it associated itself entirely with John and myself. Except for our men, it would allow no Africans to approach our possessions, growling at them if they tried to come nearer than four or five yards and attacking them if they did so. We had to warn strangers to keep away.

Throughout this journey we slept on the ground in the open, since we had no tent, and Shillingi kept guard over us. Not infrequently hyenas came close to where we were lying and Shillingi chased them away. I was glad to have him there for I knew of several cases where hyenas had grabbed sleeping men by the face. We tried whenever possible to cut enough bushes to make some sort of *boma* to enclose the donkeys at night and slept downwind of it so that Shillingi would know if any lion or hyenas approached them.

Next morning we went down to the soda lake at the bottom of the crater where there were flamingos and duck, and the following day we climbed to the 12,000-foot summit of the nearby mountain, Loolmalasin. On the march in bush country I went ahead with the heavy rifle and John brought up the rear, sometimes a considerable distance behind. At intervals, Shillingi would race up to the front to see that all was well, stay with me for a bit and then drop back again and rejoin John. Loaded donkeys travel no faster than about two miles an hour; consequently we seldom covered more than ten or twelve miles a day, since this gave the donkeys time to graze. John also had a rifle and shot for food an occasional Grant's gazelle and impala, or guinea fowl, with his shotgun. After a time the donkeys' slowness exasperated John, so I remarked to him provokingly, 'I suppose you'd rather be in a car?'

There was always something to see. Though there was not the abundance of animal life found in the Serengeti, we did see a few giraffe, oryx, zebra, gerenuk and duiker, and periodically the tracks and droppings of elephant and rhino. John was knowledgeable about the vegetation and gave me much interesting information about the plants, shrubs and trees along the way. Some people had criticized him, saying he neglected his job as a Pasture Research Officer by having too many other interests, especially his interest in the Maasai. We encountered Maasai at intervals and on most days some of them turned up in our camp. Once, when I was some distance ahead of the others, five elephant emerged out of the thick bush on to the track a short distance ahead of me and disappeared into it on the other side. Even though I had hunted elephant in the southern Sudan, I never failed to be impressed by how noiselessly they moved, even when pushing their way through thick cover.

A month after we had left Ngorongoro, we arrived at the Namalulu wells. Here the wells had been excavated to a depth of thirty feet, and, inside, sloping trenches gave the cattle access to the water. The trenches were kept clean; when a cow dropped a pat, someone picked it up and put it on her back so that she carried it out of the well with her. Two days later we arrived at Ngasumet wells. Here, three Maasai stood in a well-shaft drawing water. One stood above the other, the man at the bottom filling a leather bucket and throwing it up to the one above, and so on until it reached a fourth man who emptied the water into a trough for the cattle to drink. These men were naked, except for a skin-covering like a helmet which kept their plaited and ochred hair dry. There were a great number of these wells, and making them must have involved much labour; now only a few of them were in use, but even so it required constant work to maintain them. Other deeper wells in the area, for instance at Kitwi and Makami, involved a four-man lift. In such places a very considerable number of cattle were being watered.

A fortnight later, when we were camped beside a dam, many

elephant came down to water. The first herd, including three big bulls, cows and calves, stayed drinking and bathing until sunset. More and more elephant kept arriving and went on doing so until well into the night. We built up a couple of big fires and lying in bed we could just make out their dim, silent shapes drifting past in the firelight.

We were now more or less at the southern limit of the Maasai country. We went south for a few more days before we turned back and here we encountered a group of very unusual people whom the men with us called Wandorobo – a term which is extensively used for hunter-gatherers in Kenya and Tanzania. Maddeningly, I can neither remember nor find in my diary any reference to what they called themselves. They lived on berries and wild honey, and what they shot with bows and poisoned arrows; they kept no animals, not even dogs. They cut out small clearings in dense beds of *Sansevieria*, a tall, green, aloe-like plant with clusters of leaves as sharp as bayonets, from which, by fastening the tops together, they made tiny little shelters. I thought they must be very like the Bushmen of the Kalahari from descriptions I had read, but these people appeared to be taller. Their faces resembled those of Bushmen I had seen in photographs. Some of the girls were apricot-coloured; two fifteen-year-old boys had large projecting buttocks, the characteristic *steatopygia* of the Bushmen: the men had assumed Maasai dress. During the night we spent with the Wandorobo, a lion came close to where we lay and growled angrily at a hyena that was following it.

From here, we went back north to Moshi which we reached a fortnight later, after following the Ruvu, a large river in which there were both crocodiles and hippo. Our journey along the west bank of the Ruvu led through the most attractive country. There were patches of forest with big trees on both banks, and the view across the river with open plains and the Pare Mountains in the distance was spacious. As a result of continuous over-grazing by Maasai cattle, the plains on this side of the river were bare and animals were few in number. We saw oryx, gerenuk, Grant's gazelle and impala; and we frequently crossed the tracks of elephant which had presumably come down to drink each night from distant bush-covered hills.

from *My Kenya Days*

During my years in the Desert, the Yemen had for me the fascination of hostile and forbidden territory, its tribes constantly at war with the Rashid and other tribes among whom I lived. For years I had wanted to travel in that distinctive mountainous country in the south-west of Arabia. Many parts of northern Yemen had been seen by few if any Europeans before the Civil War which broke out in 1962. It was the Civil War which gave me my opportunity to go there in 1966.

My sympathies, naturally, were entirely with the Royalists, and in June 1966, at the invitation of the Royalist Government, I visited Prince Hasan bin Hasan, a cousin of the Imam Badr, at his headquarters at Qarra in north-western Yemen. The Prince was about thirty years old and spoke good English. Intelligent and well-informed, he worked far into the night, despite poor health, hearing petitions and judging cases. Among his staff were two British wireless operators, also a strange character called Bruce Condé, who had accompanied me to Qarra from Qizan, on the Red Sea near the border between Saudi Arabia and the Yemen. American by birth, with an extraordinary craving for self-aggrandisement, he had assumed the title of Major-General Prince Bourbon Condé, and the designation of Postmaster-General in the Royalist Government.

I had expected to be restricted in my travels, and was delighted when Prince Hasan assured me he would be only too pleased for me to see as much as I wished of the country under his control. The United States and most of Europe had recognized the Republican Government, whereas the British still recognized the Royalists. This was very largely due to Colonel Neil McLean. Since the beginning of the war he had spent months in the Yemen with the Royalists, and as MP for Inverness till 1964 had successfully championed their cause in Parliament. He had encouraged me to visit the Yemen and had put me in touch with the Royalist leaders. I soon realized that I was being accorded a semi-official status to which I had no claim, but this had its uses.

We stayed in one shattered town after another, and I watched men and boys dancing in triumph amid the ruins of their houses, celebrating the expulsion of the invader whom they hated and despised. The *Sayid* sent word ahead that the Englishman was coming, and the Governor of the town would come out to meet me, and I would be greeted with a war dance and volleys of rifle-fire. A long column of warriors would escort me to the town; ahead of us three or four boys would dance, their drawn daggers weaving round their heads; behind them came the drummers. Then town dignitaries and even schoolboys would make speeches of welcome. One small round-eyed boy asked me shyly, 'Are you Winston Churchill?' I was sorry to have to disappoint him.

I enjoyed it all enormously but it nearly ended prematurely at Mahabsha. I had been invited to inspect a captured anti-aircraft gun. Accompanied by a large crowd I climbed a steep hill, chatting on the way to two friendly young men from a neighbouring town. We reached the gun and they urged me to take photographs. Since the barrel was pointing at me I moved a pace or two aside to get a better angle, and they stepped into my place as I did so. I noticed that someone was sitting in the gunner's seat. The next moment the gun fired straight at us. Both my companions were killed; my clothes were spattered with their blood.

I returned to Qarra where I had to wait a month till Prince Hasan returned from Saudi Arabia. Then, escorted by one of his guards and with a boy and two donkeys, I went north along the escarpment. We stayed two days at Dhahir, where tribesmen from the surrounding villages and from the coastal plain crowded the streets for the weekly market. Here local boys, as old as sixteen, wore their hair cut like haloes round their heads; while others, from the lowlands, had a broad strip shaved through their hair from ear to ear. Both styles indicated that they were still uncircumcised.

We stayed again in Haidan where after dark men and boys danced and drummed late into the night under a full moon. A small colony of Yemeni Jews lived here, gentle inoffensive people, distinguished by their ringlets.

We came to Saqain where seven-storeyed houses were built of mud and resembled the *kasbahs* of the High Atlas; but the centre of the town had been bombed to ruins. Next day we followed the Wadi Badr, where the tribesmen had taken a bloody vengeance, ambushing and destroying a large column of Egyptians; anyone who tried to escape had been hunted down and killed. I had become accustomed to burnt-out tanks, armoured cars and lorries. There were many here. At nearby Qalat Razih the walls still bore evidence of where the defenders had been wiped out; young men pointed with pride to the faded blood-stains where they had killed.

From Kitaf I visited Najran just across the Saudi border. The town, unrecognizably enlarged since 1947, was the main base for the forthcoming offensive in the eastern Yemen. From there on my way to the front at Sanaa, I was given a lift as far as Haidan in a lorry carrying arms and ammunition. Convoys travelled by night but were attacked by aircraft using flares. We spent a day in the Jauf among the Dahm. They had been our bitter enemies when I travelled with the Rashid in the Sands. Now I was happy to be among them, for they were Bedu; even their voices reminded me of those bygone days. On a later occasion I stayed in their tents and there I met men who had known Musallim bin al Kamam and who spoke of bin Duailan, 'The Cat', who had died not far from there in his last great fight against the Yam. 'Are you the Christian who travelled with the Rashid? Welcome! Hey, boy, hurry and milk the red one. Hurry!' It was all so familiar; lawless as ever, the Dahm looted arms from Royalist convoys when chance offered, but I knew that while I was with them I was safe. I never felt as confident with the highland tribes, among whom treachery was not unknown. The Republicans offered large rewards for Europeans serving the Royalists.

I spent a month in the country round Sanaa, travelling on foot from one Royalist position to another. I looked across the stony, sun-scorched plain from Jebel Jamima to Sanaa, the Royalist goal, now tantalizingly close after four years of war. During those days I stayed with various Princes and tribal leaders, sharing their cheerless quarters in caves among the hills. In November 1966, after five months in the Yemen, I went back to England. There I had the cartilages removed from both knees; apparently I had worn them out.

While I was in England Egypt suffered an overwhelming defeat by Israel in the Six Days War, and in consequence Nasser withdrew all his troops from the Yemen. I went back there in November 1967 and arrived at the headquarters near Sanaa of Prince Muhammad al Hussain, Commander-in-Chief on the southern front. With him I found my old friend, Colonel Neil McLean, and Mark Lennox-Boyd. Prince Hussain's camp was dispersed among the barren rocky hills and there was a constant coming and going of tribesmen affirming their allegiance, and of camels and donkeys bringing supplies from Wasada at the foot of the eastern escarpment. It resembled settings and scenes from *Seven Pillars of Wisdom*.

In the morning four days later the camp was attacked by aircraft that bombed, rocketed and machine-gunned the area. Hearing the planes, McLean, Lennox-Boyd and I had taken shelter in a shallow watercourse. I was watching the first Mig sweep low down the valley when it opened fire. A shell burst on a nearby rock and a splinter nicked my head. I dropped further into cover. A little later I heard McLean say in an irritated voice, 'Damn it, look what you've done, Wilfred.' Blood from my head had soaked the box of cigars he had brought with him for safe-keeping.

The attacks continued into the afternoon. Four people were killed and twelve badly wounded. These included the Prince's coffee-boy, a child of perhaps thirteen; his foot was almost blown off. I could have removed it and done something for the others if my box of medicines had not been abandoned in a cave on the way here, owing to lack of transport. The wounded were lifted into a lorry and laid on the bare boards for a nightmare journey to Najran; not one of them made a sound.

Two days later the Royalists shot down a Mig and we went

254

to look at the wreckage. The pilot was an unidentifiable mess, but his map and various notes were in Russian. The Egyptians had gone but the Russians had arrived.

The Prince moved closer to Sanaa and established himself in a large cave. McLean, Lennox-Boyd and I were handicapped throughout because we had no transport, no servant and no provisions, and I was not yet fully mobile after my operations. It was very cold at night. We each carried a couple of blankets and fed and slept where we could. We ate with the Prince if we were in time for a meal; his cave was always packed with retainers and it was hard to find anywhere to stretch out at night. I often went forward to join the French mercenaries where they were mortaring the camps round Sanaa with their 4-inch mortar. They were congenial and being French fed well. Above all, there was room for me to sleep in their tent, which they had dug down for protection from the shelling. Snug after dark, they would roar out the marching songs of the Legion, while mortar bombs exploded around them in the valley. The Royalists frequently attacked at night, and then flare after flare went up from the Republican lines; the flash of guns and the arching tracer flickered along the horizon. Time and again the tribesmen would capture a position, only maddeningly to abandon it and go off with their loot.

McLean and I visited the pass at Nagil Yasla two days after the battle in which Prince Hasan Ismail, yet another of the Princes, had managed to throw back a large force from Taiz attempting to open the road to Sanaa. He had done this although the Republicans had artillery and tanks, whereas the Royalists were armed only with rifles, machine-guns and a single 4-inch mortar. The villagers had turned on the fleeing Republicans and hunted them down: the mountainside and plain below were littered with corpses, many stripped of their clothes; each of these had been left with a tuft of herbs between its legs for the sake of decency.

I had feared Sanaa would fall before I got there. Now it looked as if this inconclusive siege would go on indefinitely. It had all been an interesting experience but I could not stay there for ever. I had plans to travel in northern Kenya, and in January 1968 I returned to England.

from *Desert, Marsh and Mountain*

Meanwhile, Frank Steele had been posted to the High Commission in Nairobi and urged me to return to Kenya, which I did in August 1968.

In mid-September I returned to Maralal and, having bought six camels from the Rendille, set off from Baragoi. As well as two Rendille camelmen, I had Ekwar, Ibach, Neftali – a young Kikuyu who was energetic, enjoyed travelling and got on with the others – and another young Turkana called Lowassa who cooked for us. Rodney Elliott provided me with a Game Ranger called Longacha. He was a Samburu, authoritative, intelligent and physically powerful. We had a dry march through the Samburu Hills and an exhausting struggle across the Suguta Valley, guided by Longacha through small dunes of soft sand, which took about four hours. When we reached the far side, the others said, 'We will go anywhere else with you, but never again across the Suguta.' I was reassured by this since I had felt quite exhausted, but had attributed this to having had a cartilage removed from either knee before I went on my second journey to the Yemen. There, this had proved a handicap when I had had to squat down as Arabs do to pee.

Sometimes we started to load as early as four in the morning so as to get away at dawn. Lowassa would boil some water to make tea, while the camelmen, helped by the others, fastened the *herios*, the hides and four poles which make up the baggage-saddles of these tribes on to the protesting camels. We usually travelled for about four hours. We would stop whenever it began to get unpleasantly hot or we felt like a rest, for even after the river had dried up there were wells every mile or so in the sandy riverbed, and plenty of shade for us and food for the camels on either bank. Then, if we felt like it, we went on again for another couple of hours in the evening.

We camped next day on the nearby Kerio and travelled slowly down the riverbed through thick forest to Lake Turkana, as Lake Rudolf was now called. At the mouth of the Kerio, dense reed beds prevented us from seeing the lake, but we were just able to glimpse it through the reeds when we reached the nearby mouth of the Turkwel. We followed the Turkwel up to Lodwar. At Lodwar, I found the DC and other African officials both welcoming and friendly, and neither here nor anywhere else in Kenya did I meet with tiresome demands for permits or restrictions of any kind on my journeys. Longacha told me that there was a young Turkana here who had walked up by himself from Loiengalani to join his father who had been serving as a policeman in Lodwar but had since been transferred to Mandera. The boy had been here for some time and knew nobody. Longacha asked if he could come with us to Maralal, from where he would be able to get back to Loiengalani. I told Longacha to fetch the boy and he came back with a naked young Turkana who appeared to be about fourteen. He was a powerfully built, cheerful-looking lad with an engaging smile. I said he could certainly come with us and gave him a few shillings to buy a *shuka*, promising him more when we got to

Maralal if he was useful on the journey. He said his name was Erope, which in Turkana means 'spring rains'.

We left Lodwar on 14 October travelling up the bed of the Turkwel. The forest still came down almost to the town. Here the river was dry, but the forest on either side was thick and green from recent rain and, except in a few places, impassable for loaded camels.

I always went on ahead with Ibach and the Game Ranger, who was armed with a rifle. Ibach already showed a remarkable understanding of wild animals. Once he noticed some elephant just visible on a small island in the middle of the river. To move them, so that we could pass, I fired off my shotgun. The herd milled round for a second or two and then scrambled up the bank and disappeared into the forest. A large bull with a smaller bull in attendance remained behind and came forward to face us. The smaller bull then made a demonstration charge towards us before withdrawing to join the bigger bull. Realizing that we should have trouble if we tried to pass them, we turned back down the riverbed looking for a way round them, but the forest was so thick that we had to go back perhaps a mile before we succeeded in doing so. We then had difficulty in getting back through the forest on to the Turkwel. Further up the Turkwel we came on some running water which became more and more abundant as we went upstream until it was two feet deep. Eventually we turned south across bush-covered country by the route we had followed in 1961 and crossed the Kerio.

We had met few Turkana on the Turkwel except for occasional groups of men carrying hide shields, something I had not seen them do before. The country here was in a disturbed state. One group called the Nyoroko, who were troublesome even under British rule, had now acquired some modern rifles from the Sudan and were raiding other Turkana and the neighbouring tribes. The name 'Nyoroko' became synonymous with outlaws. They were also fighting with the Pokot, their traditional enemies. Two months previously this tribe had surprised some Turkana while they were watering their herds on the Turkwel, and killed nine of them, wounding another seven and driving off their cattle, camels and other animals. The Turkana had pursued them and recovered their stock, killing one Pokot. Since then, there had been intermittent raids and I expected the Turkana to stage a big counter-raid before long. When we passed through the Pokot country on our way to Maralal, we found that their warriors, too, were carrying shields as well as spears. In this setting of tribal unrest, my journey could easily have been like one undertaken in the last century.

I had met Bill Woodley, the park Warden of Mount Kenya and the Aberdares, before I went to Meru and told him that I was anxious to go up Mount Kenya. I explained to him that although I had travelled extensively in the Karakorams and the Hindu Kush, I was not a mountaineer, having only been on a rope once in my life. I had been up Kilimanjaro and now wanted to see Mount Kenya, the second-highest mountain in Africa. When I asked for his advice, Bill suggested I should spend a day walking right round the top of the mountain and volunteered to find me an efficient guide. He had the guide, a middle-aged, active man, waiting for me when I went to his headquarters in the Aberdares in February 1971. Bill said, 'He knows every corner of the mountain. When he was with Mau Mau, I spent weeks trying to capture him.' The man grinned and said, 'Yes, but though you tried very hard, you never did catch me!' They reminded me of two men who had played football for different schools and were now reminiscing about a famous match in which they had both played. During the thirty years I have lived in Kenya, I have never encountered resentment of Europeans or latent hostility towards them as a result of Mau Mau. I attribute this to Jomo Kenyatta's insistence when he became President that the past must be forgotten and forgiven and everybody in the country must work together to build a new independent Kenya. Fortunately, those Europeans who felt unable to accept this left the country and the remainder have identified themselves with the Kenya of today.

With Erope, Lowassa and Kibo I motored through the rain-forest by the Naro Moru park entrance to the bottom of the so-called 'vertical bog', an area of steep mountain bog, where we left the car. Then, with two porters we had collected at Naro Moru and accompanied by our guide, we laboured across the 'vertical bog' and then walked up among the giant groundsel and lobelias, vegetation unique to African mountains, to Two Tarn Hut which Bill Woodley had reserved for us.

Lowassa had started to cough and I felt anxious about him, knowing how often people developed high-altitude pulmonary oedema, a severe congestion of the lungs, on this mountain. This can be fatal unless the victim is promptly taken down to a lower altitude. As yet, Lowassa showed no symptoms; even so I decided that next day he must rest quietly in the hut, while with Erope, Kibo and the guide I made our circuit of the mountain. This disappointed Lowassa and he protested, but I insisted that he should remain behind with the porters.

We were on snow before we reached Lenana, the third-highest point on Mount Kenya, and on ice before we reached its summit. We went cautiously, having neither crampons, nor an ice-axe with which to cut steps. Fortunately, it was a clear day and there was a spectacular view all round from the summit. Though we had put on our warmest clothes, at this altitude, 16,355 feet, it was bitterly cold and so we did not linger.

It was hard-going once we were off Lenana. We kept as high as we could but we had to cross a succession of steep valleys running down the mountain, their sides covered with loose scree. Immediately above us towered the sheer-sided, snow-capped peaks of Nelion and Batian, riven with gorges, and below an expanse of lesser mountains and desert country extending indefinitely to the north. We passed the wreck of a helicopter which had crashed when attempting to rescue some injured mountaineers. Here there was no other evidence of human activity. For me, this mountain with its fascinating variety of peaks, glaciers and gorges was more exciting than Kilimanjaro which was at its best when seen from a distance.

Lowassa was all right when we got back to Two Tarn Hut, nine hours after leaving it, and we went down the mountain again the following day. I felt a personal sense of achievement having circuited Mount Kenya in a single day.

Baragoi was on the road to the north and I motored through there every now and again, partly to find out for Rodney Elliott about the movement of poachers in the area between there and Marsabit. There was a small primary school at Baragoi and most of the boys in it were aged between seven and twelve. On my way through Baragoi I used to stop my car under some trees near the school and the boys would come over and ask if they could play boxing. At Erope's insistence I had bought two pairs of gloves and we carried these in the car. One small boy in particular caught my attention and he invariably came over to greet me whenever I stopped near the school. Once, when I looked about for him, I couldn't see him anywhere. Feeling anxious in case something had happened to him, I went over and asked one of the children, 'Where is Lawi?' The boy replied, 'He's in your car.' I went back to it and found Lawi sitting in the front seat. I said, 'What are you doing in the car, Lawi?', to which he replied, 'I don't know. I'm leaving school and I'm going to stay with you,' and so we drove off together. This was in 1972, and Lawi was perhaps eleven or twelve years old at the time; he has now been with me for over twenty years. His parents were in Maralal and seemed quite happy that he should join me. He had until then been living at Ololokwe with his grandmother, to whom he was devoted.

In 1988 Lawi was elected a member of the Maralal Urban Council and the Council elected him their chairman. Consequently he was known as the mayor. He acted in Harry Hook's film, *The Kitchen Toto*, in my opinion the best feature film to come out of Africa. Lawi played the part of the corporal who picks the dead kitchen-boy out of the river.

More and more I found myself based on Maralal, camping at a variety of sites on the outskirts of the town. Erope and Lawi were permanently with me. Erope was a Turkana from Lodwar, whereas Lawi was a Samburu whose *manyatta* was close to Maralal. Increasingly I found myself involved with Lawi's family.

In July 1976, initiation ceremonies marking a new Samburu age-set began. These ceremonies took place on average every fourteen years and began after the Lmasula clan had killed a bull on Mount Nyiru, the sacred mountain. Lawi, who belonged to the Lkuwono, or blacksmith's clan, always the first clan to be initiated, was now old enough to be circumcised. On my journey with Frank Steele in 1960, I had seen groups of boys wandering about in the black cloaks which they wore for some time before and after they had been circumcised: they were the 1960 age-set. But as yet I had seen none of the ceremonies themselves. Now I was so closely involved with Lawi's family that as one of them I witnessed not only the circumcisions of the initiates but the ceremonies which went with them.

Like all the other clans, the Lkuwono selected a site for their *lorora* or circumcision camp. Each *lorora* was situated if possible near woodland where there was also sufficient water and grazing. The *lorora* comprised an extensive area enclosed by a thorn fence inside which the women of each family built a windowless, flat-roofed hut made of sticks and branches. These huts were covered with grass and the walls and roof plastered with cow-dung; a hole in the roof let out the ever-present smoke. There was an enclosure for their cattle and each hut stood adjacent to the next, sited round the perimeter of the fence according to the family's lineage. Each family had a separate gateway for its cattle. At the centre of the *lorora* was a fire where the elders gathered in the evenings and talked, argued incessantly, and prayed to the Samburu god, Nkai. This fire was not allowed to die out.

Perhaps two months before his circumcision, Lawi put on his goatskin cape made of three skins dyed black with charcoal mixed with animal fat. Then, with a group of boys, he went off to gather a suitable stick to make the shaft of his bow from one place, sticks for his arrows from another and gum, with which to blunt the points of eight arrows, from yet a third place. Each of these was collected from certain traditional areas, often far apart, such as South Horr, Baringo and Marsabit. The initiates might be gone for a week or more, particularly when collecting gum.

The day before their circumcision, all the boys in the *lorora* went off at a run, each carrying a gourd to fetch water from a traditional permanent spring – in Lawi's case to Kisima, a distance of at least twenty-four miles there and back from his *lorora*. Before their circumcision the boys wore their hair in a circular tuft; but now, on their return with the water, their mothers shaved their heads and two men who were the sponsors for each boy made him a pair of sandals from the skin of an ox that had been killed the day before. A few families circumcised their boys that evening, all the others the following morning. Throughout the night the initiates sang the *lebarta*, the circumcision song. This mass singing was immensely moving and impressive in the dark. There were only a few men in the area who knew how to circumcise. Some were really competent at performing this peculiar and intricate form of Samburu operation, others were less so.

The boys to be circumcised might number as many as two hundred in a *lorora*, and the circumcisions began almost before it got light. Any man or boy could watch, but no woman was allowed near. The boy, who was naked, sat on a fresh ox-skin, leaning back against one of his sponsors, who held his shoulders, while the other sponsor held his right leg; another man, usually a close relative, held his left leg. That year I saw many boys being circumcised; they remained absolutely motionless throughout the operation, barely blinking. They would have been permanently disgraced if they had shown the slightest sign of pain. If a boy had flinched, his family's cattle would have been driven out of the *lorora*, smashing through the perimeter fence; then cow-dung and, on top of this, hot ash would have been rubbed in his mother's hair. After a boy's circumcision, a man beat his right thigh twice and said, 'Stand up, you are now a man.' Before standing up, the boy would sing a *lebarta* asking for an ox from his family. The ox was shot in its jugular vein with a blocked arrow and the boy drank its fresh blood mixed

264

in milk. The arrow wound was then smeared with dung and the ox was sent off to graze. For two weeks the boys were not allowed to drink water and were given meat, blood and milk for food. They were not allowed to wash in water until the ceremony of the arrows a month later.

The day after circumcision, the boys' sponsors fashioned their bows and arrows and in nearly every case fastened a black ostrich feather on either side of the boys' heads. A day or two later, using four of the eight blunted arrows, they started shooting small birds, skinned each one, stuffed it with grass and hung it down from the back of their head. They were also entitled to chase and shoot at uncircumcised girls as they ran away from them, aiming at their ankles, unless the girls ransomed themselves with beads. A senior Samburu official standing beside me on one occasion said, 'You will never realize how important all this is to us. It is the most important event in our lives.'

Perhaps a month later, there followed the ceremony of *Lmuget Loolbaa*, the casting away of the arrows; after this ceremony, the initiate became a *moran*. All the families killed and roasted an ox over an open fire. Each boy then attempted to break the ox's hip-bone with one blow of a club. He then took a piece of the roasted rump, stuck on a knifeblade, gave it to his mother and said to her, 'Mother, this is the food I was eating when I was young. I am returning it to you. Never give me food again.' They gave the traditional strings of beads they had worn to their mothers and were rubbed all over with red ochre. From now on, as long as they were *moran* they might never eat in the presence of women, indeed anywhere where women were in sight. These ceremonies involved the slaughter by the family of a succession of sheep and oxen. At the conclusion of the ceremonies, the Lmasula clan killed another bull on Mount Nyiru.

* * *

In June 1978 I flew back to Kenya. Before leaving in 1977 I had got Lawi a job with Myles Burton's safari firm; Myles had taken him on sight. I had given Erope my tent and enough money to buy some animals, since I was thinking of perhaps staying on indefinitely with a tribal people in India after I left the Yemen. The day after I got back to Nairobi I ran into Lawi driving one of Myles Burton's safari lorries past John Seago's house. He jumped out of the lorry, came over, embraced me and called out to his co-driver, 'Take this lorry back to Myles and tell him I've left him and rejoined my father.'

Myles Burton understandably thought that Lawi had treated him rather badly, but I felt that nothing had mattered to Lawi except being back with me. We drove back to Maralal from Nairobi and a day or two later Lawi said to me, 'Why do we go on living like this in tents, *mzee juu*?' – *mzee juu*, 'top elder', had been my nickname over the years – 'Why don't you build a house?' I said to him, 'I own no land here, so how can I build a house?' and he replied, 'I can put one anywhere I like.' We were camped in a valley a mile or so east of the town with a hill immediately above us. The next morning, we walked up this hill and chose a site for the house under some wild olives with a spacious view. The day after, with the help of Lawi's father, we started to build the house. At that time we could see some Samburu *manyattas*, but nowhere any tin roofs which now unfortunately are becoming commonplace. When I had come here in 1961 all the country below us had been forest. Now, except for an occasional tree, this forest has all been cut down or burnt. For some years we were able to use the treestumps for firewood.

We levelled a small patch of ground under some of the trees and dug a shallow trench outlining the house. In the trench, we set up nine-foot-high cedar poles adjacent to each other, for the outer wall, and divided the house into three rectangular rooms of roughly equal size, ten feet by twelve, each with a window but with only one outer door in the central room. We obtained the roof timbers from Siddiq Bhola, and employed a local builder to put on a pitched roof of corrugated iron which was admittedly unsightly but conveniently weathertight. We concreted the floor and plastered the inside walls with a mixture of mud and cow-dung. We then bought some basic furniture in the town and put up a shelter outside the house for the kitchen, where we cooked on three stones. We also fastened gutters to the roof to catch water in drums when it rained. We built a verandah in front of the house and after that started to plant a garden. Today this garden is very colourful; the bougainvilleas especially are magnificent.

By now Lawi was six feet tall, with very broad shoulders and narrow hips, an attractive open face, and even in his later teens he had an air of self-possession and quiet authority. When he got married he wore Samburu dress and said to me, 'Anyone who is ashamed of his tribal customs is a slave.'

One day when Lawi and I were still camped near Maralal, two young Samburu turned up and helped us by fetching wood and making the fire. Lawi said, 'Let's keep that one with us'; but I opted for the other one. I asked him what his name was and he said, 'My father called me Tommy-Gun.' His father had been wounded and lost a leg fighting with the King's African Rifles in the Abyssinian campaign. I said, 'You can't be called that, it's a ridiculous name,' and he replied, 'All right, you give me a name.' I thereupon called him Laputa after the Zulu leader in John Buchan's *Prester John* and since then that has always been his name, even on his identity card and other official papers. A tall, slender figure, he has a rather sombre face with large, expressive, perhaps wistful, eyes.

As I got to know him, I discovered Laputa had a strongly artistic temperament. Some years later when I was living in Lawi's house, I gave Laputa the money to build a house for himself, which he did, on a hillside outside the town from which there was a spacious view across the valley to the Maralal Safari Lodge. It seemed to me that Laputa had selected the most pleasing site in the neighbourhood.

Below the house, the hillside sloped down to a wide shallow valley where water lay after heavy rain; beyond, the intervening ground, covered with acacias, rose gradually to a rim of low forest-covered hills. The slopes opposite the house were frequented by tame zebra, occasionally by eland and a herd of buffalo and sometimes by elephant, especially at night. Fortunately, both the road into the town and the town itself were out of sight, but after dark there was a ring of lights from the small Maralal Safari Lodge and a few houses opposite which were scarcely visible in the daytime. There is still some superb forest near Maralal. The most numerous trees are the junipers, generally called 'pencil cedars', some of them magnificent trees. There had been many on the slopes where Maralal Safari Lodge is situated. Most of these junipers are now dead and the remainder are dying. I first noticed this happening some ten years ago.

At first the very top of the tree dies and this spreads down the tree until just a leafless skeleton remains. It has been suggested to me that this is caused by mites. By now, nearly all the junipers in this neighbourhood are dead and even some of the trees in the forest six miles away to the west of the town are affected. I have a feeling of despair that this blight may eventually destroy the junipers throughout the magnificent forests in Kenya, as has happened to the elms in England. I doubt if anything can be done about it. With the demand for charcoal by an ever-increasing population in Maralal, and since no alternative fuel is available, more and more trees are being cut down to provide it. Neither can I see any solution to this problem.

A year after joining me, Laputa produced Ewoi Ekai, a Turkana of approximately his own age. He had worked for a while in Bhola's garage and was already a capable mechanic. Bhola had nicknamed him Kibiriti, or 'match', by which name he is now almost universally known. He is six feet two inches tall, powerfully built and has aristocratic features marred only by the absence of his four front teeth. He now joined us as a permanent member of our small society. Laputa had spent five years in a primary school and could read and write, whereas Kibiriti had never been at school and could do neither. Nevertheless, he has been recently elected as the chairman of one of the primary schools in Maralal, a job which he does conscientiously and very efficiently. He has sent his two small sons to this school; they have tried, but to their exasperation failed, to teach their father the alphabet.

I am very fond of Kibiriti who is kind, thoughtful and utterly reliable. His pleasant voice is curiously distinctive and I can pick it up as soon as I hear it. Kibiriti is not only industrious but has a head for business. He is generally popular not only with the Turkana but also with the Samburu. Kibiriti eventually ran a bus, the only public transport between Maralal and Baragoi, but this became uneconomic due to the heavy expense of constantly replacing burst tyres. He has a three-ton lorry which he contracts out, as well as a general store in Baragoi, his home town.

Though he is a Turkana, from a country much too arid for cultivation, Kibiriti has designed and laid out an extensive and attractive garden round his house; this is situated on a flat plain between the hill on which Lawi's house is visible, and the town. A number of poison trees of a uniform shape, a thick, bare trunk crowned by a compact mass of dark-green leaves, are scattered singly on this plain. A deadly poison can be brewed from the roots of this tree, yet elephant and children eat its small, yellow fruit. The Wakamba and Wagiriama among others use this poison with their powerful bows to kill elephant. It is interesting that in a comparatively small area at a very similar altitude, these poison trees are confined to Kibiriti's vicinity.

When Laputa and I had made our garden, Kibiriti, who proved to be a surprisingly knowledgeable, practical gardener, would advise us what to plant and how to prune. Being half-way down a slope there was little soil above the underlying rocks, whereas Kibiriti's garden was planted on richer soil in the valley bottom. We planted bougainvilleas and when these were in flower they attracted sunbirds which are always a delight to watch. Laputa hung a birdtable in one of the trees and flight after flight of starlings, mostly the spectacular Superb starlings, among others, arrived as soon as they saw him going to it in the morning. Weaver birds would be already waiting in the tree. The dawn chorus of birds, as it begins to get light, is varied and unforgettable; and after that comes the sound of approaching cow-bells.

After Lawi got married I moved into Laputa's house. One evening he said to me, 'I want to try and draw.' He told me this was something he had always wanted to do but had never done. I gave him a large sheet of paper and went off to bed while he sat there starting to work by the light of a hurricane lamp. In the morning he showed me a pencil drawing he had made based on photographs of three lion. I was astonished not only by their life-like realism and accurate proportions, but also by the originality with which he had drawn details such as the lion's mane.

Recently an Irish artist, Colin Watson, came out to Kenya to paint my portrait, which now hangs in the Royal Geographical Society. Laputa watched him doing this for some time, then borrowed a brush and oilpaints and did a study on board of a camel's head based on one of my photographs. He had never handled a brush before, yet the result was quite staggering and might have been the work of a professional artist. It hangs in the Yarre Lodge near Maralal for anyone to see. Among other things, Laputa has also produced a pen-and-ink portrait of me which is probably the finest work he has done to date. This portrait has been said to do everything but speak.

Both Laputa's and Kibiriti's houses were built on the same basic pattern as Lawi's, with three adjacent rooms; but whereas Kibiriti's house is on flat ground, Laputa had dug his into the hillside. Overlooking the valley, he had constructed an open verandah with a partially enclosed, roofed area behind it. At one end of the verandah he had another sitting room, its windows enclosed by broad wire-netting and low enough to afford a comfortable view. At the other end of the verandah there was a fully enclosed kitchen. Five concrete steps led down from the verandah to the drive below. The only fuel to be had in Maralal is charcoal and we cook with this over a small brazier called a *jiko*. Water is always a problem and, except during the rains when we catch what rainwater we can off the roof, we never have enough. The British had constructed a dam to supply Maralal and normally we could get water from the town when our water ran out. But in the 1979 drought, the dam dried up and water had to be brought to the town in tankers. We fetched water for ourselves in jerry-cans from twelve miles away.

Consequently a bath here was, and always is, a real luxury.

In 1988 Laputa married a Samburu girl called Namitu. Namitu is unusually large, tall and placid, unfailingly cheerful and always eager to help. She is unobtrusively well-educated and speaks good English. She herself keeps the house clean and tidy and, unlike so many of these educated women, is prepared to turn her hand to anything, such as fetching water or wood.

My father kept no dogs in the Legation during the years we were in Addis Ababa. When we were at The Milebrook, the first dog I owned was a golden cocker spaniel but it died of distemper after I had had it for a year. I was then ten years old and at prep school. I still remember my grief when I heard the news. I had two other spaniels; the last one I taught to retrieve and I took it everywhere with me, even to Scotland, when I was shooting. When I was stationed at Darfur, no government officials kept dogs. I understood that this was because sometime in the past, when the District Officers had gathered at El Fasher for Christmas, a dog which many of them handled and played with developed rabies. In consequence they had to be evacuated all the way to Khartoum to be inoculated, leaving the province with almost no one to administer it. I never checked this story but the fact remains that officials did not keep dogs. After this, my nomadic life gave me no opportunity to keep a dog until I came to Kenya.

With my failing sight I need someone to look after me and a cousin of Namitu's, Lopego, has constituted himself my bodyguard and sleeps in my room. One night when Lopego was not there, I was woken by a crash. Five men had arrived, smashed open the outside door with a rock and a few seconds later were in my room, the door of which was always open. The key of Laputa's room, directly opposite mine, was always kept on the outside of his door and was only used to keep his two-year-old son, Sandy, out of the room in the daytime. As the men came in, they turned this key locking Laputa, his wife and baby son in their room. That night only the Bushboy and Talone were sleeping in the central room. I turned over and saw three hooded figures in the doorway by the light of a torch which they had briefly switched on. For a second or two I assumed it was part of a bad dream, but then, realizing what they were, I hoped they weren't going to use pangas. Instead they carried thick, heavy sticks and two of them rained blows on me, luckily missing my head. In the dark, I sensed one of them beside me, rolled over, shouted, 'Get out of here, damn you!', kicked hard with my heel and started to get out of bed. I evidently got the man where it hurts most. He dropped his stick and next moment they were all gone. It was strange that our dogs had not barked or attacked these men. It has been suggested that they gave them meat to keep them quiet, or that one or more of them was well-known to the dogs. It was curious that while they were beating me, I could sense the blows but felt no pain. Two days later my left arm and both legs above the knee had turned completely black. The whole thing was an interesting experience but one which I have no desire to repeat.

The police said they were sorry I had not killed one of my attackers so that they would know who they were. Lopego never ceases to regret that he was away and was unable to kill at least one. Had he been there I am sure that he would have succeeded, using his ironshod club.

We always eat dinner in the kitchen, nine or ten of us together, in a comparatively small space. The five- and six-year-olds, even Sandy, Laputa's two-year-old son, perch wherever they can sit, to eat the food which one or other of us will have been cooking. The food does not vary, though it tastes different

273

depending on who has cooked it, perhaps Namitu, or Lopego or even the Bushboy. They cook a large bowl of white maize-meal cake called *ugali* and chapattis which are eaten with a goat stew containing grated potatoes and carrots, chopped cabbage, onions and tomatoes, flavoured with chillies and a mixed spice called Roiko, all floating in a thick and generally delicious soup. People have said to me, 'We can't understand how you can eat the same food for dinner day in and day out'; I answer, 'But, after all, the Scots eat porridge every morning for breakfast,' though admittedly we don't have the pipes to help it down. I do run to porridge or cornflakes, sometimes an egg for my breakfast, which I eat in the sitting room, and Kibiriti most often gives me lunch in his house which is usually an excellent and very filling chopped liver in a thick soup with a bowl of rice. Or the ever-hospitable Siddiq Bhola gives me a more varied Pakistani meal in his house in Maralal. In our house, tea is the staple drink, or water, though I sometimes have coffee for breakfast, which I eat by myself or with any friends who are living with me. For breakfast the others eat bread which is included in the rations we buy each day in the town.

Some visitors enjoy being taken by the children to spend a night in their dark, smoke-filled *manyattas* nearby and thus see Samburu life at close quarters. Before they go there I tell them to buy a goat for the evening meal their hosts provide. When the goat is killed, children usually take it in turns to drink the blood as it gushes from its throat. One or two young tourists have done the same, something I myself could never have done.

Looking back over my life I have never wanted a master and servant relationship with my retainers. Even in the Sudan as an Assistant DC when I travelled with camels, I instinctively and invariably slept and sat on the ground and shared my food with those who were travelling with me. This, of course, is what I did in Arabia and in the Marshes of Iraq and I have continued to do so in Kenya.

In Arabia and in the Marshes I had a very close relationship with some of the people with whom I lived; this I cherished. While I was with the Rashid I would gladly have been assimilated by them; but I would never have wished that I had been born an Arab instead of an Englishman, for I am proud to be English and could wish to be nothing else. Similarly, family pride, rather than any form of religious conviction, would forbid me from becoming a Muslim. What I valued was their companionship. Here in Kenya the people among whom I am living are involved in my life and I am involved in theirs. I pay them no wages and have never regarded them as servants, but as part of my family. I have endeavoured to help them establish themselves and this has often involved me with considerable expense; it has, however, been my pleasure to do this.

Ever since I left Oxford in 1933, I have never spent more than three, or occasionally four, months in England in any one year. I returned to London to be with my mother and to see my many friends, and acquaintances I have met abroad. For this reason, when I am in England now, I have no desire to be anywhere but in London; anyway, the English countryside means little to me. If I lived in the country I should really be confined to meeting my neighbours. Mollie Emtage had been with us for almost forty-five years. Until my mother died Mollie looked after her with devotion; and she looked after me with the same devotion until she died in 1991. Now to live alone in an empty flat, unable to read because of my failing sight, would be very desolate.

When I first came to Kenya, I intended to spend perhaps two

years in the country travelling with camels in the Northern Frontier District, but since then I have come to regard Maralal as my home. It is here, among those whose lives I share today, that I hope to end my days.

from *My Kenya Days*

EPILOGUE

Looking back, I realize that my exciting and happy childhood in Abyssinia, far removed from direct contact with the Western world, implanted in me a life-long craving for adventure among untamed tribes in unknown lands.

I knew Abyssinia in all its traditional splendour, with its age-old ceremonies and a pattern of life that had not changed in centuries. As a young man, I achieved a boyhood dream of hunting dangerous animals in the wilds of Africa. Then and later, I travelled in unexplored regions, and spent years among tribesmen who had no conception of any world other than their own. Yet I might so easily have been too late.

Even as a boy I recognized that motor transport and aeroplanes must increasingly shrink the world and irrevocably destroy its fascinating diversity. My forebodings have been amply fulfilled. Package tours now invade the privacy of the remotest villages; the transistor, blaring pop music, has usurped the place of the tribal bard. While I was in the desert with the Rashid, they would light a fire by striking a dagger blade against a piece of flint: now they hear the world's news on their radio, or watch it on their television set. Twenty-five years ago, their concern was on account of tribal raiding: now,

277

it is on account of superpower dissension over arms control, and 'Star Wars' of the future. The Rashid today, like the rest of us, know they face the possibility of nuclear annihilation.

In any case, if we survive, the future of serious geographical exploration must be in outer space or in the ocean depths. Moreover, the means to carry it forward can only be attained by modern technology, and at enormous expense; the participants in each venture will inevitably be limited to the selected few. The surface of the globe, having now, thanks to the internal combustion engine, been thoroughly explored, no longer affords scope for the adventurous individual in search of the unknown.

Journeying at walking pace under conditions of some hardship, I was perhaps the last explorer in the tradition of the past. I was happiest when I had no communication with the outside world, when I was utterly dependent on my tribal companions. My achievement was to win their confidence. Among my many rewards was, in Abyssinia, to have been the first European to explore the Sultanate of Aussa; in Arabia, to have reached the oasis of Liwa, and to have found the fabled quicksands of Umm al Sammim; and, in so many of my travels, to have been there just in time.

from *The Life of My Choice*

INDEX

279